trouble
e intro-
language difficulties, Shula Chiat explores
the stumbling blocks which lie behind their struggle. The
uniqueness of this book lies in its focus on individual children,
the extensive and intriguing examples which illustrate their
problems, and the step-by-step search for the source of those
problems. Difficulties with words, verb structures, function
morphemes and meaning are examined and illustrated by
detailed case studies.

This book provides a clear overview of what children with
language difficulties say and do, and introduces a logical
approach to analysing children's language problems. It will be
welcomed by students of linguistics, psycholinguistics and
speech and language therapy; researchers in the areas of
language development and language disorders; therapists and
teachers working with children with language and communication impairments; and lay people with an interest in how
children discover their language.

Dr Shula Chiat is Senior Lecturer in Linguistics at the Department of Language and Communication Science, City University,
London. She has authored and co-authored papers in *Journal of
Child Language, Cognition, Linguistics, British Journal of Disorders
of Communication, Clinical Linguistics and Phonetics, Aphasiology,
Language and Cognitive Processes, Journal of Psycholinguistic Research, Journal of Neurolinguistics* and *Brain and Language.*

Understanding Children with Language Problems

Cambridge Approaches to Linguistics

General editor: Jean Aitchison, *Rupert Murdoch Professor of Language and Communication, University of Oxford*

In the past twenty-five years, linguistics – the systematic study of language – has expanded dramatically. Its findings are now of interest to psychologists, sociologists, philosophers, anthropologists, teachers, speech therapists and numerous others who have realized that language is of crucial importance in their life and work. But when newcomers try to discover more about the subject, a major problem faces them – the technical and often narrow nature of much writing about linguistics.

Cambridge Approaches to Linguistics is an attempt to solve this problem by presenting current findings in a lucid and non-technical way. Its object is twofold. First, it hopes to outline the 'state of play' in key areas of the subject, concentrating on what is happening now, rather than on surveying the past. Secondly, it aims to provide links between branches of linguistics that are traditionally separate.

The series will give readers an understanding of the multi-faceted nature of language, and its central position in human affairs, as well as equipping those who wish to find out more about linguistics with a basis from which to read some of the more technical literature in textbooks and journals.

Also in the series

Understanding Children with Language Problems

SHULA CHIAT

City University, London

PUBLISHED BY THE PRESS SYNDICATE OF THE UNIVERSITY OF CAMBRIDGE
The Pitt Building, Trumpington Street, Cambridge, United Kingdom

CAMBRIDGE UNIVERSITY PRESS
The Edinburgh Building, Cambridge CB2 2RU, UK
http://www.cup.cam.ac.uk
40 West 20th Street, New York NY 10011-4211, USA
http://www.cup.org
10 Stamford Road, Oakleigh, Melbourne 3166, Australia

© Shula Chiat 2000

First published 2000

Printed in the United Kingdom at the University Press, Cambridge

Typeset in Photina 10/12pt [VN]

A catalogue record for this book is available from the British Library

Library of Congress cataloguing in publication data

Chiat, Shula.
Understanding children with language problems / Shula Chiat.
   p.   cm. – (Cambridge approaches to linguistics)
Includes bibliographical references.
ISBN 0 521 57386 6. – ISBN 0 521 57474 9 (pbk.)
1. Language disorders in children Case studies. 2. Speech disorders in
children Case studies. 3. Children – Language.
I. Title. II. Series.
RJ496.L35C46   2000
618.92'855 – dc21   99-23267 CIP

ISBN 0 521 57386 6 hardback
ISBN 0 521 57474 9 paperback

Contents

Part IV Hidden meanings, baffling meanings

14 '[æ] you don't tell nobody this?': strengths in
    pragmatic processing   243
15 'I can speak Chinese. But I can't speak Chinese':
    problems in pragmatic processing   251

    Endpoint and springboard   262
    Further reading   267
    References   269
    Index   279

Acknowledgements

I would like to thank: the children and young adults who contributed to this book, as well as parents and teachers, for letting me into their world so willingly; Sarah Connolly and Anthony Robertson, for their readiness to talk about their experience; Elizabeth Auger, Linda Brett, Dorothea Cave, Rebecca Lacey, Gwen Lancaster, Mary Solomons, Pauline St Leger, Jane Speake, for introducing me to children in their language units and clinics, and for making me welcome as an observer and a researcher; Norma Corkish, Chief Executive of AFASIC, for involving me in AFASIC activities which gave me the opportunity to meet and talk with many children and young adults with language disabilities; John Richards, AFASIC Activity Week Co-ordinator, for putting up with me on AFASIC trips and for the privilege of learning from his experience and understanding; Isabelle Barrière, Dorothy Bishop, Joyce Brown, Alison Constable, Rosemary Emanuel, Peter Hobson, Susanna Martin and Penny Roy, for their helpful comments on sections of this book; Bob and Maggie Fawcus, for opening the doors which led me to children with language disabilities; Sally Byng, Head of the Department of Clinical Communication Studies, and colleagues, for their support, particularly for enabling me to take a sabbatical in order to complete the book. I am indebted to Jean Aitchison for creating opportunities, and for her active editorial support, careful reading of drafts and perceptive feedback. I am also indebted to Maria Black and Jane Marshall for extensive and insightful comments on the text. To both, and to Eirian Jones, I owe special thanks for sharing in the irresistible pursuit of questions about language processing and therapy.

Illustrations by Jon Hunt.

Sample cards from the game 'Guess who?' are reproduced with kind permission of GUESS WHO? © 1999 Hasbro International Inc.

Shula Chiat
July 1998

Glossary of text conventions and symbols

input   Forms in bold highlight technical terms which are accompanied by a definition or clarified by examples.

cap   Forms in italics are used to cite word *forms* as opposed to word meanings.

'cap'   Forms between inverted commas are used to cite word *meanings* as opposed to word forms.

/kæp/   Items between slashes identify forms phonologically, i.e. in terms of the sound categories of English.

[kæp]   Items between square brackets identify forms phonetically, i.e. in terms of their auditory or articulatory characteristics.

Italics are also used to mark emphasis in the text.

An asterisk * before a word or sentence is a convention used by linguists to indicate that the word or sentence is not well-formed.

Sound symbols

The sounds corresponding to symbols are illustrated by words as pronounced in *Southern British middle-class English*. Some examples would not be appropriate illustrations in other accents of English.

Consonant symbols	Example	Vowel symbols	Example
p	*p*ie	i	*seat*
t	*t*oe	ɑ	*tart*
k	*c*ar	ɔ	p*aw*
b	*b*ee	u	m*oo*n
d	*d*ay	ɜ	b*ir*d
g	*g*uy	ɪ	b*i*n
f	*f*ur	ɛ	b*e*d
θ	*th*in	æ	b*a*t
s	*s*ea	ʌ	c*u*t
ʃ	*sh*oe	ɒ	h*o*t
v	*v*iew	ʊ	p*u*t
ð	*th*ough, mo*th*er	ə	*a*bout
z	*z*oo	aɪ	p*ie*
ʒ	bei*g*e, mea*s*ure	eɪ	h*ay*
tʃ	*ch*ip	ɔɪ	b*oy*
dʒ	*j*am	ɛə	h*air*
m	*m*ug	ɪə	*ear*
n	*kn*ee	ʊə	p*oor*
ŋ	si*ng*	aʊ	c*ow*
w	*w*ay	əʊ	r*ose*
l	*l*ight		
r	*r*ock		
j	*y*es		

' as in *to'mato* or *to my* 'house   indicates that the following syllable or word is stressed

Introduction

Some children can't um – can't even um – they can't even talk or anything like that and they can't talk properly. And they get trouble by talking and um – things like that.

Ian, aged 9

Ruth: My mum and dad – dan me. And my brothers.
Adult: Your mum and dad – ?
Ruth: My daddy and mum – h – they sidan me.
Adult: They send you?
Ruth: No dand me. Beechin.
Adult: What do they do?
Ruth: Nothing!!

This exchange took place between 10-year-old Ruth and myself. After a precarious start, it appears to have come to a dead-end. But with a bit of encouragement, Ruth starts again, slowly, weighing her words:

Ruth: My mum and daddy, those two – those stand me.
Adult: Understand?
Ruth: Yes!!
Adult: They understand you?
Ruth: Yeah.

We've arrived.

Our struggle over words speaks volumes. Ruth has initiated the conversation. She is quite definite about what she wants to communicate. Behind her eventually clear assertion that her family understand her lies her implicit recognition that other people don't. I prove her point with my persistent failure to understand that key word 'understand'. Ruth is ready to give up. It is just too hard to get her understanding understood.

Damian is 21, and describes himself as 'dysphasic'. He, too, can have difficulty getting his message across. He explains how he deals with this situation:

1

> Keep going. If it doesn't work, give up. Go on something else. If someone, like if someone talks to me, and I talk back to them but not in a nasty sen just ans – answer their question and they walk off, I just look at them and, ah, hell with you, and walk off.

But what does it leave him feeling? Not anger:

> Anger is from the – your mind

he says, pointing to his head,

> A urge is from inside you, in your heart (pointing to his heart). You want to hit out.

For Damian, it is a relief to talk 'his own language', which he feels free to do with his 'dysphasic' friends – friends who share his language disability:

> Speaking English, you have to be nice and clear. But if you speak in dysphasic language – it – I ca leave all that out and so you can speak however you want . . . Dysphasics don't bother. Everyone understand.

'Some children', as Ian says, 'get trouble by talking.' They may have difficulty understanding words, or they may understand words in different ways from other children. They may have a hard time producing words, may leave them out, distort them, or use them in different ways from other children. In one way or another, these children will struggle to be understood. What they encounter is not just misunderstanding of their words. It is also misunderstanding of their problem with words. All too often, people hear their halting or unusual speech and jump to the conclusion that they are lazy, or crazy, or stupid.

For most people, everyday talk is easy and effortless. We have little awareness of what makes it happen, so we have little idea what may stop it from happening. The only steps we can register, if we actively seek to, are that we have something to say and that we move the tongue and lips to say it. We have no conscious access to the **output processes** which go on in-between: the **psycholinguistic processes** which take us from meanings in the mind to motor movements in the mouth:

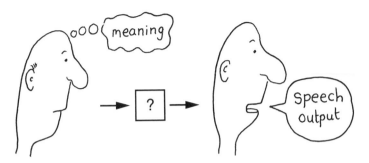

In general, we experience the connections as instantaneous. We can, by conscious effort, separate out the two ends of output processing – intending a meaning, and making sounds. But however hard we try, we cannot catch ourselves making the question-marked connection between these.

The processes by which we understand other people's utterances are equally closed to consciousness. We can make ourselves aware of hearing sound and obtaining meaning from that sound. But we cannot catch ourselves in the psycholinguistic act of **input processing**: of turning the sound which strikes our ears into meaning.

Since we are normally oblivious to the connections we make between hearing/speaking and meaning, it is easy to mistake problems with one for problems with another. Yet obstacles to speaking or hearing are clearly distinct from obstacles in their connections to meaning. Children who have problems with the auditory or motor ends of language processing may have no problems with language processing itself. They prove the point when they find some means of bypassing the barrier to hearing or speaking and their language processing is freed.

Anthony Robertson, for example, has never been able to produce speech himself, but this has not stopped him producing language. He has no problem creating language in his mind, and with communication aids which provide an alternative outlet for language, he is able to get that language out. In his early childhood, he communicated by using his eyes to point to things in the environment or to a symbol board. Then at 11, he got one of the first light pointers to indicate symbols. Now in his twenties, Anthony supplements symbol boards with a sophisticated electronic device named 'Liberator', which turns symbols into speech. In order to communicate with this, Anthony directs his headpointer at symbols, or icons, corresponding to each word he wants to produce. An infra-red sensor picks up the combination of icons he selects, and relays it to the computer. The computer turns it into synthesised speech.

Using this device, Anthony can tell us in detail about his experience of communication. The points he makes, and the language he uses to make his points, speak for themselves: Anthony's speech may be blocked, but his language processing is not.

Consider Anthony's explanation of how he uses 'Liberator':

> A: To make a word, it does take two or three icons. That's how I can say a lot more than 128 words. [There are only 128 squares on the keyboard.]
>
> SC: How would you produce the word 'language'?
>
> A: I would use 'vocabulary' because that is programmed.
>
> SC: And how would you produce the word 'word'?
>
> A: 'Word' is 'phone-God-noun'.
>
> SC: Why does 'God' come into it? Just because it's one of the icons?
>
> A: The rationale is that in the beginning God communicated the word.
>
> SC: So you had to learn what the icons were for every word.
>
> A: Yes. Like learning French, I guess.
>
> SC: It's amazing. Each word involves a couple of moves, yet you hold the whole sentence together.
>
> A: That comes with practice.
>
> SC: So you can hold the sentence in mind as you do each word.
>
> A: Somehow, yes, without thinking hard about it.
>
> SC: You don't take short cuts and miss out the 'little' words?
>
> A: Sometimes at the week-ends I do!

What would happen if Anthony did not have communication aids to express the words in his mind?

> SC: Have you come across people who didn't have your experience?
>
> A: And they are vegetables. Sorry, that is real life – if you walk into most institutions.

Anthony Robertson with Liberator

When a child cannot produce recognisable speech and does not have an alternative means to convey words, other people may wrongly assume that those words are not there. If we think of language as nothing more than speech, we are bound to see an absence of recognisable speech as an absence of language. If we make the further mistake of confusing spoken language with the meaning intentions it expresses, our judgement of a child with impaired speech may be even more devastating: the deficit in speech may be taken to reflect a deficit in thought. Anthony again articulates this experience:

SC: How do you think people saw you when you were a child?

A: I wasn't thought to be bright till when people sat down and worked with me.

SC: Was there any period in your life when people didn't find out what was in your head?

A: Yes, because of the time factor to be able to communicate. Then meant getting my board out.

SC: From when you were five?

A: Six really, because took some time to learn.

SC: Before you were six, can you remember what it was like?

A: I ought to – I used to think like any four years old person.

SC: And could you understand everything?

A: Yes. My understanding is – always has been pretty normal.

SC: Did people realise that?

A: Dad and mum knew that, and some people at school.

SC: Although you didn't use speech, when you had thoughts, were they in words in your head?

A: Yes, and in my dad's voice whenever I think of something. You must understand – I didn't get a voice like this [i.e. computer voice] till eighteen.

So, Anthony's apparent silence does not reflect a silence in his head. A disruption in the ability to move the vocal organs for speech is not to be mistaken for a deficit in language or thought. Obviously it is vital to distinguish different stages of language processing and to clarify where disruption occurs.

Deaf children face a different situation. In their case, the impairment *will* disrupt their processing of language *when that language is spoken*. However, if the barrier to auditory input is bypassed, the child's capacity for acquiring language may be freed. Lip-reading provides a Deaf person with some limited *visual* information about speech. Fingerspelling and writing provide a full visual representation of words. But the words they spell out are those of a spoken language which is not directly available. Only Sign language is entirely independent of the auditory channel, being a language which connects meaning directly to visual rather than auditory representations. When Deaf children receive normal input in Sign language, their acquisition of language proceeds along similar lines to hearing children's acquisition of spoken language (Kyle & Woll 1985).

Sarah Connolly communicates something of her experience as a Deaf person who uses different modalities to communicate:

SC: Are you completely Deaf or do you hear a little?

S: I am profoundly Deaf – 50 per cent hear nothing, 50 per cent can hear. I hear you with hearing aid.

Sarah adds the following comments in writing. These are recorded exactly as she wrote them:

> When I was born, I hear nothing which I need to learn the language of English, most imporation [presumably Sarah means *important*] is English language around me for life. Very difficult to learn the language, I am too young, actually my parents, sister and brother teach me. So I used my eyes to watch the Sign language, lip-reading and writing and when I getting older I learn the more and more English language and Sign language.

We continue in speech, supported by some use of Sign:

SC: Is it difficult to lip-read?
S: Sometimes difficult, sometimes easy . . . If I'm very tired, I can't watch lip-read, so I use Sign.
SC: And when you're at home with your husband?
S: Sign all the time.
SC: Why?
S: Because David use Sign all the time. [Sarah adds in writing] David can do the language because his family are Deaf so they always used Sign language.

Sarah's experience at her work-place provides an example of what happens when a Deaf person enters a hearing environment:

SC: Your job was what?
S: Laboratory technician at Wellcome [Sarah fingerspells these words].
SC: What happened at work?
S: When I met them first, they don't understand how communicate with me, so I teach them how communicate – write out – or lip-read. Much improve. One person did want learn Sign language because she like involve Deaf community, I think. I think she want easy communicate with me, and help us understand language.
SC: When you meet people who don't know you, how do they respond to you?
S: Two different ways. The first one when people talk to me I say I'm sorry I am Deaf. Another one – when I talk, they know I'm Deaf because my voice or speech different. Or I tell them I'm Deaf before we talk.
SC: Do people ever think you're silly because you talk differently?

At this point Sarah switches to writing:

> Some people think that I am silly when I talked different languge because they don't know or understand the language what Deaf people used or Deaf community, some people knows already because they might have Deaf friends or family learning the language.

SC: What do you feel when people think you are silly?
S: I feel not very happy, so I feel people must learn Deaf community or the language what Deaf people using so Deaf people do learning the hearing community or language. So it is fair!

As Sarah says, her speech and voice are different from hearing people's; as the transcription of our dialogue shows, the organisation of her words and sentences also differs from a hearing person's in certain respects. These differences reflect the different routes to English which Sarah has taken in the face of her lack of hearing. They do not reflect differences in her potential for making connections between the meanings and forms of language.

Children who can't hear or can't speak can nevertheless acquire language normally. Conversely, some children can hear and can speak, yet they do not talk like other children. For these children, problems must be arising at some point beyond the processes to which we have conscious access, in those hidden processes which turn heard sound into meaning, or meaning into the motor movements of speech. This book is about these children, and the search for the hidden processes which give rise to their unusual language.

The book

Part I introduces this psycholinguistic enterprise. Its focus is **words**. It unpicks the process of word-learning, developing a theoretical framework and techniques for exploring a child's difficulties with words. With these theoretical and methodological tools in hand, individual children's difficulties with words are followed up. Preliminary observations of their language give rise to a hunch about their difficulties which leads into detailed investigation.

The inquiry then turns to different types of words, in particular, those on which sentences depend. Part II looks at children's processing of **verbs** and the **syntactic structures** which they demand. Part III focuses on their processing of **function morphemes**.

Part IV steps back from connections between sound and meaning, and digs deeper into **meaning and function** in language and their relationship to the ways in which human beings process experience.

Throughout the book, individual children are centre stage. The point is, first, to bring their language to life: to show how it is limited, or odd, or baffling, but also expressive, or moving or, paradoxically, articulate. Where is it coming from? Focusing on the individual child, we explore the particular ways in which language processing is limited or blocked, and the particular ways in which the child has negotiated the obstacles. This is illustrated by in-depth case studies in each section of the book.

This book is both introductory and searching. It spells out the thinking behind much of the research into the nature of speech and language impairments in children. At the same time, it serves as a springboard for investigations which delve deep into aspects of language processing in children who are or are not developing normally.

The book is for those who want or need to know more about what is going on in the mind of a child with a language disability. It is also for those who are fascinated by the language of children, normally developing or otherwise. They may be practitioners or students in speech and language therapy, students in linguistics or psychology, parents, or teachers. Researchers in the field may find fresh insights and questions in the extended evidence and discussion of specific aspects of language processing.

In a different sense, the book is for children with language disabilities. It is an invitation to listen to what they tell us and to understand better what lies behind what we hear, bringing us closer to children's individual experience of language. The book does not deal directly with therapy or therapeutic techniques. But its insistence on exploring and understanding the individual child's language is integral to the therapeutic process. The more sense we can make of the child's language processing, the more we can respond and initiate in ways which make language more comfortable for the child, and optimise her potential for processing it.

Note: To clarify my use of gender-marked personal pronouns when referring to 'the child': I use feminine and masculine forms in alternate chapters throughout the book.

Part I
Problems with words

1 What's in a word?

Seven-year-old Steven struggles to name a microphone:

> S: Oh this is tricky . . . when you on . . . it's when you're on
> . . . like on a concert . . . and you get this . . . micro . . .
> scope . . . no . . . like thing when you speak into it and it's
> even louder. (From Hayman 1996)

Six-year-old Eamonn requests a favoured toy:

> E: I want that . . . deepersiper.
> SC: The what?
> E: [jəʊ] (= you know) the deeper . . . Where deedeepsiper? I dunno
> deedeepsiper is. Where's the deepbersiper? The deepdeepsiper?

Eamonn's search is for the deep-sea diver.

Children who have problems with language have problems with words. Typical descriptions of such children state that they are unable to understand words, find words, or say words, or that they omit words or use words in odd ways.

Such descriptions are no more than a starting-point for looking at their difficulties. To probe these further, we need to consider *what* it is the child can't understand, find, say or put in the right place. This means knowing what words are. We can then consider what is involved in coming to *understand*, *find*, *say* and *combine* them, and what might stop a child from doing one or more of these things.

While it seems obvious that intact language users know words, it is by no means obvious what it is that they know. Once we go beyond the obvious to question what it is that we know, we find that words are not simple things. Each word is a collection of rather special sorts of information.

Take the word 'hair'. To know the word 'hair' is to have represented in your mind a connection between the following:

- **Phonological information**: the sound pattern of the word. In this case, a single syllable containing the sequence of sounds /hɛə/ (in accents where the final *r* is not pronounced).
- **Semantic information**: the meaning to which the sound pattern can refer. In the case of /hɛə/, this is the clump of stuff that grows on the human head or in varying quantities on other parts of human beings and on animals.
- **Syntactic information**: the position which the word may occupy in relation to other words. This information would include the fact that 'hair' may be preceded by the determiner 'the' and by adjectives such as 'long', and that it will occur in certain positions within the sentence such as before a verb ('Hair grows'), following certain verbs ('He cuts hair') and so on.

Each of these pieces of information is **abstract** in the sense that it is picked out or **abstracted** from another level of information. The phonology of the word is the sound *pattern*, and not the sound signal which occurs when the word is uttered. Nor does it include every detail of that sound signal. For example, knowing the word 'hair' does not involve knowing the loudness with which it might be uttered. It *does* involve knowing the consonant–vowel sequence /hɛə/. This means picking out those features of the sound signal that differentiate it from other sequences of consonant and vowel such as /dɛə/ and /ʃɛə/ (*dare* and *share*). Similarly, the semantics of the word 'hair' does not include every detail of the thing it might refer to. Knowledge of the word does not include the number or shades or length or density of hairs on a particular head.

In summary, words are not concrete objects out there in the world. Their existence consists in a connection between phonological, semantic and syntactic information, and that information is picked out from the stream of information we receive.

Different languages, of course, have different words. Most obviously, languages differ in the phonological form which they attach to a meaning. Part of learning a new language is learning the phonological forms of words. But languages also differ in the exact semantics which they attach to phonological forms. For example, the phonological form *hair* in English refers to the clump of stuff on the head and elsewhere on the body. In contrast, French uses a distinct phonological form for hair on the head (*cheveux*) and hair on other parts of the body (*poil*).

Languages also differ in the syntactic properties they attach to particular phonological–semantic pairings. In English, 'hair' when referring to stuff on the head is not used with plural endings or with a plural verb: 'Mona Lisa's hair is long' is fine, but 'Mona Lisa's hairs are long' is not – at least not if the intended reference is to hair on the head! In French, the converse is true, so that the French version of 'Mona Lisa's hair is long' would make 'hair' plural, and in fact mark the verb ('are') and the adjective ('long') as plural.

Each word, then, is a phonological–semantic–syntactic complex. To know words is to have stored such complexes in our minds, in what is termed our **mental vocabulary** or **lexicon**. But knowing words involves more than knowing each such complex. Our **mental vocabulary** is not an undifferentiated collection of such complexes. Words share properties with other words. They may be phonologically similar to each other. *Hair*, for example, is phonologically similar to *fare* and *chair* and *bear* in sharing the ·rhyme /ɛə/ (the variable spelling of that rhyme being irrelevant). It is phonologically similar to *house* in sharing the initial consonant /h/. It is phonologically identical to *hare*, though spelled differently. Words such as *hair* and *hare*, which are phonologically identical but semantically distinct, are known as **homophones**.

Phonological relationships between hair *and other words*

Homophone	hare
Shared rhyme	fare, chair, bear . . .
Shared initial consonant	house, hat, hen . . .

Semantically, 'hair' is most similar to words which refer to parts of the body such as 'skin' and 'nail'. It has more in common with words referring to concrete *substances* such as 'wire' or 'soil' or 'bread' than to concrete *entities* such as 'table' or 'book'. It has even less in common with words referring to abstract things such as 'idea' or 'message', or to places such as 'library' or 'park', or to states such as 'joy' or 'poverty', or to events such as 'revolution' or 'accident'.

Syntactically, though, 'hair' shares properties with all these words, which belong to the category **noun**. This means they may be preceded by a **determiner** and **adjective**:

Det	Adjective	Noun
the	famous	skin/nail/wire/soil/bread
	weird	table/book
	new	idea/message
		library/park
		joy/poverty
		revolution/accident

But of all the above nouns, 'hair' has most in common with 'skin', 'soil' and 'bread', which are distinct from other nouns in certain respects. These nouns may, for example, occur without a determiner where other nouns may not:

Hair should be kept clean
Skin should be kept clean
*Table should be kept clean
*Library should be kept clean

Nouns like 'hair' (as on the head) form a subcategory known as **mass nouns**. They are distinguished from other nouns, known as **count nouns**, in a number of ways, one being the possibility of occurring without a determiner.

Looking at just the word 'hair' illustrates amply the idea that a word consists of connections between phonological, semantic and syntactic information, and is connected to other words by virtue of sharing some of that information.

2 The child's road to words

In acquiring language, children acquire thousands of words. What they are doing is establishing thousands of connections between phonological, semantic and syntactic information.

The first evidence of this process emerges around 9 to 12 months when children make a consistent connection between a form they hear and a thing or action to which it refers. They may point to the appropriate creature on hearing the word 'tiger', or move their hands appropriately on hearing the word 'clap'. By the time they understand 50–150 words, around 1 to $1\frac{1}{2}$ years, they start producing words (see Ingram 1989). Their lexical acquisition then proceeds apace. It is estimated that they know some 8,000 root words by the age of 6, which works out at an average rate of five new words a day, assuming they kick off at 18 months (see Carey 1978 and Clark 1993).

Children absorb words like sponges. How are they doing this? They are not presented with vocabulary lists which pair phonological forms and meanings. They start from the scenes they observe and participate in, and the stream of speech they hear. In order to acquire words, they must segment that stream of speech, separating out the sound pattern of each word. They must segment the scenes in which the speech occurs, separating out the aspects of the scene which are picked out by the words. And they must **map** the one onto the other, making connections between the sound patterns they have segmented and the aspects of scenes they have segmented.

Construed in this way, the child's task looks daunting. Imagine a child hearing the utterance 'There's a tiger' as he looks at a striped creature strutting round (see illustration).

How does the child know which aspects of the scene are the crucial ones, without already having the word to pick these out for him? How does he know that 'tiger' refers to that type of striped creature (i.e. 'tiger') rather than to just any creature (i.e. 'animal') or that particular creature (i.e. its name), or something else in the scene (such as 'fence'), or even the entire event (i.e. 'strutting', or 'tiger strutting' or 'animal strutting')? Equally, how does the child know which chunk of sound is the crucial one? How does he know that *tiger* is a sound pattern with a meaning as a whole, rather than *tige* or *atiger* or *theresatiger*? And how does he know which chunk of sound maps onto which chunk of meaning? How does he know that the chunk of sound corresponding to the striped creature is *tiger* rather than *theresa*? These questions are crucial pieces in the puzzle of word acquisition: how does the child segment the form from the stream of speech, segment the category from the scene, and map the one onto the other?

Perhaps the puzzle isn't that hard if we take into account the contribution of those who provide the language input to children. Perhaps, when people talk to children, they smoothe their path to words by removing some of the complications we have found along that path. Suppose that, instead of being bathed in streams of speech, children are presented with isolated word forms and a clear indication of what they refer to. In this idealised situation, the child hears just *tiger* as the speaker points out a tiger. This would seem to solve the problem of phonological segmentation, since the sound pattern is separated out for him. It would seem to solve the semantic segmentation problem, since the relevant creature has been picked out for him. And it would seem to solve the mapping problem, the connection of one to the other, since there is just one form and one meaning to connect up. But how does the child know that the speaker has helpfully isolated the whole form of the word, and know not to segment *tiger* into two words *tige* and *er*, with just *tige* referring to that striped creature? And how does he know that the speaker's gesture indicates the whole creature, not some part of the creature, or something it is doing, in which case 'tiger' might mean 'black and white stripes on ginger background', or 'strut about'? Presenting a single word may appear to hold out a linguistic hand to the child, but it is only helpful if the child knows that it is a single word. Such knowledge could not itself come from the environment. Hence it would have to stem from the child. Through this example, we expose a logic in the process of word learning: any adaptations in the environment can only cue the child if he is sensitive to those adaptations. He can only take advantage of a cue if he notices it (see Newport, Gleitman & Gleitman 1977 and Gleitman, Newport & Gleitman 1984).

The child's task is still more awesome when it comes to words encoding abstract things, or events, or relations. Here the segmentation and mapping problems are even more striking. Take words which refer to abstract notions such as 'friend' or 'idea', or events such as 'chase' or 'persuade', or attributes such as 'huge' or 'peculiar', or spatial relations such as 'at' or 'across'. Such words are rarely uttered in isolation, and cannot be pointed out. Words which mark time relations such as 'has' in 'He has escaped' or possessive relations such as 'my' in 'my tiger' or specificity such as 'the' in 'the tiger' never occur in isolation (unless they are being cited), and it is impossible to imagine what pointing them out would mean.

It follows that the majority of those thousands of words which emerge over a few years of a child's life are acquired from exposure to streams of speech and streams of events. The puzzle remains. If the environment is not simplified for the child, the child must come prepared in some way to deal with the complexities it presents. He must arrive at the word-learning task with some built-in clues about what to extract from the environment.

Turning to the child, what sensitivities does he bring to word learning and what cues might he notice? Research has revealed a variety of expectations which children have about word semantics and word phonology, which go some way to explaining how the child overcomes the semantic and phonological segmentation problems. They lead the child to focus on certain aspects of the stream of speech and stream of events, and to filter out infinite other aspects.

Filtering scenes

Children are not blank screens registering every feature of the scenes which pass them by. They constantly filter the myriad stimuli they receive, attending to certain aspects rather than others. This filtering process leads them to 'make sense' of what goes on around them; it also leads them to respond and interact with their environment in ways which make sense to others.

The process of filtering scenes is itself quite involved. Even children's very early use of words shows them talking about things from different perspectives (Clark 1997). It is true that their words seem to favour certain components of scenes, evident from the order in which they acquire different types of words and the meaning they attach to words. But they are not confined to these favoured components.

Dominant amongst their earliest words are labels for familiar objects, people and animals. This indicates that they have focused on these entities. It also indicates their preferred assumption that a word refers to a *whole* entity, and not to some part or property of it. Experimental evidence confirms that children make this assumption. Young children who are presented with labels for parts of unfamiliar objects treat the part-label as a label for the whole object (see Clark 1993 for evidence and discussion).

It has also been observed that children start out with what have been identified as **basic-level** terms (see Markman 1989 for a review of the evidence). These terms pick out categories which lie between the very specific and the very general, 'dog' for example being a basic-level term relative to the more specific 'spaniel' and the more general 'animal'. These are, of course, the terms that adults most typically select when talking to children (Brown 1958). We are much more likely to label the thing in the garage as a 'car' than as a 'hatchback' at one extreme or a 'vehicle' at the other. But any such bias towards basic-level terms cannot account for the child's acquisition of these as basic-level terms. Every time children hear a basic-level term, its reference is ambiguous. They could justifiably conclude that the terms refer to a more general or a more specific category. And occasionally they do. For example, they may **overgeneralise**, using a term such as 'dog' for animals other than dogs. Or they may **undergeneralise**, restricting 'dog' to just one particular creature. However, such misconstruals are not that frequent, and tend to apply to children's earliest acquired words (Rescorla 1980). This shows that children are themselves prioritising basic-level categories, and assuming that terms used by adults refer to these.

But biased as they may be towards words which pick out basic-level categories of things, they are open to other possibilities. They do not assume that all terms refer to basic-level categories. Their earliest words typically include names for significant individuals – 'Mummy' or 'David' or 'Fido'. Again, mistakes are not unknown. For example, children at an early stage may use 'daddy' to refer to any man. They may utter 'mummy' to express something like 'I want . . .' as they reach for something. But such misconstruals are rare and brief. In general, children restrict these terms to the appropriate individual. This suggests that certain individuals in certain relationships are as salient to the child as basic-level categories. The individual 'mother' is not primarily perceived as one of the category 'woman', but as an individual in a specific relation to the child. Children typically focus on things and people, but they are not limited to one perspective on these.

Nor is their focus entirely restricted to things and people. They also notice events, states, and relations in which things and people participate. This is evidenced by their early use of terms such as 'there', 'more', 'mine', 'hot', 'broken', 'open', 'gone', 'down', 'here you are'. These terms refer to the location, state or possession of an entity, or to changes in such states of affairs. (See Nelson 1973, Greenfield & Smith 1976.)

If children are attentive to different aspects of scenes, how do they know *which* aspect of a scene is the focus of the words they hear? Perhaps this is where others step in and help the child, by highlighting in some way the relevant aspect of the scene. At first sight, studies of adult–child interaction in a variety of cultures lend support to this possibility.

One of the commonly observed features of child-directed language is that it relates to the here-and-now. Adults talk to toddlers about what has just happened, is happening, or is about to happen in their immediate environment, not about events which are removed in time or space: 'Oh no, the tower's fallen over', 'Look Sam, there's an aeroplane', 'We're going to have lunch in a minute'. Children are much more likely to attend to what we are talking about under these circumstances than if we talk about what will happen when they grow up or what we watched on TV while they were asleep, and their attendance is crucial. It is a prerequisite for working out the possible meaning of the utterance and hence of the words it contains.

But adults might direct children to meaning in more precise and subtle ways than this. The timing of adult utterances has been put forward as an important cue to the child. An early assumption was that simultaneous occurrence of words and what they refer to would afford the child the most straightforward evidence of what the words mean. If the child hears 'That's a tiger' when there is a tiger present, it should be most obvious what 'tiger' refers to. This assumption can be investigated by checking out whether children do acquire words more easily if they are presented in this so-called **ostensive** condition (pointing). It turns out that they do if the words are object labels. An even more effective version of this learning condition is the **joint attention episode**, where the adult's label for an object follows the child's focus on that object, rather than directing the child's attention to a different object. For example, if the adult says 'What a beautiful tiger' when the child is already looking at or playing with a tiger, the child is likely to learn the word more easily than if the adult says 'Come and see this tiger' when the child is playing with an elephant. (See Tomasello & Todd 1983, Tomasello & Farrar 1986, Tomasello & Kruger 1992 for evidence and discussion.)

But not all words are learned best under ostensive conditions where the word is heard and its meaning pointed out at the same time. Evidence is emerging that verbs may be learned more easily in non-ostensive conditions, and that the best conditions for learning verbs may depend on the event to which the verb refers. In an experiment where children were taught a new verb under different timing conditions (Tomasello & Kruger 1992), it was found that the verb was learned better when it was presented *before* the event than at the same time as the event. The novel verb in this experiment was 'plunk', and the novel event was the pushing of a button to make a doll roll down a ramp and into a car or helicopter seat. Children who heard an utterance such as 'Look, Jason, I'll plunk the man' before pushing the button were better able to understand and produce the new verb 'plunk' than children who heard an utterance such as 'Look, Jason, I'm plunking the man' as the doll began to roll down the ramp. From this, we might infer that an utterance heard *before* a noticeable event occurs will alert the child to look for a verb referring to the event.

The timing cue may be more complicated than this, however. Perhaps what is crucial is a combination of the timing of the utterance and what is salient in the scene. If children hear an utterance when an event has been initiated and is happening, they might focus on the event and take little notice of the utterance. Suppose, though, that the event is such that it produces an effect which is still observable following the event. Under these conditions, children might take more notice of an utterance which refers to that event after it is over, when the effect is salient. An investigation into children's learning of two new verbs supported this possibility (Ambalu, Chiat & Pring 1997). Children were presented with a novel event in which the experimenter used an office stamp to print on different types of paper. The novel verb 'bock' was used to refer to this event. Children who heard utterances such as 'Look, I bocked the paper' learned the novel verb 'bock' better than children who heard utterances such as 'Look, I'm going to bock the card'. The same children were also presented with a novel event in which the experimenter spun an object on a spinning wheel, and which was labelled by the novel verb 'pog'. In this case, where the salient feature of the event was the causing of movement rather than the causing of an effect, children who heard the verb before the event ('Look I'm going to pog the ring') learned the novel verb better than those who heard it afterwards ('Look, I pogged the flower').

Who tunes into who?

It seems that variations in the timing of utterances relative to events can make it more or less easy for children to find out the connection between the two. This finding is just one in a rapidly growing jigsaw of findings regarding the cues children exploit to discover the reference of words. The picture which emerges from these findings is that children are doing much more than simply connecting words they hear to what they are currently looking at.

A key piece of evidence is the way they react when they are focused on one novel object, and the speaker focuses on and labels a different novel object (Baldwin 1993). In this situation, children of 1;6–1;7 who heard the speaker use the novel label *peri* took this to refer to the object of the speaker's focus rather than their own: this was the one they selected when they were confronted with both objects and asked to point to the *peri*. This shows that they knew to use the *speaker's* visual focus as a cue to the reference of a novel word the speaker produced.

But children do not use this cue indiscriminately. They can pick up cues that the object the speaker is looking at is *not* the intended focus, and *not* what a word refers to (Tomasello, Strosberg & Akhtar 1996). They did just this in an experiment where they heard the experimenter announce 'Let's find the gazzer', then saw her pick up an object, frown, and reject it, before picking up the intended object with glee. Children of 1;6 learned the word 'gazzer' just as well in this situation as when the experimenter found the target object straightaway. Two-year-olds picked up similar cues that an *action* they observed was not the speaker's intended focus

(Tomasello & Barton 1994). Here, the experimenter announced 'Let's hoist Big Bird', performed an 'accidental' action and said 'Woops', then performed the target action and said 'There'. Again, children recognised that the new verb *hoist* referred to the second action rather than the first. They learned the verb just as well when they had to pass over the first 'accidental' action as when they saw the intended action straightaway. These findings indicate that very young children can use non-verbal expressions of disappointment and glee and verbal expressions such as 'Woops' as cues to a speaker's intended focus.

These studies show children picking up a variety of clues to the speaker's focus of attention. They leave us in no doubt that very young children know a word refers to what the *speaker* is focusing on, regardless of their own focus. They find out the meanings of words by identifying what the speaker is focused on at the time of using them. They will do this most easily if they already share the speaker's focus. This explains why it is easiest for them to learn an object name when they and the speaker are jointly attending to the object. In the absence of such joint attention, it is they who tune into the speaker's attention and thereby find out what the speaker means. (See chapter 14 and Tomasello 1995 for further discussion.)

Filtering speech

Filtering scenes to pick out likely word meanings is not enough to acquire words. Children face the further challenge of picking out speech forms. Words usually occur in a stream of speech rather than in isolation. Children are no more blank tapes registering every aspect of that stream of speech than they are blank screens registering scenes. Again, their earliest words provide evidence of the ways in which they filter the spoken input they meet.

Children do sometimes produce a chunk of words with no indication that they have separated out the words it contains (Peters 1983). These are rather like adult routines such as 'Thank you', 'How do you do', 'Good morning'. The evidence that they are chunks is their rigid use. The child attaches them to a scenario as a whole, never varying the words inside them. This can result in inappropriate use:

Sit my knee (child wanting to sit on adult's knee)
I carry you (child wanting to be carried)   (Clark 1974)

Good girl (said to father as he lays down to sleep)
                              (A. Hirson, personal communication)

But as they break chunks down, which they rapidly do, children prove very adept at segmenting words (Brown 1973). The vast majority of their early words are appropriately segmented. Almost without exception, the forms they produce correspond to the phonology of just one word, no more and no less. Children might hear the form 'tiger' in something like the following contexts:

Look, a tiger
Where's your tiger?
There's a tiger and an elephant

as well as in isolation. This does not lead them to connect *atiger* or *yourtiger* or *tigerand* to the striped creature they pick out. We know that they segment just the chunk 'tiger', since this is the chunk they attempt to produce when they refer to that creature (even if they do not produce it perfectly).

A striking characteristic of children's early words in English is that they are **stress-carrying** words. They are words which hold prominent positions in the rhythm of an utterance and which must contain full vowels, rather than unstressed words whose vowels can reduce (be shortened). They are words like 'teddy', 'car', 'stop', 'broken', 'there', 'mine', 'up', 'off', rather than words like 'a', 'the', 'he', 'at', 'from', 'must' which can be reduced giving [ə], [ðə], [ɪ], [ət], [frəm], [məs]. In addition, these words frequently occur as the last item of a phrase or sentence, or in isolation, as in

That's *mine*
Do you want to get *down?*
Take it *off*
Oh, it's *broken*
There

In these positions, they are most likely to carry the greatest stress in the utterance. So, it looks as if children are initially picking out words which are themselves stressed and which are likely to be the most stressed word in utterances they hear. This opens up the possibility that children are sensitised to stress, and that stress serves as a cue to key phonological units. If they home in on the most prominent part of the utterance, and treat this as the start of a word unit, they will successfully break into the stream of speech and segment their first words.

A variety of empirical evidence supports the inference that stress is a significant cue in children's early speech processing. For example, when children imitate sequences of syllables or words, they tend to imitate selectively, and it is the stressed items which they reproduce (see Chiat 1979 for examples and discussion).

Evidence also comes from the errors children make. When they omit or group syllables incorrectly, this generally involves an unstressed syllable. For example, when children meet words which begin with an unstressed syllable in English, they are prone to produce the word from the stressed syllable onwards, omitting that initial unstressed syllable. This gives rise to familiar childhood forms such as 'mato, 'raffe, 'nana, 'jamas for to'mato, gi'raffe, ba'nana, py'jamas.

Though errors in word segmentation are rare, where they do occur, they appear to involve the attachment of an *unstressed* syllable. In some cases, the child fails to separate out an unstressed syllable which is a separate word and incorrectly treats it as part of a word. For example, a child is observed to use *that a* as a unit, treating 'a' as part of a word which it frequently follows. As a result, 'a' occurs in contexts where it should not:

> That a dog
> That a book
> That a my book
> That a Uncle Clyde
> That a screws   (Brown 1973)

Conversely, an unstressed syllable which *is* part of a word may be treated as separate from it:

> Adult: Behave!
> Child: I am being have

We can be in little doubt that children are biased to notice stress in utterances. But this is just the tip of an iceberg which stands out sufficiently in the child's own speech to be readily noticed by observers. The iceberg is much more than this visible tip. When we look below the surface it becomes apparent that children are able to register whole rhythmic patterns and to discriminate fine differences in rhythmic timing which go well beyond the discrimination of the most prominent element. Such subtle discrimination is necessary to distinguish between single words and groups of words, reflected in contrasts such as:

tomato vs. *to my toe*
agree vs. *a tree*
forget vs. *for good*
idea vs. *I do*
packet vs. *pack it*
bacon roll vs. *they can roll* vs. *steak and roll*

While children are obviously not set the task of sorting out pairs of utterances as similar as these, they *are* required to separate out word units which occur in less prominent positions and rarely in isolation. They rapidly accumulate such words, for example verbs which they will necessarily hear with other constituents:

You *spilled* your juice
I'm *cooking* your dinner
Will you *put* your toys away

and prepositions which they will hear not only with other constituents, but unstressed and often in reduced form:

Your tea's *on* the table
I'm going *to* the shops
Keep away *from* the fire

Research is beginning to produce evidence that children are as finely tuned to rhythmic patterns as they would need to be to grapple with these less salient elements of speech. Ingenious experiments have been carried out to see how very young infants respond to subtle distortions of rhythm. These rely on a **preferential listening technique** which checks whether children prefer to hear speech with normal rhythmic patterns preserved, rather than speech whose rhythm is disrupted. Children's preference is measured by the length of time they focus on loudspeakers producing normal or disrupted rhythms. In this way, it has been shown that children as young as $4\frac{1}{2}$ months prefer speech with pauses at clause boundaries to speech with pauses in the middle of clauses (Jusczyk & Kemler Nelson 1996). By 9 months, they show sensitivity to units within clauses as well, preferring to listen to speech where pauses occur at phrase boundaries rather than within phrases (Jusczyk & Kemler Nelson 1996, Hirsh-Pasek & Golinkoff 1996).

Infants of $7\frac{1}{2}$ months have been found to pick out even smaller units: words. These infants were familiarised with certain words by hearing them repeated, and were subsequently played passages which either did or did not contain the familiarised words. They were found to listen longer to passages which did contain the familiarised words than passages which did not (Jusczyk & Kemler Nelson 1996). The same thing happened when the sequence of presentation was reversed, with words played first in passages and then in isolation. Infants listened longer to words which had occurred in the passages than to those which had not. The indications are that very young infants can pick out rhythmic units, and smaller rhythmic units within these, and can recognise further details within these units.

A complementary finding is that 9-month-old (American) infants listened longer to words which followed the predominant stress pattern of English and began with a stressed syllable than to words which began with an unstressed syllable (Cutler 1996). Six-month-olds did not show this difference. This finding is particularly significant. It indicates that by 9 months infants are sensitive to the stress patterns in their language which they must notice if – as we have suggested – they are to use stress as a cue to word units.

Although the segmentation of words depends crucially on the child, the process may be facilitated by highlighting the cues to which the child tunes in. Studies of adult–child interaction in many (though not all) cultures have found that adults use higher pitch and more marked stress when talking to children. They have also found that children attend more to speech with these characteristics (see Snow 1995 for a review of the evidence). Attendance to speech is clearly a prerequisite to segmenting it. But heightened pitch and stress can aid the segmentation process in more subtle ways. If children use stress as a signpost to word units, magnifying stress differences will magnify the signpost. So, while adults do not actually separate out the words – they do not, for example, pause between words – they seem to extend the cue which children use to separate out words themselves.

Connecting speech and scenes

So far, we have looked at the child's filtering of scenes and of speech as if these were independent of each other. Up to a point, they must be. No amount of information about the structure of the scene could reveal the structure of the speech relating to that scene, and vice versa. This means that the child must have the capacity to interpret each in its own right. It does not mean, though, that the interpretation of each is wholly independent of the other. The child's target is, after all, to discover the connection between the two, rather than to process speech or scenes as ends in themselves. To make these connections, children must have access to *possible* units of speech and *possible* units of meaning. But their search for connections may aid their discovery of what the *actual* units are, through what have commonly come to be known as **bootstrapping** processes. These are processes whereby one type of information acts as a 'bootstrap' which helps children get hold of another type of information.

Children's identification of a particular focus in a scene may lead them to look for a phonological form which accompanies that focus. Suppose, for example, that they have experienced scenes where the focus is a small very cold transparent block which can go in the mouth. This prompts them to search for the common phonological form in utterances such as

Ooh, feel the ice!
Do you want some ice?
The ice is melting
I dropped the ice

Here, we may view the child as using **semantic bootstrapping** to reach for phonology: the picking out of the object helps them to notice the form *ice*. Conversely, children's encounter with an unfamiliar phonological form will alert them to find out what is focused when they hear that form. If they hear the new form in the presence of an object for which they do not yet have a label, they will assume it refers to that object. If, on the other hand, they already have a label for that object, they will assume that the new form refers to something different. This will push them to look for a different aspect of or angle on the object as the meaning behind the form (Clark 1993, 1997). Meeting the forms *mug* or *handle* or *china* in the presence of something they call a *cup* will trigger a search for a different and relevant perspective on cups, and lead them sooner or later to focus on its shape, its parts, what it is made of. When phonology drives a search for meaning, the child is exploiting **phonological bootstraps**.

These bootstrapping processes can only operate if children have a powerful capacity for holding in mind scenes and speech simultaneously. It is only by holding the two simultaneously that shared or distinct speech–scene combinations can be noted. It seems that children are highly sensitised not only to certain aspects of scenes and certain aspects of speech, but *also* to connections between these.

The further we search for cues in the input which guide children's discovery of words, the more we reveal how rich and subtle those cues are, and how finely tuned children must be to pick them up. Children end up as the key players, demonstrating their extraordinary sensitivities. These sensitivities are wide-ranging yet highly specific, targeting: the rhythmic patterns of speech; components of scenes such as entities, events and states; the speaker's focus within the scene; and, crucially, co-occurrences between these: between a focus on a component of a scene, and a unit within a rhythmic pattern.

When adults talk to children, they may heighten the rhythmic contrasts in their speech and so highlight the word units. They may heighten their use of gesture, eye gaze and facial expression and time their utterances in ways which highlight the aspects of scenes focused by their words. By exaggerating the cues to which children are sensitive, they play into those sensitivities. But children cannot attain normal control of words without those sensitivities. This will become increasingly apparent as we explore children's negotiation of different kinds of words.

3 Blocks on the road to words

What of children who are not developing language normally? For such children, words are in some way a problem. They do not come to understand and produce words as rapidly or reliably as their normally developing peers.

Their difficulties may show up in tests of word comprehension such as the British Picture Vocabulary Scales (Dunn, Dunn, Whetton & Pintilie 1982) or Peabody Picture Vocabulary Test (Dunn & Dunn 1981). These tests present the child with a set of pictures from which she must select the one which matches the word that she hears. A child of 5 who makes the number of correct choices typically made by a 3-year-old demonstrates a problem with understanding words. Similarly, a child may perform at a level lower than expected on a test of word production, such as the Word-finding Vocabulary Scale (Renfrew 1980) or Test of Word Finding (German 1986). Some children may be up to the mark on tests of word comprehension and production, but fall down on an assessment of the way they say words, for example on the Edinburgh Articulation Test (Anthony, Bogle, Ingram & McIsaac 1971). They may also score below par on a test such as Wepman's Auditory Discrimination Test (Wepman & Reynolds 1987), in which they have to tell similar-sounding words apart. Shortfalls in any of these formal tests suggest the child has some sort of difficulty with words, and may also suggest what sort of difficulty. (For further examples and details of such clinical assessments, see Lees & Urwin 1997, Stackhouse & Wells 1997.)

Difficulties with words are also revealed in experiments where children are taught new words and subsequently tested on their

33

comprehension or production of the words. Such experiments explore children's ability to form a representation of a word after limited exposure to it, an ability which has come to be known as **fast mapping**. In one such experiment (Rice, Buhr & Nemeth 1990), children were shown a video which incorporated unfamiliar words within a narrative, and then tested for their understanding of the new words. For example, the children heard one story which included the words 'viola' and 'trudge' in utterances such as 'He takes the viola and trudges down the road . . . Billy keeps trudging down the road . . .' After they had watched the video, the new words were presented to them in arrays of four pictures, and they were asked to point to the one named. One of the groups of children tested had been identified as language-delayed. This group came out with lower scores on the comprehension test than a group of younger children who were at a similar level of utterance production (being matched on the average length of their utterances) but were developing language normally. This language-matched group in turn achieved lower scores than a group of children older than them but matched in age to the language-delayed group. Clearly, the language-delayed children had greater difficulty in acquiring the new words than their younger language-matched and their age-matched counterparts.

Reduced speed and scale of word learning in tests or experiments provide some indication of problems with words. There may be other more overt evidence. As they talk, children may show signs of struggling for words. They may stall, or grope for a word, or make repeated attempts at it (see German 1987, German & Simon 1991 on 'word-finding' characteristics). They may resort to a roundabout form of words, a **circumlocution**, to express their meaning. Michael, aged 7, exhibits all these signs of struggling for words in his response to a picture of *handcuffs*:

> key . . . oh what do you call them . . . oh yeah . . . you put . . . you put . . . with your . . . with your . . . oh . . . with your . . . when you . . . when someone's stole something . . . and . . . what do you call them . . . necklace? . . . no . . . I just don't know the word
>
> (Constable, Stackhouse & Wells 1997)

In attempting to produce words, children may make actual errors.

They may substitute a different word, or produce the appropriate word but mispronounce it, or produce an unrecognisable form. Eamonn, Joseph and Ruth provide examples:

Substitution for target

    Eamonn: I got this motor bike, er, motor bike, motor bike.

    SC: A motor bike?

    Eamonn: Motor bike, er, boat.

Mispronunciation of target

    Joseph: [ˈaɪ ɒʔ ə ˈwæsɪʔ ɒʔ ɪʔ ˈaɪz]

    = I got a rabbit but it died

    [ʔəˈʔɒs ʔɪʔ ʔɒʔ ˈʔʌŋʔɪŋ ˈwɒŋ wɪs ɪʔ]

    = Because it got something wrong with it

    [ˈwɛnʔ ɒʔu ˈɛzən]

    = Went up to heaven

Unrecognisable realisation of target

    Ruth: There is [ˈbʌzə] bar.

    SC: Huh?

    Ruth: [ˈmʌzə] bar there.

    SC: Bar?

    Ruth: Yeah me – tal bar.

    SC: Oh, metal bar.

All of these children are clearly attempting to produce words and know something about those words, but are having a problem somewhere along the way. What is stopping them from hitting the target?

Where the blocks may lie

Our consideration of what goes into word learning provides a starting-point for thinking about what might go wrong with it. We are talking about a child who can hear and produce sounds crisply. The problem with words must then lie somewhere beyond hearing and articulation, in the processes which connect these to meaning. We start with a preliminary analysis of what these processes are. We will refine this analysis as we venture into children's processing of different sorts of words.

Input processing

Having heard the input, the child may have difficulties:

- picking out those features of the speech signal which are crucial in segmenting the stream of speech into word units
- storing the sound patterns of words which have been identified
- picking out those aspects of scenes which are crucial to the meanings of words
- mapping sound patterns onto meanings

Problems could arise in just one of these components of processing or in more than one. Where one is necessarily dependent on another, we would expect problems in one to affect the other. For example, a problem in processing the stream of speech must surely affect the establishment of phonological representations. It is hard to see how you could identify the sound patterns of words if you could not process the sound patterns of speech in the first place. We might also expect problems in phonological processing to affect the identification of word meaning, since this involves the mapping of phonology onto aspects of scenes. As we investigate children's difficulties, we will be considering possible interdependencies between different components of processing, and possible effects of one on another.

Figure 3.1 represents components of input processing which may be impaired, and expected or possible relationships between these.

Output processing

It may be that input processing is intact, and problems arise only in output. The child may have difficulties in:

- picking out relevant aspects of scenes
- selecting aspects of scenes corresponding to word semantics
- accessing word phonology corresponding to word semantics
- planning articulation of word phonology

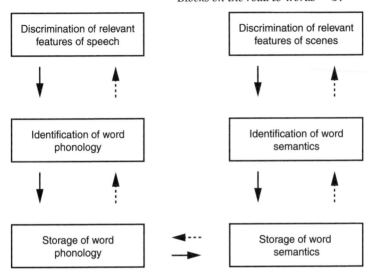

Figure 3.1 Components of input processing

As with input, problems could conceivably arise in one or more of these components, and problems in certain components would be expected to affect others. It is hard to see how you could find the phonology for what you want to say if you cannot work out what you want to say. If you did find word phonology without first selecting word meaning, it could not be the phonology for a meaning you intended. We would therefore expect a problem in selecting word semantics to affect accessing of phonology. But accessing of phonology could be an obstacle even if selection of word meaning is not. You might know what you want to say, but hit problems in finding the phonology to say it. If you did have difficulties in accessing word phonology, we would expect these to disrupt your articulatory planning, since you can only articulate what you have accessed. The reverse effects – such as the effects of difficulties with word phonology on word semantics – are less predictable.

Figure 3.2 represents components of output processing which may be impaired, and expected or possible relationships between these.

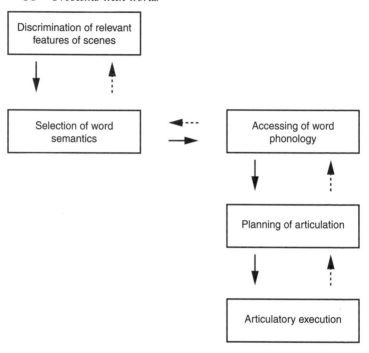

Figure 3.2 Components of output processing

Repercussions for lexical development

The processes we have been considering are **on-line**: they are processes which take place as the child receives an utterance or produces one. Through these on-line processes the child discovers words, stores them, and has them available for her own use. They are therefore necessary stepping stones in the child's acquisition of new words and development of her **mental lexicon**. As the child acquires words, the relationship between on-line processing and the mental lexicon reverses. Instead of processing utterances to get to words, the child can draw on her previously established knowledge of words to process utterances. She can pick out familiar phonological chunks within the utterances she hears, and retrieve the meaning she has already attached to these chunks. She can use her knowledge of words to package her thoughts into word-size meanings, and access the phonology corresponding to these.

Where the stepping stones to words are lacking, there will be repercussions for lexical development. The child who has yet to learn words is in a different position from someone who has already established a mental lexicon when she acquires a deficit in on-line processing, as a result of, say, a stroke. Such a person may have stored information about words despite severe difficulties with recognising words in input or accessing words for output. Not so the word-learning child. (See Chiat, Law & Marshall 1997 for further discussion of differences in the effects of developmental and acquired processing deficits.) As we saw above, if a child has difficulty extracting information from the stream of speech, this will inevitably affect her establishment of word phonology, and may also affect her establishment of word meaning. The representation she stores in her mental lexicon will be correspondingly limited. We may expect the child to learn new words slowly, and even when words make it into her lexicon, we may expect them to be unreliably specified. The limitations in her lexical development will rebound on her on-line processing. She will have less ready-made information about words to help her pick out words from incoming utterances and select words for her own utterances. So we may expect to see a spiral from inadequate on-line processing giving rise to inadequate lexical representations giving rise to inadequate on-line processing.

Depending where a child's problems arise, the repercussions between on-line processing and representations will vary, with varying effects on the child's lexical development. This will become apparent when we look at children whose problems arise at very different points in processing.

4 Exploring the blockage

Thinking about where problems *could* arise begs the question of how we find out where they *do* arise. Not only are there many possible stages at which breakdown may occur. There are also many possible effects of breakdown at one stage on another stage. It is no mean task to identify stages at which breakdown occurs, and disentangle the source of the breakdown from its effects.

Consider the following difficulties exhibited by Eamonn:

1. E: Daddy [fɪɪn] the cat (describing picture of a man feeding a *horse*)
   SC: Who's hungry?
   E: The [k] – the horsie.
2. E: [əju] pick him up, he get [fi nɜəs] (= 'if you pick him up, he gets very nervous', talking about a robot).

The first appears to be a semantic confusion, with Eamonn selecting the word 'cat' which is related in meaning to his target 'horse'. Here we might infer a problem in *semantic* processing. The second appears to be a phonological confusion, with Eamonn producing the forms [fi] and [nɜəs] related to the sound of his targets 'very' and 'nervous'. Here we might infer a problem in *phonological* processing.

However, neither confusion is transparent: both are open to alternative accounts. In the first case, it may be that Eamonn could not access the phonology for 'horse', picked a word close to his intended meaning, and ended up with a different animal name. In the second case, it is conceivable that Eamonn was hazy about the semantics of the words 'very' and 'nervous' and this made his access to phonology precarious. To get below the surface of these sorts of problems with words, we will need tools for digging deeper. The purpose of those tools will be to tap particular stages of processing, separating these out from other stages.

The starting-point for probing a child's difficulties is a hunch. This will not be just any hunch, but a well-informed hunch based on initial observation of the child. The richest source of information at this point is the child's spontaneous output. This can be tapped by obtaining a sample of language the child produces in a naturalistic situation, where he is at ease and talking as he normally does. If any tests of word comprehension or production have been carried out, these may also generate a first hunch.

The key to that hunch is noticing what is or is not all right about the child's words. What sort of words are produced appropriately, and what sort of words are omitted or produced inappropriately? If words are produced inappropriately, which aspects of those words are nevertheless appropriate, and which aspects are responsible for their inappropriateness? The aim at this stage is to identify a possible pattern. First observations may suggest that the child's words are semantically fine, but phonologically distorted. Or the initial impression may be the reverse, that the child's words are phonologically on track but that they are not quite right semantically, or even more strikingly, that they are completely inappropriate for the context. The initial hunch about the area of difficulty will drive further investigation. That investigation will check out whether the hunch is right: whether the child does have a problem with the aspect of words which is suspected. It will go on to explore where that problem arises in input and output processing, and how it might relate to other aspects of the child's processing.

At this point, we need more refined tools of investigation. The tools available to us are a range of techniques for tapping particular aspects of processing. These techniques have endless variations and continue to develop as new questions are posed about children's language processing and novel methods are devised to address these. However, they have certain things in common. They all present the child with some deliberately selected input, such as pictures, or actions, or combinations of speech sounds, or words, or a mix of these. They all elicit a response to that input which may involve producing speech or words; making a judgement of right/wrong or same/different; pointing to a picture; or carrying out an action. What is presented to the child and what is required in response crucially determine what aspect of word processing is being tapped.

Such psycholinguistic investigation starts with and is led by the child. It draws on an understanding of what is involved in language processing in order to focus on and delve into a particular child's comprehension and production of language. The child is not a passive recipient, subjected to a gamut of predetermined psycholinguistic tests. The aim is rather to pursue questions which arise from observations of the child, where it is appropriate to pursue those questions, using activities which are responsive to the general concerns, needs and interests of the child. With these assumptions as a starting-point, we turn to some examples of the tasks which may tap different stages of processing.

From hearing speech to phonology: phonological discrimination tasks

To find out whether children are able to pick out relevant aspects of speech, we need a task which taps just their discrimination of speech, and does not involve knowledge of words. This means asking children to make judgements about speech. Eliciting such judgements might run along the following lines:

> I'm going to say two words, and I want you to tell me whether they sound the *same* or *different*. Here they are . . . *cap – tap*. Do they sound the same or different? . . . Now here are two more. See if they sound the same or different. *tap – tap* . . .

The only way the listener can make this judgement is to notice the sound difference between *tap* and *cap*. You may notice that *tap* and *cap* are different words with different meanings, while *tap* and *tap* are the same word – if your language processing is intact you probably will. This may make the judgement easier. But the point is that you do not need to notice this. You could make the judgement just on the basis of the sound of each pair, and this is something you must anyway do in order to register whether the words are different or the same. It is also what you must do if you are presented with pairs of **non-words** rather than words, as in the following:

> I'm going to say some funny words, and I want you to tell me if they sound the same or different. *tep – kep* . . .

Here, the input consists of phonological forms which you have not met or stored, and which have no meaning. By using non-words in a discrimination task, we can ensure that the judgement is made on the basis of sound only.

Such tasks can be used to check whether a child is able to recognise particular phonological distinctions. The distinctions one chooses to investigate will depend on the initial hunch which motivates the investigation. This may be an observation that the child is not making certain distinctions in his own speech. Suppose that words beginning with /t/ and /k/ both sound as if they begin with /t/ in the child's speech, and words beginning with /f/ and /v/ both sound as if they begin with /b/. In this child's speech, members of word pairs such as *tap* and *cap*, *tea* and *key*, *fit* and *bit*, *vase* and *bars* would sound the same. In this case, the point would be to check whether the child **perceives** the differences he is not making. A discrimination task will check this. Can he tell that *tap/cap*, *tea/key*, *fit/bit*, *vase/bars* sound different?

In this example, certain initial consonants were at stake. A discrimination task can be used to check other aspects of speech suspected to present difficulty, and quite subtle ones. The child may produce particular consonants differently depending where the consonant occurs within the word. For example, he may produce /k/ and /g/ correctly at the ends of words, but not at the beginnings of words. Or he may leave out consonants at the ends of words, but not at the beginnings. If it looks as if the position of a consonant affects the way it is produced, it will be important to control the position of the consonant in the words used in a discrimination task in order to see if this affects discrimination of the consonant as well. We might want to present the child with judgements about consonants in final position as well as initial position:

Discrimination of /k/–/t/ in word-initial position	Discrimination of /k/–/t/ in word-final position	Discrimination of consonant in word-initial position	Discrimination of consonant in word-final position
key–tea	sit–sick	eat–beat	bee–beat
tea–tea	sit–sit	eat–eat	beat–beat

Children may make errors in sequencing consonants, in which case the task could present pairs such as *lost/lots* which differ in this respect.

More unusually, a child may show problems with producing vowels, in which case a discrimination task would present pairs differing in the vowel they contain:

Vowel discrimination
bit–bet
bit–bit
car–core
car–car

Problems may affect whole syllables rather than just sound segments. In this case a discrimination task could present pairs differing by a whole syllable:

Discrimination of syllable structure
but–button
win–window

All these examples illustrate how discrimination tasks may be used to find out whether problems in producing speech are due to problems in picking out the relevant features of speech. This means checking out discrimination of not just any speech distinctions, but the particular distinctions which are affected in the child's output.

On the other hand, initial observations of a child's speech may point to difficulties with word phonology but not with any specific phonological distinctions. We would still want to know if the child's errors in production may be related to his discrimination of speech. The most revealing way of checking this would be to feed back the child's own incorrect forms paired up with the correct forms to see if the child can discriminate these.

What can such discrimination tasks tell us? If the child *is* able to make the judgement, a great deal. It is only possible to differentiate 'same' pairs from 'different' pairs if you can discriminate the feature which distinguishes these. So, if the child can judge *cap–tap* and *kep–tep* to be different, and *tap–tap* and *kep–kep* to be the same, he must have the /t/–/k/ distinction at least in initial position within words.

But suppose the child does not make correct judgements, responding randomly to all pairs, or always giving the same response whether the pairs match or not. Can we conclude that the child is unable to discriminate between the relevant sounds? Not necessarily. Any discrimination task involves more than just phonological discrimination. For example, it entails an understanding of the task itself, which means understanding what is meant by 'same' and 'different'. It entails a willingness to listen to the input, and to attempt a judgement. These demands are taxing for children under about 4. So, if the child appears to 'fail' at the task, this could be due to these other requirements. He may lack the same/different concepts. Or he may simply hate the task and refuse to co-operate. In either case, we have no further information about the child's phonological discrimination.

This brings out a general point about the use of tasks designed to tap a specific aspect of language processing. If someone *succeeds* on these tasks, we can be sure that they can process the relevant distinction. They could not respond reliably unless they appreciated the specific aspect of language they are being required to process. If, on the other hand, someone does not respond reliably, we cannot draw firm conclusions. All tasks involve more than just the language processing under investigation, and other 'task variables' may be responsible for the person's difficulty with the task.

We must therefore be cautious about interpreting 'failure' on a task such as discrimination. We need to explore further what may lie behind the child's responses. Here, the key will be any *pattern* in the child's responses: any evidence that the child can do the task in some cases but not in others. Suppose, for example, that the child can make reliable judgements on /p/–/k/ pairs but not on /t/–/k/ pairs:

/p/–/k/: judged correctly	*/t/–/k/: judged incorrectly*
pat–cat	*tap–cap*
pea–key	*tea–key*
pes–kes	*tep–kep*

This would be proof enough that the child understands the task, including the concepts 'same/different', and that he can discriminate certain speech differences. We could then infer that there *is* a specific problem with discriminating /t/–/k/. In the absence of such evidence, it may be important to establish that the child *can* make same/different judgements using input of a different kind. For example, if we can establish that a child can make a same/different judgement about visual stimuli such as shapes and sizes, we at least know that the concepts 'same/different' are understood.

From phonological discrimination to word phonology: lexical decision tasks

This detailed introduction to discrimination tasks sets the scene for tasks tapping other stages of processing.

Once relevant features of speech are discriminated, the child must pick out and store the chunks of these features which constitute words. How can we check whether the child is storing words appropriately? One way to go about this is to see if the child can decide whether a string of sounds is a word or not, using what is known as a **lexical decision** task. Here, the child is presented with phonological forms, some of which are words, and some not. The child must indicate whether these forms sound right or not. One way of eliciting such a judgement is with the help of a puppet:

> I've got a puppet. Looks like a clown, doesn't he . . . This clown is having a bit of a problem. Sometimes he says words and they sound right. But sometimes they sound silly. I wonder if you can help him. Can you tell him when he says something right and when he says something funny? . . .

Alternatively, the child's interest might be engaged by inviting him to judge the speaker:

> I'm going to say some words now. Sometimes I'll get them right, but sometimes I'll get them wrong. When I get them right you can give me a tick, and when I get them wrong you can give me a cross. Then at the end we can see how many I got right . . .

The materials used in the task would be determined by the observations of the child which motivated the task. Suppose the child is producing incorrect forms of words, and we want to check whether he has stored the forms correctly. The ideal check is to feed back the child's own 'errors' to see if he can recognise them as such, and distinguish them from the appropriate forms. For example, a child who was producing /k/ and /g/ at the beginning of words as [t] and [d] might be presented with the correct forms and the incorrect forms:

Words	*Non-words*
card	tard
carrot	tarrot
carpet	tarpet
girl	dirl
garden	darden

Another child may produce variable and more distorted forms for a word. With such a child, we might feed back all these forms along with the target word in a lexical decision task.

A rather different case for using a lexical decision task would be with a child who is producing correct forms of words, but whose range of words is unusually limited. We may want to find out whether the child recognises a wider range of word forms than he is using. This could be done by presenting the child with words and non-words, to see how much the child knows about the phonology of words.

This is precisely what a lexical decision task is getting at. It need not involve the meaning of words at all. If you do know the meanings of the words in a lexical decision task, this may help you to recognise and 'approve' them as words. But the lexical decision task does not require this. The minimum you have to do is to discriminate the phonological forms and compare them with phonological forms you have stored. Suppose a child can make lexical judgements reliably, accepting the words and rejecting the non-words. We can then be sure that the child has discriminated and stored the phonological form of the words correctly. If the child can reject non-words such as *tarrot* and *darden* which we hear him produce, then he must have not only noticed the difference between /t/ and /k/ and between /d/ and /g/, but also stored the words 'carrot' and 'garden' with the correct initial consonant.

What if the child cannot make reliable judgements? As we saw with discrimination tasks, apparent 'failure' is not clear-cut. There are many reasons why a child may have difficulty with this task. A problem with storage of word forms is just one possible reason. The child may actually have the correct forms stored, and still make errors in lexical decision. The task is, after all, very taxing in other ways. In order to accomplish the judgement, the child must have grasped the notion of something 'sounding right'. He must hold onto the form he has heard (e.g. *carrot*) and must check to see whether he has this form in his mental lexicon. A tall order. One would not expect a child under 4 to cope with these demands. Even at a later age, we would need to consider whether the child was having difficulty with the task demands rather than the words themselves. Again, a *pattern* of response would be the key. For example, suppose we can show that the child *is* able to reject non-words except where the difference from a word involves /k/ or /g/. This suggests that the child has grasped the concept of judgement, and that he has correctly represented most sounds in words. We then have stronger evidence that there *is* a problem in the storage of words with /k/ and /g/ – assuming that we already know the difficulty is not due to discrimination.

The lexical decision task may be easier for the child if meaning is brought into the picture, and the judgement is not a purely phonological one. Instead of just asking the child to judge whether a form sounds right, you present him with a picture of the target word and ask him to judge whether a form is right for the picture:

Is this a carrot?
vs.
Is this a tarrot?

The presence of the picture may provide a more meaningful context for making phonological judgements. Instead of just judging the sound of the word the child must think if it sounds like the word for that picture. Yet the task still requires a phonological judgement. If the child is able to make consistent judgements that *carrot* is right for the picture but *tarrot* is not, we can be sure the forms are correctly stored.

However, because the task asks the child to make a phonological judgement in relation to a picture, any problem in responding could be due to the picture and its meaning rather than the phonology. For a start, the child may be distracted by the semantics. He may look at the picture, recognise the vegetable, and decide that *tarrot* is clearly aiming for the right word semantically and so accept it as appropriate, even though it doesn't sound exactly right. Or the picture may be more than a distraction from the phonology. It may itself present a problem. Suppose the child's difficulties lie in semantics, or the connection between semantics and phonology. Such a child may have difficulty deciding whether *carrot* or *tarrot* are right for the picture, even if he knows that *carrot* is a word while *tarrot* is not. This knowledge might show up on a purely phonological judgement task, and be obscured once meaning is introduced.

From phonology to semantics: word-to-picture matching tasks

Making the leap from phonology to semantics might be seen as the key stage of word processing. The main function of words, after all, is to act as a vehicle for conveying a meaning. Not surprisingly, this is the aspect of word processing that's focused in traditional approaches to children's problems with words. It is also the aspect that's targeted in traditional methods for assessing children's word processing: picture-pointing tasks. In such tasks, the child is presented with a set of pictures and asked to point to one of them. For example, given pictures of a bear, spoon and dress, he might be asked to 'show me the bear'. Here, the child must discriminate the phonology of *bear*, recognise it, and connect it to the appropriate animal. What will we find out about the child's processing from this traditional sort of assessment?

This will depend crucially on the content of the task. If we present the child with a random set of pictures to choose from, the task will not tell us much. On the one hand, it involves all aspects of input processing, from phonological discrimination to meaning. On the other hand, that processing need not be very precise. Since *bear* sounds nothing like *spoon* or *dress*, you could pick out the right picture even if you registered its phonology only loosely. Similarly, since 'spoon' and 'dress' belong to quite different semantic categories, if you knew nothing more about 'bear' than that it was an animal, you could pick out the right picture.

But suppose the selection of pictures is more calculated. Suppose the pictures include one which is phonologically similar to the target, such as *pear*, which acts as a **phonological distractor**. The child must then discriminate the phonology quite precisely if he is to pick the pear rather than the bear picture. Similarly, the pictures might include a **semantic distractor** which is semantically related to the target, for example a picture of a wolf. This ups the semantic stakes for the child: his semantic information about 'bear' must be precise enough to rule out other animals. Where both phonological and semantic distractors are combined with the target, the child must have phonological and semantic information well specified if he is to home in on the correct picture.

So, with careful selection of the pictures, a picture-pointing task can reveal just what a child knows about the phonology and semantics of the target words. If the child is consistently able to pick the right picture, we can be sure he has at least the phonological and semantic information about the target word needed to distinguish it from the phonological and semantic distractors. If he sometimes picks the phonological distractor, but not the semantic one, this would suggest some difficulty with phonological processing. We could follow this up by looking at his phonological discrimination and representation in more detail. If he sometimes picks the semantic distractor, but not the phonological one, we might infer that his semantic representations are not fully specified, and follow this up by looking at his semantics more closely.

From perception of the world to semantics: picture-sorting tasks

One means of tapping semantics, as we have seen, is a word-to-picture matching task with semantic distractors. This necessarily taps semantics via phonology. If the child has a problem with the recognition of a word's phonology, this could block access to its semantics even if the semantics would not itself be a problem. How can we tap the child's semantic categories without involving phonology?

One way would be to rely entirely on visual materials, and to ask the child to do something which involves picking out some aspect of the visual materials but not saying anything about them. We could, for example, elicit judgements about the relationship between a set of pictures. The pictures would represent meanings which were or were not related in particular ways. For example, we might want to know if the child categorises objects in semantically relevant ways, that is, in ways which correspond to words. Does the child group together different items which would be identified by the same word? We could check this by presenting the child with sets of pictures to decide which ones went together, or which one was the odd one out. Each set of pictures would represent distinct examples of the item along with an item which was different (even if it looked quite similar):

Sets of pictures could be selected to tap all manner of distinctions, from distinctions between different members of a general category such as clothes:

to distinctions between members of different 'general level' categories such as vehicles and buildings:

They might represent properties such as shape, or colour, or temperature, or emotion:

This sort of task could even be used to look at the categorisation of events. The child might be presented with a picture of one event, then given pictures of two more events to choose the one which matches the first event:

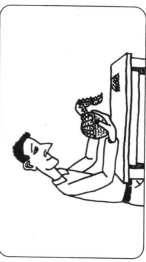

First published in J. Marshall, S. Chiat & T. Pring, 'Event Perception Test', in Marshall et al. 1999.

(see Marshall, Pring & Chiat 1993, Marshall et al. 1999 for further explanation and examples). Or the task might look at the child's recognition of what sorts of things are involved in different events. You might present him with a picture of an event, such as cutting, and a set of pictures of objects which can or can't participate in the event, such as paper, cloth, bread, pencil, iron, milk.

An alternative to picture materials is **acting out**. This is particularly appropriate for investigating semantic aspects of events, to see if the child is picking out those aspects of events which are encoded by words. Because events are dynamic and occur over time, their features are more easily picked out from a dynamic representation, such as an acted-out scene, than from a still picture. Imagine, for example, representing a girl pushing a car. If this event is acted out, the girl's pressure on the car and the car's movement are directly observable. In the case of a still picture, on the other hand, the action and movement must be inferred.

Now, suppose we act out an event in front of the child or show the child a video of the event, and then ask the child to do the same thing. For example, we might show events involving movement in different manners, such as rolling/spinning/throwing a stick, or in different directions, such as pushing/pulling a car, dropping/lifting a book. We could then give the child a different object from the one used in the modelled event, and ask him to do the same thing. Will he act out the event with the same manner or direction even though the object is different, spinning a ball if the model was spinning a stick, pushing a box if the model was pushing a car? We might want to check other aspects of events such as their effects. If we model events which produce different results, such as opening and closing a box, or emptying and filling a jug, and give the child different objects to carry out the same action, such as a bottle or a drawer to open or close or fill or empty, will he produce the same result? If he does act out the relevant manner or direction or result, he must have noticed those aspects of events which differentiate verbs from each other and so are semantically relevant. But if he doesn't? Can we infer that the child is not picking out relevant aspects of events? Not necessarily.

Yet again, if the child does pick out features which distinguish different verbs, for example manner or direction or effect of movement, we can infer that the child has noticed those features. But if the child responds differently, this doesn't necessarily mean that the child is oblivious to those features. It may be that he has based his response on a different criterion from the one we have focused on. He may sort pictures according to which things or events look most similar, or which might occur at the same time or in the same place. These similarities may override knowledge of other shared properties which the child nevertheless possesses. The task should therefore be seen as an exploration of *how* the child groups representations of things or events, rather than a test of semantic knowledge about those things or events. We would be looking to find patterns in the child's responses – for example preferences for certain sorts of features in grouping pictures or actions – rather than scoring them as right or wrong.

As with other tasks, the child's response will depend on his understanding of the task as well as his ability to process the distinctions it focuses. We may well use such tasks with a child whose semantics cannot be tapped through phonology because he is known to have problems with phonological input. But his problems with phonological input will make it difficult if not impossible to explain the task verbally. In this case, we may have to present the task non-verbally, by giving the child examples of how pictures might be grouped. We would then be relying on the child 'getting the idea' of grouping the pictures and attempting to group them in his own way.

From lexical semantics to lexical phonology: internal judgement tasks and cued naming

Suppose we know that a child's processing of words in input is fine. The child has no problem understanding words, so must have discriminated and recognised their phonology and matched their phonology to semantics. Yet he has problems producing words. Where does the difficulty arise? Is it in accessing the phonology of the word for output? Or is the word accessed appropriately, with difficulties arising in its articulatory production?

One of the toughest challenges for the psycholinguist is to tap the child's *accessing* of words separately from his saying of words.

This separation is necessary if we are to find out whether the phonology he has in his head is different from the phonology he produces. Imagine a child who, presented with a picture of a cap, can't name it, or names it as *tap*. In either case, he may actually have the form *cap* in mind. How can we find out what he has in mind without asking him to say it?

With some ingenuity, it is possible to probe the sounds in the child's mind. The relevant tasks are quite challenging for the child: they require the child to make **internal judgements** about sound rather than produce it. By way of illustration, take the following materials:

(a)

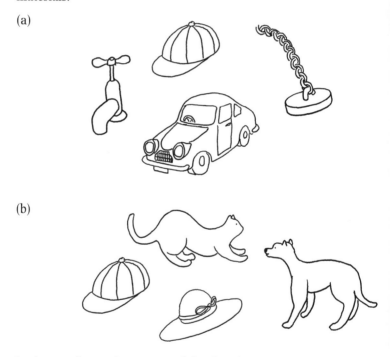

(b)

Look at each set of pictures and decide which two begin with the same sound. Now decide which two rhyme with each other. Now consider how you arrived at your decisions. You were presented with purely visual materials, no words. You had to recognise the objects in the pictures to select the semantic target. You had to match that semantic target to a phonological representation – /kæp/, /tæp/, /kɒ/, /plʌg/, /kæt/, /kæp/, /hæt/, /dɒg/. Then you had to hold the phonological representations in your head and compare them to see which shared the relevant phonological feature – the initial sound, or the rhyme. So, in order to make the judgement, you had to access the word phonology, but you did not have to speak it.

A phonological judgment task like this may be carried out in a variety of ways. One of the simplest would be to present just two pictures, and ask for a yes/no judgement. Do the following pairs rhyme?

(a)

(b)

Do the following pairs begin with the same sound?

(a)

(b)

Here, the child must hold just two words in mind. Another way of reducing the load on the child is to present one picture at a time, and ask the child to make a judgement about just that picture. You might give the child a heap of pictures illustrating words beginning with /k/ or /t/, and ask the child to post each picture into either a [k]-box or a [t]-box. In this case, the child has only to hold the phonology for one picture, and compare it with the two target sounds. More demanding is a task which presents more pictures, and includes distractors as in the *cap, tap, car, plug* set. This included a **phonological distractor** picture whose name was phonologically similar to one of the target pair; and a **semantic distractor** picture which was semantically similar to one of the target pair.

Whatever the particular mode of presentation, this sort of task involves an internal judgement about word phonology. If the child is able to make the judgement reliably, we can be sure that he is accessing the particular aspect of word phonology to be judged – the initial sound or the rhyme of the words. But if the child responds randomly? As usual, we must think again.

This task is particularly taxing. It requires the accessing of word phonology, but it requires a good deal more than this. Suppose we have asked the child to say whether a 'cap' picture rhymes with a 'tap' picture. First of all, the child must interpret the pictures as we intend – if the child sees the cap as a hat he is already out of the running. Once he has the appropriate semantic targets, he must access the correct forms *cap* and *tap*. But that is not all. He must then hold onto *cap* and *tap*, and pick out the rhyme part of each in order to compare them. So even if the child has accessed *cap* and *tap* he may make a wrong judgement for other reasons. He may be unable to hold onto the two forms to compare them. Or he may not understand or recognise rhyme, and so be unable to see the similarity between the words.

To some extent, we can check out these components of the task independently, and we should do so before using it. After all, there is no point doing an internal rhyme judgement if the child does not understand rhyme. But if we have checked that the child recognises rhyme when we *say* pairs of words such as *cap/tap, cap/car*, we know he has the concept of 'rhyme'. We can then rule this out as the source of difficulty with an internal judgement task. However, other difficulties with the task may still account for the child's responses. It may be that he simply doesn't understand what he's supposed to be trying to do. After all, making a judgement about sounds corresponding to pictures is a pretty obscure and demanding activity.

In some cases, there may be no need to resort to such devious methods in order to probe what is in the child's mind. We may be able to elicit evidence more directly. Returning to the scenario of the child who is presented with a picture of a cap and cannot name it, or struggles to do so, we might see whether we can prompt the child to produce the word with **cued naming**. Suppose we give the child a **phonological cue**. We may try just the initial consonant of the target: '[kə-]?'. If this makes no difference, we may extend the cue to the initial consonant + vowel: '[kæ-]?'. Where the target is more than one syllable, we may offer more. With a word such as *candle*, the cue may be gradually increased from initial consonant [kə] to initial consonant + vowel [kæ] to initial syllable [kæn]. The question will be whether, and at what point, the child succeeds in producing the word. Success implies that the child *does* have access to the word form and *can* produce it. But gaining that access is difficult. The amount of cuing the child requires will indicate just how difficult.

If cuing makes no difference to the child's output, this may be because the child has nothing to cue: he has no further information about the word. But it may also be because accessing information about the word is not the problem anyway. The barrier to producing the word lies elsewhere.

From phonological input to phonological output: repetition tasks

Internal judgement tasks separate out the accessing of word phonology from the articulation of the word. They provide a roundabout way of getting at a child's phonological representation of a word without the child having to articulate it. How can we do the reverse? How can we tap children's articulation of words without them having to access the phonology of the word first?

Repetition tasks fit this bill. Again, puppets can help to introduce the task:

> So, we've each got a puppet. My puppet is going to say a word and I want to see if your puppet can say the same thing. Let's see if your puppet can say *dog*.

Here, the child is given the word form, so he does not have to access it. All he has to do is discriminate the phonology of *dog*, hold it, and plan its articulation. If the word is familiar, he will inevitably recognise the phonology and access the semantics. Assuming he recognises the form *dog* and has it connected to the category 'canine creature' this information will surface when he is asked to say *dog*. But it is not required. If the child's phonological processing is intact in both input and output, it will be possible to repeat *dog* without recognising its form or meaning. The test case for this is repetition of non-words:

> Now my puppet is going to say some funny words. See if your puppet can say them. *deg* . . .

In repeating a form such as *deg*, which is not a word, the child will have to rely on purely phonological processing. (See Gathercole, Willis, Baddeley & Emslie 1994 for their *Children's Test of Nonword Repetition* which includes non-words of 2–5 syllables.)

So, if a child has shown difficulties in producing words, repetition allows us to check whether this difficulty is due to problems in articulatory planning. We can ask the child to repeat words which he has produced incorrectly himself. Or we can select words or create non-words to check out articulation of particular phonological targets. For example, if we suspect the child has difficulty with planning articulation of /s/ *before* a stressed vowel but not *after* a stressed vowel, we might ask the child to repeat words and non-words with /s/ in both positions:

/s/ *before stressed vowel*	/s/ *after stressed vowel*
sea	horse
sock	face
seven	castle
sandal	message
decide	listen
cassette	basin

Then we could do the same thing with non-words:

/s/ *before stressed vowel*		/s/ *after stressed vowel*	
['sɒ]	sah	['lɔs]	lorse
['sæb]	sab	['veɪs]	vace
['sɛfəl]	sefal	['tɒsəm]	tahsem
['sæmpən]	sampen	['nɛsət]	nesset
[gɪ'saɪt]	gissite	['rɪsəl]	rissel
[tə'sɛp]	tessepp	['geɪsɪl]	gayssil

The implications of this task? Where the child repeats the target appropriately, we can be sure that he has no problem in its articulatory planning and execution. Where his repetition differs from the target we need to think further. First, we need to establish that the child understands the task. With a repetition task, this should be obvious. If the child is attempting to repeat the words, he clearly does. In this case, we might need to go back to input processing and consider whether this is responsible for difficulties in repetition. If the child is falling down in discrimination of sounds, this will inevitably affect repetition. But if we know that the child's discrimination is adequate, we have to focus on his output and dig deeper. What we'll be digging for is patterns in the child's repetitions – contexts where the child can repeat correctly versus contexts where he can't.

Suppose the child given the above words with /s/ behaves as expected, repeating /s/ correctly only in words and non-words where it follows a stressed vowel. This implies that the child does have difficulty with articulating [s], but only when it occurs before a stressed vowel.

Or suppose that the child repeats non-words correctly, but not real words. His correct production of the non-words shows that he can discriminate and produce the sounds in these words. So the problem with the real words must be something to do with their being stored. This suggests that the child has faulty representations of the words, and is using these faulty representations when he repeats them. The problem does not arise with non-words because they are not stored.

So, with an astute search for factors which influence the child's repetition, guiding an astute selection of targets to repeat, we can make inroads into the source of a child's difficulties in producing word phonology.

Reviewing psycholinguistic tasks

Setting out from questions about the difficulties children may have in processing words has opened up many possible paths of investigation. We have seen how tasks or activities may present particular aspects of words to which children are asked to respond in particular ways. They may present word meanings (represented as pictures or acted out) or word forms. The child may be asked to make a same/different or right/wrong judgement about the stimuli; or to group those which are similar or pick out one which is different; or to copy one. The nature of the stimuli we present and the response we elicit – whether we present pictures to judge or phonological forms to repeat or phonological forms to judge – will determine which aspect of input or output processing we are tapping. The selection of stimuli will determine how finely we tap the child's processing. If the selection of stimuli to be judged or grouped includes distractors which are very distinct from the targets, the skills required by the task will be limited. If, on the other hand, the stimuli include distractors which are similar to the targets in some way, the task will require more refined skills. In working with a child, we will be designing tasks to suit the level and detail of processing we are aiming to tap. This will depend on our previous observations of the child, and the psycholinguistic hunches we derive from our observations.

These psycholinguistic tasks should be regarded as a means of exploring, rather than testing, the child's processing. With each task, we have seen that the child's responses will be open to different interpretations, and will not necessarily lead to definitive conclusions. In general, if children 'succeed' in a task, we can infer that they are able to carry out the aspect of processing that task taps. This conclusion will only be justified, though, if we have given the child enough examples to be sure that the responses are *reliably* correct, and not just correct by chance. In informal exploration with a child, we may not have enough examples to be sure.

In this case, any conclusions must be tentative, and must continue to be checked out, perhaps in different ways.

If children have difficulties with a task, we cannot draw conclusions directly. We have to think about what is involved in the task, and might be responsible for the child's difficulties with it. This might lead us along new paths of inquiry. We might check out whether the child can carry out the same type of task with a different type of materials, or with less demanding materials. Or we might generate a new hunch about the child's difficulties and a fresh line of investigation.

In any case, psycholinguistic tasks should not be viewed in isolation. Comparison between tasks is crucial. Where we find better performance on one task relative to another, we can make inferences about what is a problem and what is not. Where different tasks give rise to the same inferences, we can be more confident that we are on the right tracks.

The tasks presented here are by no means exhaustive. They simply illustrate psycholinguistic methodology using unsophisticated and readily available materials and activities. There is no end to the properties of words which may be investigated, and the methods for investigating them. Different insights into the properties of words, semantic, phonological and syntactic, open our eyes to different aspects of words to be investigated. Different technologies open up all sorts of possibilities for presenting materials and responding to them. Videos and computers, for example, can be harnessed for interesting presentation of visual or auditory input. They also offer different modes of response, such as pressing a button or moving a curser. The psycholinguistic logic will be the same: we will still be starting from the processes we are aiming to tap, devising a task which calls on those processes, and analysing the child's pattern of response to the task. The possibilities for pursuing this logic are myriad once the psycholinguistic imagination is stirred.

All the way along, the psycholinguistic journey will be directed by the child. The goal is *not* to carry out every psycholinguistic task one can think of, or to carry out a task for the sake of it. The goal is to explore, with the child, what he can and can't do with words, and what he might yet be able to do.

5 'Dant always day dings': problems with phonology

Listening to some children for the first time is a bit like trying to see when you've just moved from bright sunlight into an unlit room. When they talk, you hear a stream of speech in which it's difficult to find any familiar, meaningful forms. But gradually, with further exposure, the flow begins to take shape. Words begin to step out, and as you differentiate them, you find you can recognise and understand what the child is saying.

Stephen is a chatty 5-year-old. Presented with a bunch of miniature toys, his play is inventive and he keeps up a running commentary with utterances such as

[a 'dɒʔ wʌn əz 'ðiz bʌʔ ɪʔs 'nɒʔ ə 'daɪgə ɪʔs ə 'laɪjən]
I got one of these but it's not a tiger it's a lion

['wɒʔ ə ðiz 'dɔld ə'dɛn]
What are these called again?

[ɪ 'dɒ̃ʔ 'dɛd ə 'deɪsɪz ɒn]
He can't get the cases on

With a bit of exposure, the listener has no difficulty recognising that

[dɒʔ] = got
['daɪgə] = tiger
[dɔld] = called
[ə'dɛn] = again
[dɒ̃ʔ] = can't
[dɛd] = get
['deɪsɪz] = cases

66

Joseph, like Stephen, has normal 5-year-old conversations as he plays with miniatures or beats you hands down in a computer game. His utterances are even more opaque:

['aɪ ɒʔ ə 'wæsɪʔ ɒʔ ɪʔ 'aɪz]
I got a rabbit but it died

[ən aɪ 'ʌlər ɪʔ 'ɪn 'ɜrs]
Can I colour it in first?

Yet even his utterances gradually take shape for the listener, revealing that

[ɒʔ] = got
['wæsɪʔ] = rabbit
[aɪz] = died
[ən] = can
[ɜrs] = first

How is it that you come to pick out shapes which you could not pick out before? Somehow, you have adjusted to what is blurred in the child's speech, and you can get through that blur to recognise words. This is only possible because the child's blurring of sounds follows certain patterns. The child is not producing words in random ways. What we find is that there is a systematic relationship between the word forms produced by the child and the form of those words in adult English. Once the listener unconsciously recognises that relationship, she can adjust to the child's system and can, in most cases, translate each of the child's word forms into corresponding adult word forms. Where there is more than one possible correspondence between child and adult forms, context will usually eliminate all but one of the alternative adult forms. There will be instances where a word remains unidentifiable, leaving the listener in the dark. But in general, initially unintelligible children like Stephen and Joseph become unexpectedly coherent.

To illustrate the point, consider first the small sample of speech from Stephen. He appears to have difficulties with certain sounds of adult English which he pronounces inappropriately at least some of the time. /k/ and /g/ are often realised as [d]:

cases ['deɪsɪz]
again [ə'dɛn]

Once we have been exposed to a number of words in his speech which show this connection to adult speech, we adjust to the possibility that Stephen's production of [d] may be targeting /d/, /k/, /g/ and also /t/, and we select the one which yields a word appropriate to the context. So, when we hear [dɒʔ] in the above sample, we are open to the possibilities *dot, tot, cot, got,* and we go for the only one of these which is an English word fitting the context, in this case, *got.*

The listener's adjustment to the child's speech will depend partly on how closely it corresponds to adult forms. The more distinctions a child makes in her speech, and the closer those distinctions are to adult speech, the easier it will be to adjust. Stephen, for example, is easier to follow than Joseph. This is because there are many more speech sounds which Joseph fails to produce. In the sample above, the only consonants which he *does* produce are [s], [z], [m], [n], [w], [r], [l], [ʔ]. Where other consonants are required, he either omits them altogether or he pronounces them as [s] or [z]:

died [aɪz]
rabbit ['wæsɪʔ]
colour ['ʌlər]

Yet even in Joseph's case, the listener can often work out which consonant would yield the most appropriate word for the context, and so identify the words which he is targeting. Even though [ɒʔ] could be, for example, *pot, tot, dot, cot, got, shot, jot,* we are rapidly able to home in on *got* in the above sample.

It is only possible for us to do this because the child's output is perfectly appropriate in other respects. For a start, most aspects of the child's words are fine. Even phonologically, his words preserve much of their adult targets. They almost always have the same number of syllables and the same stress pattern. Their vowels are virtually always correct. Note, for example, the correct number of syllables, stress and vowels in Stephen's *tiger* and *again,* and Joseph's *rabbit* and *colour.* Distorted as their speech might at first appear, we find that it is only certain consonants that are systematically affected.

The fact that important aspects of word phonology are unimpaired is partly what enables us to identify the words the child is targeting. For the rest, we rely on context. We can do this just because the child's words are syntactically and semantically appropriate. Syntactically, the combinations in which they occur are normal, with words virtually never omitted or misplaced. Semantically, they convey meanings which are compatible with each other and make sense. We might also note that the child's combinations of words have appropriate rhythmic patterns. For example Joseph's utterance

[ən aɪ 'ʌlər ɪʔ 'ɪn 'ɜrs]
Can I 'colour it 'in 'first?

has stress on the words 'colour', 'in' and 'first', leaving 'can', 'I' and 'it' unstressed as we would expect them to be, with the vowel /æ/ of 'can' reduced to [ə] in its weak form.

Phonological problems

We have narrowed down Stephen's and Joseph's difficulties to the area of phonology, rather than syntax or semantics. We have further narrowed it down to the phonology of words. Even more specifically, we have identified consonants in words as the culprits, these being vulnerable to substitution or omission. Such a problem has come to be described as a **phonological problem**. The problem is so described for two key reasons which are connected to each other.

The first is that it is the child's **phonology** – her sound system – which is affected. This means that sounds are not randomly omitted or replaced. Rather, it is certain *classes of sound* within the sound system of the language which are affected. They are replaced with related sounds or omitted. This results in a smaller range of sounds and sound contrasts, at least in some places in words. The sort of substitutions and omissions which occur have come to be described as **phonological processes**. These are processes which affect target consonants in particular ways. For example, we have seen that Stephen often realises targets /k/ and /g/ inappropriately. These sounds of adult English share certain characteristics: they are both produced by forming a closure between the back of the tongue and the soft palate, or velum, so that the air flow through the mouth is momentarily blocked. This means they have the same **place of articulation** in the mouth. Stephen, however, replaces /k/ and /g/ with a sound which is made by forming a closure further forward in his mouth, between the front of the tongue and a point in the hard palate known as the alveolar ridge: a sound which we hear as [d]. Thus, he has shifted the place of articulation of the target. This not unusual substitution is captured by a phonological process known as **fronting**, whereby velar /k/ and /g/ are fronted to [t] or [d].

Producing the sounds [t], [d], [k], [g] involves a complete closure in the mouth, a characteristic also shared by the sounds [p] and [b]. This means they have the same **manner of articulation**. The set of sounds produced in this manner are known as **stops**. They contrast with another set of sounds where the lower lip or the tongue moves towards the upper lip or palate without forming a complete closure. Here, the airflow through the mouth is partially but not completely obstructed, causing friction. Sounds produced in this manner are known as **fricatives**. In English they include [f], [v], [θ], [ð], [s], [z], [ʃ], [ʒ]. These sounds share their manner of articulation with each other, but vary in their place of articulation. Some children have difficulty with fricatives, and replace them with stops. This alters the manner of articulation of the target. Karl exemplifies this in the words *share, for, some* which he pronounces as *dare, bor, dum*:

Karl: (playing with a box of keys)

[aɪ 'dɒə 'dɛəwəm 'dʊʔ]
I gotta share them out

['wʌm bɔ 'mi] ['wʌm bɔ 'ju]
One for me   One for you

['aɪm 'dɪɪn 'ju dʌm]
I'm giving you some

This substitution is described by the process of **stopping**. Typically, when Karl targets a fricative, he uses the stop which is produced at the same or nearest place in the mouth. He replaces /s/, an alveolar fricative, with [d], an alveolar stop. And he replaces /f/, a fricative involving the lower lip and upper teeth (**labio-dental**), with [b], a stop involving both lips (**bilabial**). As well as stopping, Karl shows the fronting process we met in Stephen, so that /g/ in *giving* is realised as [d].

The class of fricatives and stops divide into pairs of sounds which share their **place** and **manner** of articulation, but which differ according to whether the vocal cords vibrate during the closure to produce what is known as **voice**. /d/, /g/, /v/, /z/, for example, are voiced. Their voiceless counterparts are /t/, /k/, /f/, /s/. Both Stephen and Karl show difficulty with this voicing contrast. They both exhibit a process known as **voicing**, whereby voiceless stop targets are voiced. So, Stephen not only fronts /k/, which would result in [t]; he also voices it, resulting in [d], so that the word *cases* sounds like *dases*. Karl not only stops /s/, but also voices the stop, resulting in [d], so that *some* sounds like *dum*.

As with Stephen and Karl, the deviations in Joseph's speech affect particular classes of sounds. But the effects are more far-reaching. They involve a wider range of targets, and more extreme deformations of those targets. In some cases, he omits stops and fricatives altogether, showing a process of **consonant deletion**. This is what happens with the /k/ in ['ʌlər] (*colour*) and the initial /d/ in [aɪz] (*died*). In other cases, he does produce a consonant where one is expected, but it turns up as [s] or [z]. We see this with the /b/ in [wæsɪʔ] (*rabbit*) which becomes [s], and the final /d/ in [aɪz] (*died*) which becomes [z].

While the extent of these deformations varies, the fact that they are systematic, affecting particular classes of sounds in particular positions in particular ways, leads them to be classified as phonological. The implication is that the child's problem is not with individual sounds, but with classes of sounds which are related to each other and which contrast with other classes of sounds.

A second reason for identifying the problem as phonological draws on evidence of a different type, but leading to the same conclusion. This evidence is that the child is physically able to produce the sound which she is failing to produce. There is no organic obstacle which prevents her from moving her articulators as required to produce the target. Indeed, in some cases the child is able to produce the very same sound in isolation, or in certain positions. Stephen, for example, does produce [k] and [g] in some positions – in words such as *tiger*, *monkey*, *take* and *back*. This proves he is physically capable of moving his tongue in a manner appropriate to produce velar stops. But if articulation is not responsible for the problem, what is? Proposed answer: phonology. What this says is that the problem is somewhere in the child's mental organisation of speech sounds into classes, rather than in the physical execution of those sounds. According to this interpretation, the child is capable of producing the gestures for velar stops, and it is a difficulty with sorting out the contrast between alveolar and velar stops which leads her to realise velars as [d].

This is how children such as Stephen, Karl and Joseph have come to be labelled as **phonologically delayed** or **phonologically disordered**. If the child's system of sound contrasts appears to be similar to that of a much younger child, phonological development may be described as delayed. On the other hand, the child's system may show patterns of substitution or omission which are rarely if ever observed in the majority of children, even at an earlier stage. Or the child's system may be out of step with normal development, showing some patterns characteristic of an earlier stage of normal development and others characteristic of a later stage. Children exhibiting these **atypical** patterns may be described as not just delayed in development, but disordered. However, the distinction between delay and disorder is not a clear-cut one. Since there is considerable variation within the limits of normal development, it is not possible to draw an absolute distinction between what does and does not occur normally.

But in any case, what do these labels tell us? They tell us that the child's speech patterns differ from adult patterns, and also from the patterns observed in most other children, in certain systematic ways. They do not tell us at what point in the processes of receiving or producing speech these differences arise. This is a psycholinguistic question, and it is to this psycholinguistic question that we now turn.

Possible sources of phonological problems

Psycholinguistic investigation, as we have seen, sets out from a hunch. In the case of these children, the initial hunch leaps out. The deviations observed in these children's speech are quite specific. We have established that their language is fine in most respects. Once we adjust to their phonological systems, we discover that they have no problems with the semantics or syntax of words. We also discover that they use their words in contexts which are semantically and syntactically appropriate, and in appropriate conversational interactions with other people. Their problems are confined to word phonology, with particular aspects of speech sounds being deformed in particular ways. Our first hunch, and a pretty well founded one, will be that the child's difficulties reside specifically in phonological processing. This entails the following components in our model of word processing:

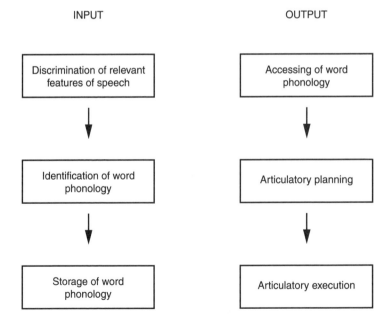

Figure 5.1 Components of phonological processing

So far, the only component of speech processing we have eliminated is articulatory execution. Since the children are physically
capable of making the sound distinctions they are failing to make,
articulatory difficulties were ruled out as an explanation for their
phonology. This still leaves a number of possibilities. Does the child
have difficulties in input which then give rise to the deformations
observed in output? If so, does the problem occur in discrimination
of words, or only in the representations of words which the child
stores? Or is the problem confined to output? If so, does it occur in
the representations which the child accesses for output, or only at
a later stage when representations are programmed for articulation?

These questions can be tackled by looking first at the speech we
have already observed, to see if this leads us to rule out certain
possibilities and suspect other possibilities. Based on the evidence
we have, our next hunch may be that the problem is confined to
output. For a start, we have not observed difficulties in comprehension which would suggest difficulties with input: all the
children appear to understand and respond appropriately to the
input they receive. If they had difficulties in recognising the phonological distinctions they fail to produce, this would surely distort
the input they receive and we might expect this to interfere with
their comprehension. This would be especially true for a child like
Joseph who is producing very few distinct consonants. If he registered so few consonants in input, he would lose a great deal of
phonological information which might be thought critical to recognising and understanding words.

But how tight is this evidence? Not tight enough. It is just
possible that Joseph does have difficulties in input, but that the
phonological information he does receive, together with astute
guesswork based on his interpretation of the non-verbal context,
enable him to understand language in context. In other words, it
may be that Joseph is receiving the same degraded input from
others that we receive from him, and that he is still able to pick out
words and retrieve meaning in others' speech just as we do with
his. Evidence of comprehension in context is not precise enough to
rule out input difficulties. We need to dig deeper for more reliable
evidence. To do this, we must turn to the sort of input and output

tasks we met in the previous chapter. Such tasks have been carried out with groups of children and with individual children who have phonological problems. What do they reveal?

Evidence from tasks tapping different components of input and output

Investigations of input phonology rely on tasks which ask the child to make some sort of **judgement** about phonological forms or to classify them in some way. The forms used in these tasks are chosen to test just those phonological distinctions which appear to be problematic for the child. Take the case of Stephen, who fronts velar stops so that they sound like alveolar stops. Can he tell the difference between these two types of stop? To check this, a classification task was introduced, in the following way:

> Look, we've got red cars and green cars and I want you to post them into this box. But you must *listen* before you post them. I want you to post a *red* car if I say [dəʊ] and a *green* car if I say [gəʊ]. So see if you hear [dəʊ] or [gəʊ], okay . . .

After introducing the task, Stephen was randomly presented with the two forms [dəʊ] and [gəʊ]. The task was then repeated with the pair [fə'dɛt] and [fə'gɛt], and the pair [də'rɛkt] and [kə'rɛkt]. He selected the appropriate car for all thirty items presented. The task was then used with three more pairs, [dæn] and [kæn], [ə'dɛn] and [ə'gɛn], [dəm'pit] and [kəm'pit], but now he was not told which car went with which member of each pair. This meant he had to decide whether [dæn] was like [dəʊ] or like [gəʊ]. Under these conditions, Stephen's judgement was still perfect. From this, we know that he could discriminate velars from alveolars, and assign them to distinct sound categories.

Another way of checking whether the child's input is different from her output is to have her listen to her own output. If we play her speech back to her, will she hear it as we hear it? Where two words sound the same to us, will they also sound the same to the child? Or will she hear distinctions in it which we cannot hear? This was investigated in a group of 3- to 5-year-olds who were making a variety of phonological errors (Dodd, Leahy & Hambly

1989). The children were played a tape of their own production of words, and had to choose the picture for the word they heard from a set of four pictures. The set of pictures included one illustrating the word the child was targeting, and three illustrating words which were the same as or phonologically similar to the child's pronunciation. When their own pronunciation sounded like a different adult word, it was found that the children chose the picture matching their pronunciation rather than their target. Suppose, for example, that their production for *tree* sounded like *tea*. Hearing this production on the tape, they would go for the tea rather than the tree picture. This shows that these children were hearing their own speech as the adult does, rather than as they intended it to be.

Such evidence allows us to rule out a problem in phonological discrimination. It does not rule out a problem in phonological *representation*, however. The child may discriminate sounds but fail to store them distinctly. This possibility was not checked with Stephen, but it has been investigated in other studies. In the research study described above (Dodd et al. 1989), the auditory discrimination task using tape recordings of the child's pronunciation of words was repeated with tape recordings of an *adult's* production of those words. For example, the child pronouncing *tree* as *tea* would hear the adult pronunciation of *tree* and have to select a picture from a set of four which included tree and tea. In order to select the correct picture, the child must discriminate the form *tree* from *tea*, but must also have that distinct form stored as the label for 'tree'. The subjects in this study were much better at identifying the adult's pronunciation of words than their own pronunciation, showing that they have both discriminated and stored the distinct forms of these words.

Where the child's responses to input tasks are reliably correct, we can conclude that she has discriminated and stored the phonological distinctions tested in those tasks. We can in turn conclude that the difficulties observed in output arise only in output processing. But at what point in output processing? To investigate this, we turn to tasks which separate out the accessing of phonological representations from the programming of their articulation.

These are exemplified by a set of categorisation and production tasks carried out with a group of 4- to 7-year-olds who were fronting velar stops, producing target /k/ as [t] or [d], so that *cap* sounded like *tap* or *dap* (Brett, Chiat & Pilcher 1987). The tasks were also presented to a group of children of the same age as the fronting children, but who had no phonological problems.

For the categorisation tasks, children were introduced to two postboxes and told that one went with the sound [t] and one with [k]. They then had some practice in posting cards according to which sound they heard. After the practice, they were given an auditory judgement task and a pictorial judgement task. In the auditory task, they heard a mixture of six words beginning with /k/ and six beginning with /t/, and they had to post a card into the box matching the sound they heard. In the pictorial task, they were given pictures of the same twelve words to post. In this case they had to think of the words themselves, and post the pictures according to the sound they could hear in their heads. The results revealed that the fronting children did not differ significantly from the normally developing children in these tasks: they were able to categorise both auditorily presented words and pictures. The children's success on these tasks shows that they do not have difficulties in input: they have discriminated and stored the targets which they are not producing. But their success on the pictorial task goes further. It shows that they know which words begin with which of these sounds even when they have to think up the word forms rather than being given them. That is, the children had in mind distinct forms for words beginning with /t/ and /k/.

Results in the production tasks, on the other hand, revealed striking differences between the two groups of children. These tasks involved naming the pictures, repeating their names, and repeating similar non-words beginning with /t/ and /k/. Here, the fronting children made significantly more errors than the normally developing children. The difference between the form in the child's mind and the form he actually produces is neatly illustrated by one child who picked up the picture of the car, said

[tɒ] [tɒ]

and proceeded to post the picture in the [k] box! This child mispronounces the word, but is not deflected by his own mispronunciation, showing that he is 'hearing' a /k/ target internally.

These findings make it clear that the fronting children had no particular difficulty in discriminating, storing and accessing the distinction between velar and alveolar stops. Their difficulty with velars must, then, arise at a later point in output processing – at the point where its articulation is planned. This component of processing is involved in all the production tasks (naming, repetition of words and repetition of non-words) but not in any of the categorisation tasks.

With these children, we appear to have come full circle. We set out with the claim that such children have the articulatory capacity to produce sounds they are not producing, and that their faulty output cannot be due to articulation. Instead, it was attributed to limitations in the speech contrasts they make – in their organisation of phonological distinctions. Yet now, having investigated their *processing* of those same phonological distinctions, we have found that the bulk of that processing is unimpaired: they make the relevant contrasts throughout their processing of words in input, and even in accessing those words for output. We have concluded that their difficulties arise in getting those words articulated. Is there a contradiction here? On the one hand, we have concluded that the child has no problem in articulation; on the other hand, that the child's failure to make certain contrasts occurs at the point of articulation. These conclusions may appear contradictory at first sight, but they are not, once we take into account the complexity of the articulatory process itself. Between the accessing of a word's phonology and its articulation lie the intricate processes of speech programming. There's room for many a slip in these processes. This emerges very clearly when we explore patterns of errors in the children's output, and their implications for speech processing.

Evidence from patterns in the child's output

We have already observed that children's difficulties with particular phonological targets are not necessarily consistent. Many children hit the target in some words but not in others. Stephen, for example, could produce velars correctly in *tiger, monkey, back, take,* but fronted them in *got, called, again, forgot, can't, cases.*

These children's ability to produce a sound in one context and not in another can prove quite puzzling:

Stephen
SC: This puppet is called Mikey. Can you say 'Mikey'?
Stephen: ['maɪgɪ]
SC: (showing a key) Can you say 'my key'?
Stephen: [maɪ 'di]

Karl
SC: Can you say 'icing'?
Karl: ['aɪsɪŋ]
SC: Can you say 'I sing'?
Karl: [aɪ 'dɪŋ]

These data reveal a curious phenomenon. Karl can say *icing* but not *I sing.* Stephen can produce a velar in *Mikey* but not in *my key.* When David is presented with *aching* and *a king,* he spots a trick:

David
SC: Can you say 'a king'?
David: [eɪ 'dɪŋ]
SC: Can you say 'aching'?
David: ['eɪkɪŋ]
SC: Now, 'a-ching' (slowed down)
David: ['eɪ kɪŋ]
SC: Now (showing a picture of a king) – 'a – king'
David: ['æʔs ə 'trɪk wʌn] (= That's a trick one!)

David's detection of a 'trick' suggests that he has come face to face with the paradox which occurs in his speech and the speech of the other two children. Each child appears to be able and yet unable to produce a particular target correctly. This apparent paradox leads to the question: what makes it possible for the child to hit the target in some words yet not in others? If we can discover the factors which affect the child's production, we may throw some light on the nature of the child's difficulties and the point at which they arise. To discover the factors, we need a good range of examples of target and non-target strikes.

We might start by collecting a sample of spontaneous speech and separating out all those words which contain incorrect

Table 5.1. *Stephen: Velar targets in spontaneous production*

Correct	ta<u>k</u>e, ba<u>ck</u>, wal<u>k</u>, du<u>ck</u>, le<u>g</u>s, Goldilo<u>ck</u>s ti<u>g</u>er, fin<u>g</u>er, mon<u>k</u>ey, fo<u>x</u>es
Fronted	<u>g</u>ot, <u>c</u>alled, <u>g</u>et, <u>c</u>ases, <u>g</u>onna, <u>c</u>ome, <u>G</u>oldilocks for<u>g</u>ot, a<u>g</u>ain

Table 5.2. *Karl: Fricative targets in spontaneous production*

Correct	you'<u>v</u>e, ha<u>v</u>e, co<u>s</u>, thi<u>s</u>, hi<u>s</u>, of<u>f</u>, he'<u>s</u>, ambulan<u>c</u>e di<u>v</u>er, e<u>v</u>en, o<u>v</u>er, si<u>s</u>ter, per<u>s</u>on, sci<u>ss</u>ors, sau<u>s</u>age<u>s</u>
Stopped	<u>f</u>or, <u>f</u>it, <u>f</u>ish, <u>s</u>ome, <u>s</u>ausages, <u>s</u>ister, <u>s</u>cissors

realisations of a target and all those words which contain correct realisations of that same target (see tables 5.1 and 5.2). At first glance, the difference between the correct and incorrect cases looks obvious: targets at the beginning of words are incorrect; targets in the middle or at the ends of words are correct. So, Stephen fronts /k/ and /g/ when they are word-initial, but not word-medial or word-final. Karl stops word-initial fricatives, but not word-medial or word-final fricatives. There is just a hint in these data, however, that the picture is not quite so simple. In *forgot* and *again*, the velar is word-medial, yet Stephen fronts these velars. Is this a random error? Or is there some difference between these word-medial velars and those which he produces correctly?

It turns out that there is. The stress pattern of these words is different. *Forgot* and *again* have stress on the second syllable – /fə'gɒt/ and /ə'gɛn/. Here, the velar stop *precedes* the stressed vowel. The words *tiger, finger, monkey, foxes*, on the other hand, have stress on the first syllable, following the more typical stress pattern for two-syllable words in English – /'taɪgə/, /'fɪŋgə/, /'mʌŋkɪ/, /'fɒksɪz/. Here, then, the velar stop *follows* the stressed vowel. Could stress be the factor which determines whether medial velars are correct or fronted?

In order to find out, we obviously need more examples of words with targets in different positions. There are unlikely to be enough

Table 5.3. *Karl: Fricative targets in repetition*

Correct	Word-final	laugh, cough, safe, dive, give, miss, dice, rose
	Word-medial after stress	offer, toffee, river, answer, easy, pencil
Stopped	Word-initial	feed, fog, fat, fall, sit, suit, safe, sock
	Word-medial before stress	before, re'fuse, deserve, cassette, decide, beside

examples of such words in the child's spontaneous output. So, we need to find a way of eliciting further examples. One possibility is to ask the child to repeat appropriately selected words. So long as the child repeats words in the same way as he produces them spontaneously, we can use repetition data to probe his difficulties.

Repetition tasks were tried out with both Stephen and Karl. The stimuli were designed to investigate production of the relevant targets in different positions within the word: word-initial, word-final, word-medial before stress, and word-medial after stress. Both children were very willing to repeat words, making it possible to sample a good range of targets. Both showed the same pattern of production. This pattern is exemplified by Karl's stopping (see table 5.3)

Word-final fricatives are correct, whereas word-initial fricatives are stopped. In word-medial position, production of fricatives depends on stress. They are correct when they follow stress, but stopped when they precede stress. In the same way, Stephen produced velar stops correctly if they were word-final or word-medial following stress, but fronted them if they were word-initial or word-medial preceding stress (see table 5.4). The effect of stress on Stephen's production of target /k/ is highlighted by the contrast between '*record* (correct) and *re'cord* (fronted).

Why should the child succeed in making a distinction in some positions but not others? Why is it possible for Karl to produce the fricative /s/ in *icing* but not in *I sing*? The observation of such differences in children's production of consonant targets offers a

Table 5.4. *Stephen: Target velar stops in repetition*

Correct	Word-final	tic̲k, duc̲k, dog̲, tag̲, cak̲e, cook̲, kic̲k, gag̲
	Word-medial after stress	mak̲ing, luc̲ky, wrig̲gle, wag̲ging, tic̲kle, tal̲king, tur̲key, tic̲ket, bak̲er, an̲gry, whis̲kers, 'rec̲ord, ac̲hing, bas̲ket
Fronted	Word-initial	̲key, ̲car, ̲go, ̲gay, ̲cake, ̲cook, ̲kick, ̲gag, ̲cat, ̲kid, ̲get, ̲gate
	Word-medial before stress	be̲cause, a̲gree, be̲gin, re'c̲ord, for̲get, o̲kay, a̲gain, be̲come, se̲cure

mine of information about how speech is processed, and which speech patterns are easiest for the child to process. One implication of these differences is that stress pattern, or rhythm, is very important in speech processing. Children like Stephen and Karl show us that the alveolar/velar distinction and the stop/fricative distinction are not produced independently of their place in the rhythm of a word, since a single one of these distinctions may come out differently according to its position in relation to the stressed vowel in the word. The stress pattern of a word appears to act as a frame on which further details of speech are hung. The stress pattern affects whether a consonant hangs onto a preceding or a following vowel, and this in turn affects the way the consonant is produced. In the examples we have met, the velar closure and the fricative closure were easier to produce when they followed from a vowel (word-final) than when they preceded a vowel (word-initial). In word-medial position, the relation of the stressed vowel determined how they behaved. If they preceded the stressed vowel, they behaved like a word-initial and were produced incorrectly. If they followed the stressed vowel, they behaved like a word-final and were produced correctly.

These rhythmic frames on which the consonant distinctions hang appear to be word-size. The evidence for this is that the stress pattern over a word affects the pronunciation of these distinctions, but the stress pattern over a sequence of words does not. Compare Stephen's production of the single word *beacon* and the sequence of words *he can*:

'beacon → ['bikən]

Here, the target /k/ comes between a stressed vowel and an unstressed vowel and in the middle of a word. This velar is correct.

'he can 'dance → ['hi tən 'dɒns]

Here, the target /k/ still comes between a stressed vowel and an unstressed vowel, but the unstressed vowel is in a *separate* word and the velar is at the beginning of that word. This velar is fronted.

Conversely, when /k/ comes between an unstressed vowel and a stressed vowel *within* a word, Stephen fronts it:

be'cause → [bɪ'dɒz]

But if the /k/ occurs at the *end* of a word in this stress pattern he preserves the velar:

back 'out → [bæ'gɒʊt]

(though he changes its voicing).

Drawing together these observations, it appears that each word in a sequence of words is produced as a separate rhythmic unit. This rhythmic unit consists of one or more vowels, which may be flanked by consonants. Whether the consonants attach to a preceding vowel or to a following vowel depends in part on the stress of the vowels, that is, on the position they occupy in the rhythm of the word.

So far, we have only looked at the processes of fronting and stopping. These involve changes in the place or manner of the target consonants. What about other aspects of speech which are affected in children with phonological difficulties? One such aspect is the voicing of consonants. In English, some consonants are voiceless, with the vocal cords open while the closure is made, as in [k] or [t] or [s]. Others have vibration of the vocal folds, as in [g] or [d] or [z]. As we have seen, some children have difficulties with this voicing distinction. For example, they may produce voice when they are targeting voiceless consonants:

Stephen: voiceless /k/ becomes voiced [g]
monkey → [ˈmʌŋgɪ]
baker → [ˈbeɪgə]

Karl: voiceless /s/ becomes stopped and voiced [d]
sit → [dɪʔ]
sea → [di]

This sort of error again occurs in certain positions only. Again, it appears to occur at the beginning but not at the end of words, at least when they stand alone. For example, Stephen does not voice the word-final stops in *walk* and *back*. But look at what happens when these words occur in phrases, with a vowel following:

[ˈi dən ˈwɔg ɒm ˈwɔdə]
He can walk on water

[ˈdʌm bægˈɒʊt]
Come back out

Here, the stop at the end of the word is correctly realised as a velar, but it is incorrectly voiced. Why should the /k/ be voiceless when *back* occurs alone, but voiced when it is followed by *out*? Could it be that a stop comes out voiced when it is followed by a vowel, even if that vowel is in a separate word?

This possibility was investigated experimentally (Brett, Chiat & Pilcher 1987). The subjects in the experiment were ten children whose speech showed voicing. These children were asked to repeat words and short phrases containing voiceless stops at the beginning, in the middle, and at the end of the word or phrase. In single words, the children did exactly as expected: they always voiced initial stops, but always produced final stops correctly. What happened when the words were combined into short phrases? Now, the word-final stops which had been correct in isolation tended to be voiced, and were almost always voiced if the following vowel was stressed as in *get ˈup, back ˈout*. This confirms our suspicion that voicing of consonants is affected by a following vowel, whether that vowel is in the same word or not. Processes altering the place or manner of a consonant, on the other hand, appeared to be affected by its position in relation to the stressed vowel *within* the word. This explains the *correct placement* but *incorrect voicing* of /k/ in Stephen's production *back out*. Velars are correct word-finally, so the velar aspect is correct. But voiceless stops are liable to be voiced before any vowel even if they are word-final, so the voicing aspect is incorrect.

Detailed analysis of the types of phonological errors which occur and the phonological contexts in which they occur has led us into the thick of speech processing. We have inferrred that different consonant distinctions are processed according to their position in relation to stressed and unstressed vowels. Place and manner distinctions were seen to be affected by vowels preceding and following them within the word, while voicing was affected by any following vowel.

Looking ahead

Drawing on a range of evidence, we appear to have nailed down the source of children's phonological difficulties. Our conclusion has been that the problem is in articulatory planning (see model of phonological processing above), and we have gone on to explore the nature of that problem. But there is an alternative possibility which we have overlooked. Throughout our consideration of the data, we have assumed – as most observers do – that the child is *failing* to make a phonological distinction such as the distinction between alveolar and velar stops, or between fricatives and stops. We have then investigated different components of input and output processing to see where this failure occurs. It is true that when Stephen produces a word such as *car*, we perceive a /t/ or /d/ rather than /k/ at the beginning. When Joseph produces this word, we perceive it as having no initial consonant at all. But is our perception reliable? Suppose these children *are* making a distinction in their speech, but one which we cannot hear. This is entirely possible. There is even some evidence that it happens. This evidence is of a different kind from any we have so far considered. It lies in measurement of acoustic properties of the child's speech.

An acoustic analysis was, for example, carried out with three children who omitted stops at the ends of words (Weismer, Dinnsen & Elbert 1981). The analysis revealed that two of the children, aged 7, were producing words differently according to whether the stop was voiced or not, even though the stop was not itself produced. The difference occurred in the vowel, which was reliably longer if the word should have ended in a voiced stop than if it should have ended in a voiceless one. In adult speech, there is also a difference in the length of the vowel according to the voicing of the following consonant. Evidence of such contrasts in the child's speech proves conclusively that the child *is* making a phonological distinction, and eliminates any explanation in terms of a lack of contrasts in the phonological system. This is consistent with our findings that some children do make distinctions in input tasks and even in internal judgement tasks where they identify *car* as beginning with /k/ even though they appear to produce it as [tɒ]. Under this interpretation, these tasks represent no problem because the child makes the relevant distinction, and the reason we don't perceive her distinction is that she does not make it in the relevant way.

The problem shifts from failure to make a distinction, and becomes failure to make an *appropriate* distinction. This puts us back to square one in considering where this problem occurs in input or output processing. Difficulty may arise in picking out the correct features from the input, or in storing them, or in accessing them, or in programming their articulation. We may hazard a guess that the problem still arises in articulatory output. It seems unlikely, for example, that a child would distinguish /s/ in input on the basis of features so different from the adult's that it ended up sounding like [t] to the adult ear. To move beyond a good guess, we would need more sophisticated psycholinguistic tools than we have so far used. If we are to check not just whether the child recognises a distinction, but what sort of distinction the child picks out, we cannot use normal spoken input which contains only normal adult distinctions. A possible way of checking the child's sensitivity to particular distinctions is to use synthesised speech. This allows us to reproduce just the acoustic distinctions we think the child may be making, to see if *she* can recognise these distinctions even if *we* cannot. If we can show that the child *does* perceive distinctions which we do not, we would have evidence that she is focusing on different features in input, which could account for the output we observe.

The questions which are now emerging and the methods for pursuing these are at the vanguard of current research. They show how psycholinguistic exploration leads to the most delicate dissection of the child's phonological processing.

Note: Stephen, Karl and Joseph were originally presented in Chiat 1983, Chiat 1989 and Chiat 1994. To avoid confusion with the subject in Chiat 1983, the name of the subject in Chiat 1989 which was also Stephen has been changed to Karl in this chapter.

6 'Stip' or 'step' or 'slip' or what?: problems with lexical processing

Eamonn is an alert and excitable 6-year-old. He engages intensely with the world around him, a willing participant and an enthusiastic initiator. He is assertive about his own interests and preferences (not least his passion for Batman) but is at the same time sensitive to other people's concerns and points of view (including their ignorance about Batman). And he loves talking: telling what's happening at home or school, expressing what touches him or those around him, finding out what's going on for other people. His words often tumble out in an eager torrent, as they do when he starts recounting a class trip into the garden:

E: We [wɛn] in the garden – get some – [wigɔ̃ə] get some soil. [bɪˈkɒ] we [nɒ] got no soil.
SC: Where haven't you got any soil?
E: [bɪk – bɪˈkɒ – bɪkɒʁ] we went in the garden – dig and [ˈkæti faɪn] – a snail – a snail. [ɪs] not a big snail [ɪsə ˈlɪʔə] snail.

Seven-year-old Michael (Constable, Stackhouse & Wells 1997) also has his wits about him. His particular passion emerges when he is asked to name the kinds of work people do and he comes up with:

> making toys, making trainsets, making steam trains, making electric trains, making diesels . . .

Michael shows considerable ingenuity and insight in his negotiations with words. Unfamiliar with unicorns, he responds to a picture of a unicorn with the label 'horse with a party hat on'. Faced with a picture of handcuffs, he does recognise what they are and strives to get this across:

key . . . oh what do you call them . . . oh yeah . . . you put . . . you put . . . with your . . . with your . . . oh . . . with your . . . when you . . . when someone's stole something . . . and . . . what do you call them . . . necklace? . . . no . . . I just don't know the word.

First impressions of children like Eamonn and Michael may be that they are quite intelligible. Many of their words sound just as they should and can be readily recognised and understood. But such first impressions may be deceptive. These children produce words inconsistently. They may produce some words correctly, while similar sounding words are produced incorrectly. They may produce a particular word correctly on some occasions, but not on others. Incorrect attempts at a word may themselves be inconsistent, with different errors occurring on different occasions. In some cases, their words may be unrecognisable. When they produce a whole stream of these, we may have difficulty making sense of what they are saying. Yet even at this extreme, we may perceive them as being in some sense 'on the ball'. Intuitively, we may feel that they have coherent meaning intentions but that these have got obscured or lost in a morass of output.

When these children talk, they present us with a much more hazy picture than the 'phonologically impaired' children followed up in the previous chapter. The deviations in their words are at once less consistent and more diffuse. This suggests that the source of their difficulties is different. To form an initial hunch about the obstacles in the path of their language processing, we need to take a closer look at the strengths and weaknesses in their language.

First observations

Eamonn's language impairment is evident. At 5, a test of sentence comprehension (Test for the Reception of Grammar, or TROG) had him performing at the level of a 4-year-old, and a word-finding test (the Renfrew) at 3. By the age of 7, the gap in performance is greater. On the TROG and on a word-comprehension test (British Picture Vocabulary Scales), he is two to three years behind his age. In contrast, a non-verbal general intelligence test (the performance section of the Wechsler Intelligence Scales for Children, or WISC) finds him average/low average for his age.

To get a feel for Eamonn's language, consider this more extended sample of his conversation about the class session in the garden:

E: We [wɛn] in the garden – get some – [wigɜ̃ə] get some soil. [bɪˈkɒ] we [nɒ] got no soil.

SC: Where haven't you got any soil?

E: [bɪk – bɪˈkɒ – bɪˈkɒʁ] we went in the garden – dig and [ˈkæti faɪn] – a snail – a snail. [ɪs] not a big snail [ɪsə ˈlɪʔə] snail.

SC: Cassie did?

E: Yeah. [ˈkæsis dɪ] – and [i] see it [ɪnə – ɪnə] thing. And then Cassie – Cassie throw it away in [ə] – in – in the pond. And then [i] – the – the snail [kæm meɪk] it. No.

SC: The snail?

E: No. Ca – We [li] the snail there. The snail – in the ground – [ðæsəʊ]– [bɪˈkɒh ɛdɪs – æwi stɪp] it, [ɪb] – it be die.

SC: If you do what to it?

E: [æjɪ stɪp] it.

SC: If you step on it.

E: Yeah. It die.

Looking at this conversation globally, Eamonn's contribution is fine. He takes appropriate turns with the other person, initiating comments and responding to questions. Each of his comments and responses relate to the topic of conversation. Eamonn comments on significant events, such as the finding of a snail, and consequences of events, such as the fate of the snail if stepped on.

In his responses to questions, we begin to see problems. Although they still relate to the topic of the question, they do not always answer the specific question that was posed. For example, to a question about place:

SC: Where haven't you got any soil?

Eamonn appears to respond with a reason, and then rapidly changes the subject:

E: [bɪk – bɪˈkɒ – bɪˈkɒʁ] we went in the garden – dig and [ˈkæti faɪn] – a snail – a snail. [ɪs] not a big snail [ɪsə ˈlɪʔə] snail.

To a later question about purpose:

SC: What do you need the soil for?

Eamonn responds obscurely and again changes the subject:

> E: Soil for we [ni ə pwæn?] the – we ['nidə] put some soil – in – in the thing – in the pot – and [ɪnə 'ɒtə'nun] we [kə] take them home. [æwi bi fi fi] good.

As well as producing some utterances which disrupt the thread of the conversation, Eamonn produces some which are unintelligible and whose relevance to other utterances therefore cannot be judged:

> . . . the snail [kæm meɪk] it

Here, where Eamonn's words are unclear, we can't decipher whether or how they relate to the context. When he goes on to say:

> We [li] the snail there

we don't know whether 'there' refers to 'in the pond' (already mentioned) or 'in the ground' (mentioned subsequently). Clearly Eamonn is saying something about the location of the snail and its fate, but the connection between the two remains obscure.

In shifting our view from the more global to the more local connections between utterances, Eamonn's difficulties emerge. When we narrow our focus even further, looking at individual utterances, his problems are very evident. His combinations of words do not always match the requirements of English sentences, sometimes missing elements such as markers of time:

> Cassie throw it away = throws? threw?
> . . . it be die   = will die? will be dead?

One or two combinations are very odd:

> Soil for we [ni ə pwæn?] the . . .

Finally, there are problems with words themselves. He gropes for a word:

> We ['nidə] put some soil – in –

and may come up with an 'empty' substitution:

in – in the thing

before finally hitting the target:

– in the pot

In some cases, he stops with the empty substitute:

. . . and [i] see it [ɪnə – ɪnə] thing

In others, he goes for the target directly, but the sound of the word is distorted, often to a point where it is unrecognisable:

['kæti] = Cassie
[æwi] = if we?
[stɪp] = step? slip? both?

His attempts at a target are not necessarily consistent, for example he produces *Cassie* perfectly on some occasions.

While the sound of word forms is often distorted, Eamonn does appear to be targeting a single word form. And the meaning of that form is generally appropriate. At worst, it is over-general ('thing'). There are no instances of words being semantically inappropriate in this sample, though semantic errors were occasionally noted in other samples of Eamonn's output:

(Describing picture of man feeding *horse*)
E: Daddy ['fiɪn] the cat.
SC: Who's hungry?
E: The [k] – the horsie.

(Talking about a *motor boat*)
E: I got this ['məʊə baɪʔ] er ['məʊðə baɪk – 'məʊə baɪk].
SC: A motor bike?
E: A ['məʊə baɪk] er boat.

From these samples, we can draw a preliminary picture of Eamonn. He appears to show problems with all aspects of utterance use and utterance structure. His utterances are not always fully appropriate to their semantic context; their syntactic organisation is sometimes wanting; and the words they contain are often hard won, or semantically vague, or phonologically distorted. The picture does not show a clear-cut mismatch between strengths and weaknesses such as we met in children whose difficulties were confined to phonology. But there is some hint of mismatches. Pragmatically and semantically, Eamonn's output is relatively strong. His utterances may be imprecise in their content and relation to the topic, but they are always in the right ball park. His word forms and combinations of words, on the other hand, show persistent deviations from those needed to express his intended meanings.

Starting from this apparent mismatch, our first hunch may be that Eamonn's difficulties are primarily with the forms and structures of language, rather than their meanings and functions. This predicts that Eamonn will show problems with words and sentences independently of, but possibly responsible for, any problems we meet in meaning and function.

Through exploration of Eamonn's spontaneous output, we have homed in on his problems with words, and primarily the form of words. The study of 7-year-old Michael (Constable, Stackhouse and Wells 1997) sets out from a similar point, though this point is reached mainly via formal assessments rather than spontaneous output. Michael's profile resembles Eamonn's in a number of ways. Like Eamonn, he comes out in the 'low average' range on a test of intelligence (the Kaufman Assessment Battery for Children). Also like Eamonn, he has good conversational understanding, but comes down on formal tests of comprehension. His score for vocabulary comprehension (BPVS) is at the level of children a year younger, which identifies him as 'low average'; his score for sentence comprehension (TROG) is more than two years below his age mates. His output, though, shows an even more striking delay, his score on the Test of Word Finding being way down for his age. These test results indicate that Michael has difficulties. To find out whether his difficulties lie primarily in semantics or phonology, some preliminary assessments were carried out.

Two of these were naming tasks. Here, Michael made a few semantic confusions similar to Eamonn's rare semantic errors:

flamingo   → octopus
moustache → [bɪjəʔ stɒʃ bʌ stɒʃ bɪjə bɪjəd stɒʃ stɒs bʌstɒs]
            = *beard + moustache?*

But he frequently described a picture using a **circumlocution**:

hammock – 'a net where you sleep on'

or a distorted form:

cigarette – [sɪʔəsɪɹɪjɛt][siːjɛt]

In these cases, he is clearly targeting a word which has the appropriate meaning. This is the strongest evidence that the source of his problem with words is their form rather their meaning. This evidence is supported by the results of two tests which focus on meaning. One, known as **Pyramids and Palm Trees** (Howard and Patterson 1992), was actually designed for adults. It presents an array of three pictures, one at the top (e.g. a pyramid) with two below it (in this case, a palm tree and an oak tree). The task for Michael was to match one of the bottom pictures with the top one (palm tree going with pyramid). In order to succeed, the child must know which pictures are related to each other. Though billed as a test of semantics, strictly speaking **Pyramids and Palm Trees** tests a person's knowledge about the world rather than knowledge of word meaning. This is shown by one of the few errors Michael made. Presented with a picture of a windmill, he selected the daffodil rather than the tulip 'cos they're in the countryside'. His wrong choice, then, is due to ignorance of the Dutch connection rather than ignorance about words. Michael's impressive score, 22/24, indicates that his world knowledge is generally good. A second test required Michael to come up with items in response to a category such as 'kinds of work people do' (Word Association subtest of the Clinical Evaluation of Language Fundamentals, or CELF). Here, Michael produced appropriate if rather limited associates, as we saw with his examples of work:

making toys, making trainsets . . .

which were cited above. The results of these tests at least indicate that Michael has made normal associations between things, and they give no hint of semantic difficulties.

Turning to phonology, a number of tests point to difficulties. In an auditory discrimination task (Bridgeman and Snowling 1988),

Michael was able to discriminate many pairs of words and non-words, but had some difficulty judging non-word pairs such as *vost–vots*, which vary the order of a consonant cluster. In a second task, Michael was asked to find words which rhymed with another word. He found this very difficult, managing just three rhymes compared with the average of 125 produced by 5-year-old children. He made imaginative attempts to respond, resorting, for example, to semantic associates or extensions such as *cow → calf, hay → hey dood*.

As with Eamonn, initial assessment of Michael has highlighted a problem with word forms above and beyond any difficulties with semantics. The question is: where do Eamonn and Michael's problems arise in the process of receiving and producing word forms, and connecting these to meaning?

Possible sources of precarious words

Our hunch so far is that both children have problems with words, and that those problems are primarily with the form of words rather than their meaning. Both children have adequate discrimination to separate out word forms. Their problems must arise in the further processing of those segmented word forms. At this point we have scant evidence of just where, in that processing, their problems reside.

As far as input is concerned, we know that hearing is within normal limits for both children (thanks to audiological testing), which rules out difficulties at the very earliest point in input. In Michael's case, we have a hint of problems in fine auditory discrimination. At the other end of the input process, both children appear to get to more or less the right meanings behind utterances in conversation, but we have seen that even in conversation Eamonn's responses are not always fully appropriate, suggesting he may have difficulties when it comes to precise understanding. Such difficulties are confirmed by the results of sentence-comprehension tests. Both children, put in a situation where wider cues to meaning are not available, perform below their age. This could be due to problems at any point in connecting the sounds they hear to meaning: in auditory discrimination, in the identification or stor-

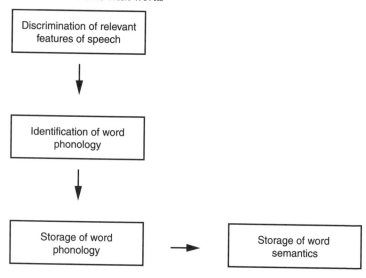

Figure 6.1 Michael and Eamonn: possible points of breakdown in lexical input

age of word forms, or in accessing their meaning, as shown in figure 6.1. All of these possibilities are compatible with our current evidence of their understanding.

Turning to output, we know that both children produce a wide range of speech sounds and sound sequences, and do so precisely. Even more telling, they may produce perfectly on one occasion the very sound in the very word which they have distorted on another occasion (as with Eamonn's production of *Cassie*). This is evidence that articulatory execution is not the problem. Their difficulties must then arise at some point between meaning and articulatory execution: connecting word meanings to word forms, accessing precise word forms, or planning their articulation, as shown in figure 6.2. All these possibilities are compatible with our evidence so far.

Exploring these different components of input and output means going beyond the limited evidence of spontaneous output and existing tests.

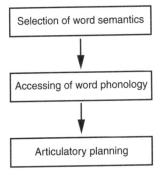

Figure 6.2 Michael and Eamonn: possible points of breakdown in lexical output

Evidence from tasks tapping different components of input and output processing

The point of further investigation is to see whether clearly identified deviations in the children's output and roughly identified constraints on their input can be attributed to difficulties in particular components of input or output processing. We turn to tasks which probe different processing components.

Each child received a range of tasks using words (or sometimes non-words) of the sort he had produced incorrectly. Keeping to the same sort of items ensures that any differences between tasks using those items reflect the processing involved in the tasks, rather than the items themselves.

The items used in Eamonn's tasks varied, but all were either words which he had attempted spontaneously and were therefore in his vocabulary, or non-words which were similar to these words. The words reflected his interests. They had cropped up in talk around favoured subjects such as Batman (hence the item 'Riddler' naming a character in Batman), and the antics and health of his cat (hence the item 'vet').

All Michael's tasks used a core set of ten items: 'hospital', 'elephant', 'crocodile', 'microphone', 'octopus', 'escalator', 'binoculars', 'helicopter', 'television', 'caterpillar'. These three- and four-syllable words were known to be in Michael's vocabulary, and were selected as suitably challenging for him. Some tasks supplemented these ten items with related items, for example non-words which were phonologically similar to the words.

In Michael's case, the same tasks were given to two groups of normal children. One group were selected to match his chronological age, averaging 7;8. The other group were selected to match his vocabulary age and were therefore younger, averaging 6;01.

Input processing

Eamonn's and Michael's difficulties are most evident in their **output**. We have, though, witnessed some constraints on **input** as well. Could it be that their impaired output is actually a mirror of what they are taking from the input they receive? To find out whether and how their processing of input may be limited, we need to investigate their ability to perceive and recognise the sorts of distinctions they are failing to make in output. To this end, **judgement tasks** were used with both children.

In Eamonn's judgement tasks, he was shown a picture which the investigator named correctly or incorrectly. Eamonn was invited to give her a tick when the word sounded right, and a cross when it sounded wrong, so he could see how well she had done at the end. The first round of these tasks presented Eamonn with ten error forms he had produced in his spontaneous output, mixed up with the ten corresponding target forms. For example, the following picture was named once as ['kæ'ru] and once as *kangaroo*:

Eamonn made *no* errors in judging these items, indicating that he could recognise and reject the forms he had himself produced.

Rounds 2 and 3 upped the stakes, focusing on just those distinctions which appeared most vulnerable in Eamonn's output. Round 2 tested the **voicing** of consonants, using the following three pairs of words and non-words which differ only in voicing:

Word	*Non-word*
boat	[pəʊt] poat
fish	[vɪʃ] vish
vet	[fɛt] fet

Eamonn heard each word and non-word three times. His judgement of these was almost always correct. He made only three errors, and all were in response to the non-word *fet* which he incorrectly accepted for the picture of the vet.

Pursuing this curious consistency, round 3 presented Eamonn with sixteen pictures of words containing [f] or [v]. These were accompanied by either the correct form, for example *fire*, *vest*, or a corresponding incorrect form which reversed the voicing of [f] and [v], for example [vaɪə] (*vire*), [fɛst] (*fest*). This time Eamonn's score was down to 72 per cent, with all but one error involving judgement of a non-word as correct. Of the sixteen non-words, eight were misjudged.

As the items have become more demanding, requiring sensitivity to fine distinctions which had appeared problematic in his output, Eamonn's performance has deteriorated. This suggests that he does have *some* problem in input. We might then ask further questions about the source and effects of this problem. First, does it occur in **auditory discrimination** or in **word recognition**? Either way, can it account for the **output** problems we have observed?

The judgement tasks provide some indirect evidence. That evidence, though, looks bafflingly contradictory. Eamonn appears to have problems with certain sound distinctions, particularly the distinction between voiced and voiceless consonants, and even more specifically, the [f]–[v] distinction. If a problem occurs with particular distinctions and *cuts across* words, the implication is that the problem is not with the words themselves, but with auditory discrimination. The paradox is that although certain auditory distinctions are especially vulnerable, they also appear to be more vulnerable in some words than in others. Eamonn's responses to words show curious mismatches. He makes consistent errors in judging *fet* for *vet*. But he makes no errors in judging *vish* for *fish*. In order to make the *fish* judgement, he must perceive [v] as different from [f]. If he can tell [v] from [f], he has the perceptual capacity to tell *fet* from *vet*. His failure to do so, then, must be due to confusion in his recognition of the word rather than in discriminating it.

So, it looks as if Eamonn's problem with *vet* is on the one hand due to general difficulties in distinguishing [v] from [f], and on the other hand due to vagueness in his representation of the specific word *vet*. Our fine-grained analysis of Eamonn's input appears to have ended up in a cul de sac. Or has it? Are our two conclusions necessarily in conflict? Or can we reconcile them?

They can be reconciled, if we assume that one component of processing may interact with another. Suppose Eamonn *does* have subtle difficulties in auditory discrimination, and may even have had more extensive difficulties at an earlier age. These will have limited the information available to be stored, and may have affected the phonological representations of words he has stored to varying degrees. The point here is that difficulties in one component of input processing have reached into another component.

If we take this still further, we might hypothesise that Eamonn's input difficulties have reached into his output and are enough to account for it. This is feasible, but hardly compatible with the evidence of his output which we already have. If we flash back to Eamonn's difficulties in 'finding' words, and his phonological distortion of words, these go well beyond any difficulties we might predict on the basis of his subtle difficulties in input. Indeed, we have seen that he is well able to reject most of his own 'errors'. This means he *perceives and recognises more about words than he is able to produce*. Explanation of his output, and its relation to his input processing, must wait on further output investigations. Before embarking on these, we turn to Michael to see how he fares in input.

Michael's input tasks consisted of **lexical decision**, presented

with pictures and **without pictures**. All tasks used his ten test words. In the easiest round, he was – like Eamonn – fed back his own errors, these being the incorrect forms he produced in naming the ten items, along with the target forms. Here, his judgement was 100 per cent. The other rounds of lexical decision were tougher, because they used specially created non-words which were much closer to the target than his own errors. The ten real words were mixed up with:

A.　Ten *non-words* created by *copying a sound* in the real word e.g. [ɛskəleɪkə]

B.　Ten *non-words* created by *swapping two sounds* in the real word e.g. [ɛstəleɪkə]

C.　Ten more *real* words which were added to keep equal numbers of words and non-words

Now, Michael's score dropped. He still judged real words perfectly. But like Eamonn, he came down with non-words – to, on average, 70 per cent in judging non-words with pictures and 60 per cent without pictures. His worst performance was with non-words in which a sound was copied (type A above) when these were presented without a picture. Here, he scored 50 per cent, which means he was performing at chance with these items. In Michael's case, we have proof that his difficulties are abnormal, because the same tasks were carried out with the age- and vocabulary-matched groups of children. Even the younger, vocabulary-matched children performed way better than Michael on the non-words, their worst average score being 89.17 per cent – on judgement of type A non-words with pictures. It seems that, like Eamonn and unlike all the normally developing children, Michael was unsure about non-words despite being sure about very similar real words.

Again we can ask whether Michael's difficulties with judgement arise in **auditory discrimination** or in his **word representations**. We know from earlier testing (the Bridgeman & Snowling test) that Michael has some auditory discrimination problems, since he could not always distinguish sequences of consonants. However, we have reason to think that these problems are not responsible for his misjudgements. First, his perfect judgement of the real words suggests that he *is* making some discrimination between these and the non-words on which he falters. Even more telling is the apparent relation between his judgement and naming of particular words. Most of his incorrect judgements occurred with words he had also named incorrectly. For example, he accepted three non-words for *binoculars* which he also named incorrectly, whereas he rejected all four non-words for *crocodile* which he named correctly. The fact that he makes errors on the *same* words in *different* tasks suggests that he is unsure about the form of these words.

We are back where we left Eamonn – with evidence of some limitation in auditory discrimination, but further evidence of limitations on specific lexical items. Before we explore this outcome further, we need to know more about how it tallies with evidence of the children's **output**.

Output processing

Words can only be produced if they have been discriminated and stored. So, if there are constraints on these input processes, we would expect constraints on output as well. Having set out from observations of Eamonn's and Michael's output, we already know they have problems. We have also seen some connections between their errors in input and output. Both had difficulty in making judgements about words they had misproduced – recall Eamonn's problem rejecting non-words for *vet* and Michael's problem rejecting non-words for *binoculars*, words which the children also had problems naming. Does this mean their output problems are just a spin-off from their input? Or do they have further difficulties in output – in going from semantics to the phonological representation, or from the phonological representation to speech?

We already have some reason to think they do. Although their judgement sometimes matches up with their production of words, both children make far fewer errors in judgement than in production. Their judgement errors involve fine distinctions such as [f] vs [v], or between sequences of sounds [n]–[l] vs [l]–[n]. Their phonological errors in naming and spontaneous speech sometimes involve rather more gross deviations such as:

Eamonn: very → [vi] [fi]
Michael: binoculars → [ˈnɒkənɜz] [ˈnɒkəmɪlɒz]

This accounts for the children's successful rejection of almost all their *own* errors when these are fed back in judgement tasks.

Their output errors, then, appear to go beyond their input difficulties. This could be because their output has been held back by difficulties in input which occurred earlier in their development. Perhaps some constraints on input have now been resolved, but have left their mark on output. Current output representations are then relics of earlier limitations on input and have not benefitted from improved input representations. In this case, the children's output is a product of their difficulties in input processing. If the deviations in output are relics of past input, they should occur only when the child produces a word from his store of words. When he produces a word without accessing a stored representation, production should be as good as input processing allows. We have tools for checking this out. **Repetition** does not require access to stored representations. In the case of **non-word repetition**, there is no representation to access. How do Eamonn and Michael fare in these tasks?

Eamonn was first asked to repeat a set of words he had named. His score on repetition matched his score on naming: both 30 per cent. All but one of the errors he made in repetition occurred on the same items as in naming. But the errors were not necessarily the same:

Target	Naming	Repetition	
guitar	[tɪˈta]	[tɪˈta]	*same*
kangaroo	[ˈkæˈwu]	[ˈkæməˈwu]	*different*
umbrella	[ˈbwɛlə]	[ʌmˈbwɛ̃]	*different*

The same thing happened in a further test of repetition. This test comprised a set of words which had proved difficult in production, and a corresponding set of non-words which altered the vowel and in some cases also the stress of the word. These are illustrated by the following examples:

	Matched non-words			
Words	Same stress		Different stress	
after	['iftə]	eefter		
garden	['gidən]	geeden		
guitar	[gə'tɜ]	geter	['gɜtə]	gerter
balloon	[bɪ'lɔn]	bilawn	['bɔlɪn]	bawlin

This repetition test was carried out twice. Eamonn's scores were similar for words and non-words, both 36 per cent first time round, 60 per cent for words and 52 per cent for non-words second time round. He sometimes responded to words and non-words in the same way

	Target		Eamonn
Word	Riddler		['wɪgələ]
Non-word	['rædlə]	raddler	['wægələ]

but did not always do so:

	Target		Eamonn
Word	guitar		[dɪ'tɒ]
Non-word	[gə'tɜ]	geter	*correct*
Word	garden		*correct*
Non-word	['gidən]	geeden	['digən]

What can we infer from these repetition tasks? First, Eamonn makes the same sort of errors in repetition as in naming and spontaneous output. And he makes the same sort of errors whether he is repeating words or non-words. These findings point to problems in production even when he need not or cannot refer to a stored representation. The implication is that Eamonn has production difficulties which are not due to inadequate representations resulting from earlier input difficulties. As with naming, Eamonn's errors in repetition exceed his errors in judgement. He makes errors in repetition of the sort he rejects in judgement. This again indicates problems in output which go beyond his input problems.

At what point in output might these errors arise? One source of evidence is a comparison between naming, where a word must be accessed from a store, and repetition of non-words, where there is no stored word to access. Eamonn makes similar numbers and types of errors whether or not a representation is accessed. The parallels in the errors he makes on these different production tasks imply that the errors arise in a component of processing common to word and non-word production. The one component common to naming, repetition of words and repetition of non-words, is articulatory planning. In line with difficulties in articulatory planning, Eamonn seems to have problems with certain target sounds whatever the production task, for example in *Ri<u>dd</u>ler*, *a<u>f</u>ternoon*, *nu<u>m</u>ber*.

At this point, we strike a paradox akin to the one which emerged in his input. While certain sounds or sound sequences appear to be vulnerable, they appear to be more vulnerable in some words than others. For example, while /f/ is consistently omitted in *afternoon*, it is consistently correct in *after*. While some words are almost always produced in the same way, for example *vet*, *very*, *guitar*, others are produced inconsistently. This variation between words suggests that some words are more stably represented than others. But this indicates a problem in representations rather than in articulatory planning. Again, we have come up with evidence for constraints on articulatory planning of words *and* vagueness in representations of words. Putting this together with the analysis of Eamonn's input, we appear to have identified constraints on *all* the components of phonological processing we have considered: on speech discrimination, on articulatory planning *and* on the representations to which these connect.

Turning to Michael, output investigations lead to a similar conclusion. Michael was given his set of twenty words and twenty non-words to repeat. His performance was weak: only 20 per cent of the words and 10 per cent of the non-words were repeated correctly. The scale of his difficulty is evident when we compare his performance with the performance of the other children in the study:

| | Percentage of correctly repeated | |
	Real words	Non-words
Michael	20.00	10.00
Vocabulary-matched children	99.17	66.25
Age-matched children	100.00	86.00

Like Eamonn, he shows problems with repetition that go beyond the problems he shows in input. He repeats correctly even fewer items than he is able to discriminate in lexical decision tasks. Since he makes errors in repeating non-words as well as words, we might again infer that there are difficulties in a component of processing common to these: articulatory planning. On the other hand, as with Eamonn, Michael's production of words varies. He produces certain words correctly even though these appear no simpler than words he produces incorrectly. This again suggests that some words are more precisely represented than other words, which points to problems in word representations. Michael too appears to have constraints on auditory and articulatory processing which cut across words *and* constraints on the representation of particular words.

Looking ahead

Eamonn's and Michael's difficulties, it seems, are quite diverse. They appear to span all aspects of phonological processing beyond hearing in input and before articulatory execution in output, including the representation of word phonologies.

Such children tell us that impairment may extend over different components of word processing. The occurrence of more diverse difficulties with phonology is perhaps unsurprising. The nature of the *connections* between those more diverse difficulties is harder to fathom. The picture which has been emerging is one of each component of phonological processing being constrained in its own right, but also constraining other components of processing connected to it. This may lead us to see components of processing in a fresh light. Rather than being separate and self-contained

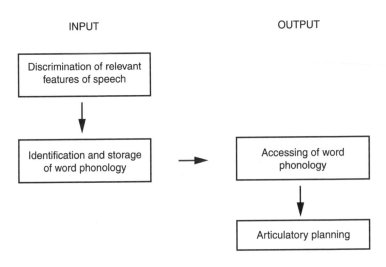

Figure 6.3 Possible forward cascade in phonological processing

'boxes', they may be viewed as collections of information which cascade forwards – and perhaps even backwards. This means that a constraint on auditory discrimination may weaken phonological representations which may undermine articulatory planning, as shown in figure 6.3.

Conversely, a constraint on articulatory planning may weaken phonological representations which may undermine auditory discrimination – though this backward 'domino effect' is likely to be much weaker than the forward effect, as shown in figure 6.4. Such cascading of information is taken on board in **connectionist** theories of processing.

For Eamonn and Michael, then, the primary impairment may lie in the flow of information from what they hear to the representations they store and the articulatory planning of those representations, and possibly back again. In contrast, the difficulties of children with 'phonological impairment' appeared to lie in very specific aspects of articulatory planning, with no observable effects on other components of processing (see previous chapter). This

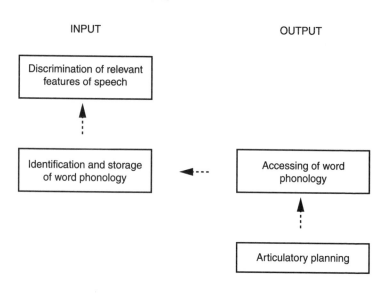

INPUT   OUTPUT

Figure 6.4 Possible backward cascade in phonological processing

suggests that the reverberations from impairment at a very late point in output processing are negligible or non-existent.

But if this rather hazy notion of cascading information is right, where and why does the cascade stop? Why does an impairment which cuts across phonological processing not feed forward, and even backward, to semantic representations, which are connected to phonological representations, as shown in figure 6.5?

The answer may be that it does. On present evidence, we know very little about Eamonn's and Michael's semantic processing. We established at the outset that their semantics was *relatively* unimpaired. But semantic errors were noted in both children. It could be that these errors are simply a spin-off from the problems with phonological processing already identified. Perhaps when Eamonn and Michael can't access the phonology they are looking for, they go for a meaning close to their target or a very general meaning for which they *can* find the phonology. So, when Eamonn can't find *horse*, he lands on another animal, *cat*; when he can't find *pot*, he falls back on *thing* until *pot* comes to him. But there is another

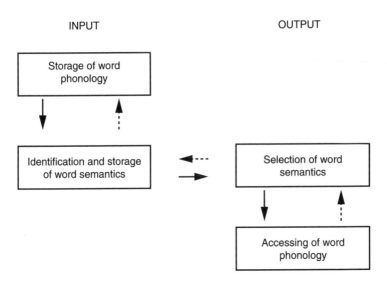

Figure 6.5 Possible forward and backward cascade in lexical processing

possibility. Recall that a word's phonology acts as a 'bootstrap' to meaning, and a 'handle' on a particular package of meaning (see chapter 2). If words' phonologies are weak for a child, perhaps this weakens the child's phonological bootstrapping and his handle on meaning. While we have reason to think that Eamonn and Michael are well able to make sense of the world, and do so in similar ways to other children, this doesn't rule out the possibility that their 'packaging' of the world into *word* concepts is affected by their difficulties with word phonology.

We find that this is more than just a hypothetical possibility when we turn to children's difficulties with the words from which sentences are grown.

Note: Eamonn was originally presented in Chiat & Hunt 1993. The presentation of Michael is based on the data in Constable, Stackhouse & Wells 1997 and draws heavily on the authors' discussion of these data, for which I am indebted.

Part II
Grappling with verb structure

7 Translating events

When children are having difficulties with sentences, the most immediate sign of those difficulties will probably be the way they struggle in everyday conversations. They don't necessarily have problems taking turns as conversational partners. But as they take their turns, they falter, producing utterances which are halting, or limited, or mixed up. Witness Eamonn's attempts to explain that he has been unwell in the night and that his teacher may have to call his mother:

> I not feel well today – sick the school – why – my mum gonna call – Mary gonna call me – Anna gonna call m – [ɪɡədə] call my mummy I sick . . . I'm getting sick in [ə] school – Anna gonna t – phone – my mum out – phone my mummy out.

Here, we see Eamonn start a sentence, stall, have another go, or change direction and start again. Each stab he makes at expressing himself consists of a run of words which comes out fluently even though it may be incomplete. Other children produce sequences of words which may be clearer but are more disjointed. Take 8-year-old Richard's attempts to explain what happens to the lambs on the farm where he lives:

> R: Um – girls, keep, boys, not keep.
> SC: What do you do with the boys?
> R: [tsɛl – tsɛ –] on – oth' people.
> SC: Sell them? So why do you keep the girls?
> R: Breeding.

A closer look at these children's utterances shows that some of them are organised in slightly odd ways. As well as leaving out certain words, they may combine words which don't go together, or which don't quite get across the meaning they seem to be aiming for, as with Eamonn's

> . . . sick the school . . .
> . . . phone my mummy out

or Richard's

> [tsɛl – tsɛ –] on – oth' people

The order of the words may also go awry, as when Eamonn tries to explain how his teachers know that he has been unwell:

> Because he write my mum – because my mum write in my book

Does he mean '. . . write my mum' or 'my mum write . . .'?

As a consequence of these children's difficulties, the listener is sometimes unsure what these children are trying to say. Everyday conversations may suggest that their *understanding* is precarious as well. When they respond to other people's utterances, it may become obvious that they have missed some detail of what the speaker was saying, or have got the wrong end of the stick entirely. Conversations with Eamonn can lead into such cul-de-sacs or tangles:

> SC: Do you like school?
> E: Like to go home.
> SC: Why do you prefer to go home?
> E: Because I dunno.
> SC: You like home better than school?
> E: No I love home.

Signs of difficulties with sentences in everyday conversations might be confirmed by formal assessments. The child might come down on something like the Test for the Reception of Grammar (Bishop 1983), where they must select one out of four pictures to match a spoken sentence, for example

> The girl is sitting on the table
> The man is eating the apple
> The girl is pushing the horse
> The man is chasing the dog
> The elephant is pushed by the boy

If they are below par on this test, it looks as if they have difficulties in understanding sentences. A wide-ranging assessment such as the Clinical Evaluation of Language Fundamentals – Pre-school (Wiig, Secord & Semel 1992) may reveal problems in the 'Sentence Structure' section, where the child has to point to the right picture for sentences such as

The bear is in the wagon
The man opened the door
The girl took some flowers to her mother
The woman caught a big fish
The boy was followed by his cat
The girl is being pushed by the boy

This would also point to problems with comprehension. Or problems might surface in the 'Recalling Sentences' section, where the child has to repeat back sentences such as

I can carry it
You can wear this old coat
I am putting ketchup and mustard on my hamburger

Here, difficulties could be arising in production.

Formal procedures for analysing children's spontaneous utterances might confirm that they are not producing the sort of structures expected at their age. Examples of such procedures are the Language Assessment, Remediation and Screening Procedure – LARSP (Crystal, Fletcher & Garman 1976) or the Bloom & Lahey (1978) or Systematic Analysis of Language Transcripts – SALT (Miller & Chapman 1982–7). (For further examples and details of clinical assessments, see Lees & Urwin 1997.)

What is it that stops these children dealing with sentences as other children do? Are they having difficulty with the sorts of *meanings* which sentences express? Or do they have the meanings, but struggle with the *words* which are needed to create sentences? Or do they have the words, but struggle when it comes to *combining* them? Whatever their difficulties, do they arise in output only, or do they show up in input as well?

To explore these possibilities, we need to know more about sentences and the sort of words that are needed to grow them.

From scenes to events

Semantically, a sentence encodes a state of affairs, or **event**. But the relationship between event and sentence is not a simple one. Sentences relate to events in a rather special way.

At any moment within the flow of our experience, we tune in to certain aspects of that experience. Looking at a scene, the sorts of things we might notice are the presence of an object; something about the object such as the state it is in; the position of an object relative to another object; the way it is moving; and so on. The scene may call to mind some other scene, which we picture in our mind's eye, and again, we attend to certain aspects of the pictured scene. Or we may be entirely oblivious to the scene in the outside world, attending only to something in our mind's eye. Sentences enable us to express and communicate what we experience in the outside world and in our mind's eye. But they can only do this indirectly. We cannot take the whole conglomeration of our experience at successive moments and encode it all in one sentence. This is because sentences are highly focused in their meaning. They pick out certain aspects from the flow of experience. To be more precise, they pick out a particular event from the flow of experience. To be even more precise, they pick out a particular angle on a particular event.

To illustrate this crucial point, take a look at this picture of Fred, Bob and an old car.

A picture, being a static representation, already limits the information we receive about a scene compared with a video or with direct experience. Yet even the frozen picture includes more than we can encode in a sentence. Looking at the picture, we might notice what Fred is doing, what Bob is doing, what is going on between them, what Fred or Bob or the car is like. If we were to encode these observations, we might come up with sentences such as:

> Fred handed over the money
> Fred paid for the car
> Bob took the money
> Fred bought the car from Bob
> Bob sold the car to Fred
> The car looked old

and so on. Each of these sentences picks out only certain aspects of the event in the picture. And that is what sentences necessarily do: they act like a 'zoom lens' (Fisher, Hall, Rakowitz & Gleitman 1994) focusing in on an event from a particular perspective.

From events to verb structures

Since the semantic heart of the sentence is an **event**, the sentence hinges on the word or words which encode that event. In the examples above, these are words such as 'buy' and 'sell' and 'take'. It is these words – syntactically the **verbs** – which give rise to the 'zoom lens' effect. If we change the verb, we change the 'camera angle' on the scene. This may change which participants in the scene are in view, and are included with the event. It may also change what it is about the participants that is in the foreground. 'Pay' focuses on the transfer of the money, and the goal of that transfer. 'Hand' and 'take' both focus on the transfer of the car, but they take different perspectives on that transfer. 'Hand' takes the perspective of the starting-point, or **source**, of the transfer (Fred). 'Take' is from the perspective of the end-point, or **goal**, of the transfer (Bob). 'Look' has an entirely different focus. It does not capture any relationship between participants in the event. Instead, it focuses on just one of the participants (the car), and says something about its state.

In some cases, the event is encapsulated in the verb alone. This is true for 'buy' and 'sell'. Some events, though, are encoded by a verb along with a further sentence constituent. Take the case of 'look old'. Here, the verb on its own has a rather general meaning: it refers to the visual state of an entity, but not to any specific state. Syntactically, it is the **adjectival** constituent following the verb ('old') which specifies the particular state.

This illustrates a pattern which commonly occurs in English. States and changes of state may be encoded by a general state verb, such as 'look', 'be', 'seem', 'feel', 'get', which combines with an Adjective Phrase specifying the state:

Verb	*Adjective Phrase*
be	sad
look	quite ill
seem	angry
feel	great
get	very wet

On the other hand, many changes of state can be expressed by a single verb which incorporates the particular state: 'tire', 'age', 'cool', 'sadden', 'freeze', 'melt', 'break' all express a particular change of state.

Some of these states can be encoded either by a single verb *or* by a general state verb with a separate Adjective Phrase:

Single verb	*Verb + Adjective Phrase*
tire	get tired
cool	get cold
age	get old
sadden	get sad

A pair of sentences such as:

The soup cooled

and

The soup got cool

express very similar states – though you may discern a subtle difference between them.

Movements, like states, may be expressed by a specific verb or by a general verb which is further specified. In this case, it is the *direction* of movement which is specified separately. Direction is commonly expressed by a curious category of words known as particles. These include prepositions such as 'up', 'down', 'in', 'on', 'out', 'off', 'away':

Verb	*Particle*
go	up
run	out
jump	in
move	off
throw	away

However, the verb and particle do not always express a movement and a direction. Often they combine to express a specific event as a whole. For example,

give up/sell out/throw up/put up/pick up/go off/put off

can all refer to a very specific event, as in

He gave up his job
The peaches went off

Again, there may be a single verb expressing the same or a similar event:

He resigned his job
The peaches rotted

Similarly, some movement events can be expressed by either a single verb or a verb with a particle:

Verb	*Verb + particle*
leave	go away
enter	come in
insert	put in
lower	put down
raise	hold up

In all these examples, we see that events are expressed by verbs, either on their own, or together with an Adjective Phrase or particle. If the *semantic* heart of a sentence is the *event*, the *syntactic* heart must be the *verb*. To understand and produce sentences in a language, we must know verbs. Knowing verbs means knowing their phonological forms, such as /baɪ/ (*buy*) or /sɛl/ (*sell*), and knowing the events which those forms encode, such as 'exchange of object for money'.

From participants in events to argument structures

But knowing verbs involves more than the connection between their form and meaning. This is because events, and the verbs which encode them, also involve participants – the 'who' and 'what' play a role in the event. The verb, in taking a particular perspective on an event, decides which participants are in view. This determines which participants can or must be included with the verb. For example, a verb which focuses on movement entails at least that which undergoes the movement. A verb focusing on possession entails at least that which possesses and that which is possessed. Returning to our original example, 'Fred bought the old car from Bob', the change of possession event involved three participants: the original possessor 'Fred', the ultimate possessor 'Bob', and the thing changing possession 'the old car'.

The participants entailed by a verb are known technically as its **arguments**. Arguments typically refer to things, as with 'the old car', or to people, as with 'Fred' and 'Bob'. They play particular roles in events, known technically as **thematic roles**. The thematic role of an argument identifies what the argument is doing in the event. One such role is the **theme.** This refers to the argument which undergoes a state, location or possession. In the following sentences, 'the car' is a theme undergoing:

State:	The car looked quite old
	Sue cleaned the car
Location:	The car stood in the garage
	Fred put the car in the driveway
Possession:	That car belongs to Mary
	Jane bought the car from Mary

The **agent** refers to an argument which causes or brings about an event. In the following sentences, 'Alice' is an agent bringing about:

State:	<u>Alice</u> broke the glass
Location:	<u>Alice</u> took the car to the station
Possession:	<u>Alice</u> sent the letter to the doctor

The **source** and the **goal** refer to the arguments which are the starting- and endpoints of a change. In the change of location

The bus goes <u>from the station to town</u>

'the station' is the source and 'town' is the goal. In the changes of possession

<u>Fred</u> sold the car <u>to Bob</u>
<u>Bob</u> bought the car <u>from Fred</u>
<u>Bob</u> received the message <u>from Fred</u>

'Fred' is the source and 'Bob' is the goal. **Stimulus** and **experiencer** are sometimes used to refer to the arguments involved in a mental or psychological state. In the following sentences, 'Sam' is the experiencer, with 'jokes' as the stimulus:

<u>Sam</u> enjoys <u>jokes</u>
<u>Jokes</u> amuse <u>Sam</u>

These labels for thematic roles by no means exhaust the different ways in which arguments participate in events, as we would find if we delved further into the vast range of events we can express. But they enable us to distinguish certain of the roles involved in certain types of events.

Since sentences express events and events involve arguments, sentences require not just the verb expressing the event but also the arguments involved. These arguments take the form of constituents which combine with the verb. And they combine in ways which indicate the role each argument is playing in relation to the verb. In English, **word order** is the main device for marking the relation between arguments and verbs. Hence the difference between two sentences containing the same verb and the same arguments but in a different order:

The dog tripped up the postman

and

The postman tripped up the dog

Both focus the same type of event – the causation of a change of location – and the same characters – the dog and the postman. But the roles played by these two characters change – while the dog is the agent and the postman is the theme in one, their roles are reversed in the other. In order to understand and produce sentences, then, we must know not only the verbs to express the events and the arguments they entail. We must also know where the arguments go in relation to the verb.

The **position** of an argument depends on the verb, and the perspective it takes on the event. Human beings show certain strong biases in the perspectives they take. These are reflected in the way verbs encode events and where they place their arguments. For example, we have a strong tendency to focus on **causation**, with vast numbers of verbs encoding the causation of different states of affairs. Verbs which take this perspective on an event always involve a causer or agent, and this agent always occurs in the **subject** position, which precedes the verb in English:

State:	Alice broke the glass
Location:	Alice took the car to the station
Possession:	Alice sent the letter to the doctor

What happens when an event involves more than one 'causer'? For example, where there is a change of possession, it may be that two parties in the exchange play roles which are distinct but which are both active in bringing it about. When we come to encode such an event, we must construe it from the perspective of one or other. Often, the language offers us both possibilities, giving rise to pairs such as 'give/take', 'sell/buy', 'lend/borrow'. 'Give', 'sell' and 'lend' take the perspective of the *source*, placing the source in the subject position. This focuses on the source as the agent bringing about the event. Conversely, 'take', 'buy' and 'borrow' focus on the *goal* as the agent of the event. They place the goal in the subject slot.

It seems that the subject of a verb encodes an agent wherever the verb entails causation. This is why we typically think of the subject as being the 'doer'. However, this is not necessarily the case. Despite our strong inclination to notice causation and causers, we are quite capable of seeing events from perspectives which do not involve causation and do not entail an agent. Where a verb's focus is not causation, the subject slot will be filled by a different role. We have already met examples where the **theme** occupies the subject position:

State:	The car looked quite old
Location:	The car stood in the garage
Possession:	The car belongs to Mary

In these examples, where there is no agent, the subject slot is filled by the entity which undergoes the event. In contrast, where the verb took the perspective of the agent and placed this in subject position, the same theme occurred after the verb, in the position of the **direct object**:

State:	Sue cleaned the car
Location:	Fred put the car in the driveway
Possession:	Jane bought the car from Mary

Some verbs can take more than one perspective on an event and, correspondingly, more than one argument structure. For example, 'melt', 'break', 'cool', 'move', 'drop' and many other verbs can express the causation of a state of affairs. They then involve an agent in the subject slot and theme in the direct object slot:

Sue broke the car
Sue moved the car

But they can also refer to the same state of affairs without causation and without an agent. They then involve just a theme, and this takes up the subject slot:

The car broke
The car moved

Other verbs take only one of these perspectives. 'Fall', for example, refers to the movement of its theme:

The handle fell off

It cannot refer to the causation of that movement by an agent:

*The child fell the handle off

Conversely, 'pull' refers to the agent causing the theme to move:

The child pulled the handle off

but cannot generally refer just to the movement of the theme:

?The handle pulled off

Knowledge of these verbs thus includes knowledge of the perspectives they allow, and the arguments which come into those perspectives.

We have now revealed fully the core of the sentence. *Semantically*, it is an event which is viewed from a particular perspective entailing certain participants, or arguments, playing certain roles. *Syntactically*, the event maps onto a verb, or verb + Adjective Phrase, or verb + particle. The arguments map onto constituents which combine with the verb. Their position in relation to the verb depends on the perspective the verb takes on the event and its participants.

Sentences, then, consist of a complex and indirect connection between events we perceive or imagine, and verb–argument structures. In order to interpret and express events in sentences, we must conceive events from the sorts of perspectives that verbs take on events. We must know the connections between particular perspectives on events and particular verb forms. And we must know the connections between participant roles in events and argument positions round the verb.

For children discovering their language, the relation between events and verb–argument structures is a key target. They must discover the verbs of the language: their forms, and the events on which they focus. They must at the same time discover the arguments entailed by the verb. And they must discover where those arguments go in relation to the verb.

From verb–argument structure to rhythmic structure

When the verb and arguments come together to encode an event, the phonological forms of the verb and arguments join to form a larger phonological unit. Those phonological forms are not simply strung together one after the other, each equally prominent. If you try uttering the sentence

Fred bought the car from Bob

you will find that the sentence has a rhythm in which some words are more prominent than others. The rhythm or stress pattern of the sentence is directly related to the way in which the words are combined. When words combine in a constituent, the last word in a constituent generally carries the greatest stress in the constituent. When constituents combine in a sentence, the most stressed word in the last constituent carries the greatest stress in the sentence. It is partly this increased stress at the end of constituents and at the end of the sentence which gives rise to the 'up and down' rhythm of the sentence.

We can see how this operates in our example:

Fred bought the car from Bob

'Fred' is a constituent, and since 'Fred' is the only word in the constituent, it carries the constituent stress. This stress can be represented by a cross above the word:

```
x
Fred bought the car from Bob
```

'The car' is a constituent, and here it is the final word 'car' which carries the constituent stress:

```
x              x
Fred bought the car from Bob
```

'From Bob' is a constituent, in which 'Bob' carries the constituent stress:

```
x              x       x
Fred bought the car from Bob
```

'Bob', being the final word in the final constituent of the sentence, also carries the sentence stress, for which we can add another cross:

```
                       x
x              x       x
Fred bought the car from Bob
```

The verb 'bought', which does not end a constituent, is less stressed than 'Fred', 'car' and 'Bob'. So, we end up with a stress pattern with 'Bob' carrying the greatest stress, and 'Fred' and 'car' carrying greater stress than the other words. This shows the prominence of certain words in the rhythm of the sentence. You might check this out by uttering the sentence as naturally as possible and tapping out its rhythm.

Because nouns frequently occur at the end of a Noun Phrase, and sentences frequently end with a Noun Phrase, nouns often carry constituent and sentence stress. Verbs are much less likely to occur at the end of a constituent or sentence, because they are typically followed by NP arguments. Verbs therefore tend to be less prominent than nouns. If you go back to the examples we have considered and say them out loud, you might notice the prominence of the nouns compared with the verb in the rhythm of the sentence.

Sentences, then, connect a verb–argument structure to a rhythmic structure in which certain words 'weigh' more than others. In dealing with sentences, we must be sensitive to the way words are stressed when they come together in a sentence.

Sentences: connections between events, verb–argument structures and rhythmic structures

We have now seen that a sentence is a rhythmic unit, made up of the phonological forms of words which receive varying prominence. The core of that rhythmic unit is the verb and the arguments organised around it. These encode an event from a particular perspective, and the participants in that event.

The route between scenes as we observe or imagine them and sentences is not a simple one. Scenes do not map directly onto sentences. If children are to understand and talk about events, they must discover the complex connections between events, and rhythmic structures containing verbs and arguments.

8 Growing verb structures

Children set out with two sources of information about sentences: the scenes which they observe and participate in, and the sound of the utterances they hear. We have just seen that the connection between scene and sound is an indirect one. The sound consists of word forms organised in a rhythmic structure, and this relates to a particular event involving particular participants. In discovering sentences, children must somehow discover which components of the sound relate to which aspects of the scene. This means identifying verb forms and the particular events which map onto those forms. It also means identifying the way arguments are organised around the verb and the event roles which **map onto** those arguments.

Most children appear to meet the challenges posed by language with ease and speed. By 16 months, they will often respond appropriately to requests such as

Give Jane the cookie
Show Jane the cookie

suggesting that they understand the verb and the roles of the arguments (Huttenlocher 1974). This is backed up by evidence of what they do when they are given peculiar requests which they are highly unlikely to have heard before, and which therefore call for active interpretation of the verb and argument roles:

Smell the dolly
Kiss the truck

Presented with bizarre instructions of this sort, children of 16–24

127

months carry out a fair proportion correctly (Sachs & Truswell 1978). Where they do, they have clearly understood the verb and the role of its object. Whether they have also understood the importance of word order is a moot point. This can only be proven by asking them to act out contrasting pairs such as

Make the car push the cow

and

Make the cow push the car

Few 18-month-olds will readily comply with such instructions to show us whether they do or don't understand them. Their likely response is to ignore the request, be distracted by something else, or wander off, leaving us none the wiser about their understanding. To get round the hazards of checking out comprehension directly, we need more subtle probes which catch them unawares.

This is what the **preferential looking** technique can do (Hirsh-Pasek & Golinkoff 1996). With this technique, the infant is seated on a parent's lap, between two video screens showing different scenes involving the same two TV characters. On one, Cookie Monster is tickling Big Bird. On the other, Big Bird is tickling Cookie Monster. The child hears a tape playing . . .

Look! Cookie Monster is tickling Big Bird! Where is Cookie Monster tickling Big Bird?

The question is whether children look longer at the screen which *matches* the utterance they hear. If they do, we can infer that they have understood how word order determines the roles of the participants in the event. When a group of children around 17-months-old were 'tested' in this way, the majority did look longer at the screen matching the utterance. It seems they understood who was tickling who.

This finding comes as little surprise when we see what infants do with their own utterances around this age. Between 18 and 24 months, most move beyond single words and start producing their first word combinations. The range of combinations they use is at first limited, and develops slowly. But by the time they have produced around 100 different word combinations – typically at about 22 months – their word combinations take off (see Ingram 1989).

Even before they actually produce word combinations, children give some evidence of communicating events or relationships. Although the majority of their early words refer to things and people, not all do. A small proportion of their words pick out states such as 'broken', possession such as 'mine', location or change of location such as 'there', 'down', 'gone'. These words picking out relations in which things and people participate are the obvious seeds of verb–argument structures. But children's use of 'thing' and 'people' words at this stage also anticipates their development of verb–argument structures. Often, these words are used not simply as labels for the thing or person, but to indicate their relation to another entity. Take the example of the child who picks up her mother's slipper and says 'Mommy. Mommy', and when asked what it is, says 'Slipper' (Bloom 1970). The child is surely not using 'Mommy' as a name for the slipper. Much more plausibly, she is pointing out a relation between an individual, 'Mommy', and the slipper. Such a relation is just the sort that verb–argument structures serve to encode – relations which later become specified as 'possession' or 'location'.

These relations become more explicit in the child's utterances as more relational words are used and as words are combined. The child's early combinations look like very limited verb–argument structures – focusing on participants in events and their relations. Strikingly, children seem to mark relations between participants appropriately from a very early stage. The verb–argument structures they use may be incomplete. But they rarely show errors. In general, their verbs match the perspective the adult language takes on events, and they order arguments around the verb as the adult language would order them.

Take the utterances produced by Alison at 2;3. Alison uses a limited range of word combinations, and the structure of the combinations she uses is very limited. Often, her utterances identify just a thing or person, such as 'Teddy', 'Shoe', 'Paul'. Often, they identify just an event or relation:

Drop (after penny dropped)
Fall out (after money falls out of purse)
Hiding (when teddy is in cupboard)
Open (trying to open purse)
Off (taking socks off doll)

Where she does combine events and participants, though, the event and the participant are ordered as they would be in adult English:

Agent – Event – **Theme**:	'Ali do it' (= open door)
	'Michelle do it' (= put doll in bed)
Agent – Event – **Goal**:	'My daddy go home'
Event – **Theme**:	'Wash teddy'
	'Open it'
	'Push me'
	'Got some'
Event – **Goal**:	'Go in there'
Theme – State:	'Teddy wake up'
Experiencer –	
Psychological state – **Stimulus**:	'I [wanə] money'

Compare Paul, at exactly the same age. Paul has much more developed word combinations:

Me play [ə] puzzles. Me want – play [ə] puzzles. Me want [ə] look at this . . . Let's do some drawing . . . My cut it out. Me want to cut it out now.

Add to this sample the following utterances Paul produced five months later:

You don't like the skin? . . . I don't like [ə] skin. I don't like it in – in – in – in – my water.

Within these samples, both Alison and Paul make reference to psychological states ('want' and 'like'). These examples of psychological states provide particularly good evidence that they have discovered the perspective English takes on certain events and the way this is reflected in verb–argument structure. The verbs they have used take the perspective of the experiencer of the psychological state, placing this before the verb, with the stimulus following the verb. Alison produces one example, and this shows the correct mapping of the experiencer and stimulus:

I [wanə] money

Paul produces more varied and sophisticated examples, again with the correct mapping:

Me want . . .
You don't like . . .

To appreciate fully the significance of the mapping the children have made, notice that it is different from the mapping which must be made by children acquiring certain other languages. In Italian and Spanish, the psychological state of liking is expressed from the perspective of the stimulus rather than the experiencer. The everyday verb for expressing this state is akin to 'please' rather than 'like'. 'I like . . .' therefore translates literally as 'To me pleases . . .'. Children acquiring these languages will therefore acquire a different verb–argument structure from that which Paul has used correctly with 'like' in English (see Bowerman 1996 and Slobin 1996 for further discussion and evidence).

In Turkish, relations between the verb and its arguments do not depend on word order, as in English, but on word endings, or **inflections,** attached to nouns. Children acquiring Turkish use these inflections consistently and productively by the age of 2;0 (Aksu-Koç & Slobin 1985). While their utterances may be short and simple in the early stages, they still convey verb–argument relations through their virtually error-free use of inflections. In Turkish, word order serves to convey the relative newness or importance of information in the sentence rather than to mark verb–argument relations. Young Turkish children already order the verb and its arguments for this purpose.

Evidently, even in their early, very limited word combinations, children are on the road with verb–argument structure. Whatever language they are acquiring, they already convey events in accordance with the perspectives that language takes on events, and with the devices it uses to mark relations between participants in those events. Children continue apace along this road. Their limited verb–argument combinations become more varied and more complete. Their range of verbs proliferates, so that they are able to refer to a wide variety of events from the particular perspectives of their language. At the same time, their verb–argument structures fill out, so that verbs are used with all the arguments they require.

The point is well illustrated by the following sample of language from Shel, taken at 2;6, while she was playing with miniatures. Shel's utterances already average four to five words:

> Can't shut that. Them get out and she – little baby's can go in there. Can't get she in. Push him. Should I push him? . . . They go [ə] fall off. Where's [ə] other girls? Look, I found two . . . Can you bend her legs? . . . Mummy, can I take my shoes off? You wanna wear my shoes? No, think they too big. Hope they're not too big for me . . .

Strikingly, these word combinations virtually always include verbs. And these verbs encode an impressive variety of events:

Causation of change of state:	'shut'
Change of location:	'get out', 'go in there', 'fall off'
Causation of change of location:	'push', 'bend', 'take off'
Causation of change of possession:	'find'
Psychological state:	'want', 'think', 'hope'

Shel also includes all the arguments required by these verbs, and in the appropriate position for their role in the event.

Children vary considerably in their rate of development, and many will not produce diverse and complete verb–argument structures as early as Shel. But the majority will get there somewhere between 2;6 and 4. The consistency of their verb–argument structures at this point is startling. They do make errors on occasion. But on the whole, their sporadic deviations from adult verb–argument structure still follow the patterns of the adult language. Far from being evidence of confusion about patterns of verb–argument structure, they provide evidence that the child has discovered these patterns.

Consider, for example, the following 'errors' produced by various children:

2;6   Mummy, can you stay this open (= make this stay open; keep
       this open)
2;8   Daddy go me round (= make me go round; spin me)
3;8   And the doggie had a head. And somebody fell it off (= made it
       fall off; broke it off)
4;2   He disappeared himself (= made himself disappear; hid himself)
4;3   It always sweats me (= makes me sweat; ?bakes me)

                                                    (examples from Bowerman 1982)

In each case, the child's verb is in the right semantic ball park. The
child is conveying the intended state (stay open, sweat) or location
(go round, fall off, disappear). The problem is that each of these
verbs is being used with one argument more than it allows. Each of
the verbs refers to a state or location, and entails a theme undergoing that state or location. In adult English, the theme is the subject:

I go round
This stays open
It fell off

In the children's utterances, this theme occurs *after* the verb, as
the direct object of the verb:

Daddy go me round
Can you stay this open
Somebody fell it off

So what has the child done with the subject slot? This is filled by
another argument:

Daddy go me round
Can you stay this open
Somebody fell it off

Intuitively, we take this argument to be an agent, bringing about
the event. There are a number of grounds for our assumption. One
is the context, which makes it likely that, for example, 'daddy' is to
bring about the event of 'going round'. Second, we know that
agents are always subjects, so if the child has created a new role for
the subject, it is likely to be an agent. Third, and most telling, we
know many verbs which can be used with an agent, expressing

causation of an event, or without an agent, expressing just the event.

Agent		Theme		Theme	
Daddy	moved	**me**		**I**	moved
Somebody	broke	**the head**	off	**The head**	broke off

The child's errors therefore follow a familiar pattern, using a verb which expresses *just* a change of state/location to express *causation* of that state/location. It is the inclusion of the agent, placed in the subject slot, which implies causation.

These are the sort of 'errors' which occur in young children's language. They hardly warrant being called 'errors', since they are not arbitrary. The children are not haphazardly adding an argument or putting it in the wrong place. On the contrary, they have discovered a pattern in the complex relation between events and verb–argument structures, and have systematically applied this to verbs whose meaning and structure do not fit that pattern. These so-called errors are therefore not a sign of difficulties in determining the meaning relations between verb and arguments, or the organisation of verb and arguments. Rather, they confirm the child's sophisticated grasp of verb–argument structures.

What is more, such errors are vanishingly rare. The utterances exemplified above are a drop in the ocean of the child's utterances which generally follow the adult model and use verbs with their required argument structures (Pinker 1989).

Filtering verb–argument structures from scenes and speech

The speed at which children move from early words through early word combinations to full and varied verb–argument structures is impressive. But even more impressive, perhaps, is the fact that they get there at all. Recall that the connections between scenes and verb–argument structures are indirect: scenes can be interpreted in many different ways corresponding to many different verb–argument structures. To identify verb–argument structures from the information provided by scenes and sound, the child must

- identify which event and participants in a scene are being focused by an utterance. The utterance may focus on a directly observable event involving things and people in the scene, for example, 'I'm giving the ball to granny'. But this is not necessarily the case. The utterance may focus on an event which is anticipated and so is not immediately observable, such as 'Give the ball to granny' or 'Kate's coming home soon'. Or it may focus on an invisible event – a perceptual or psychological state such as 'listening', or 'wanting', or 'liking' or 'feeling proud'.
- identify the verb or verb structure which maps onto the focused event: 'listen' or 'give' or 'pick up' or 'feel proud'. Verbs may occasionally be heard in isolation, in utterances such as 'Stop', 'Watch', 'Wait'. But they will much more often be buried in a string of words from which they must be segmented, as in 'Listen to that', 'I'll give you a drink'.
- identify the constituents of the sentence which map onto the arguments in the event, and the positions of those constituents in relation to the verb:

    You'll listen to the story
    You'll hear the story
    Granny will tell you the story
    The story will surprise you
    You'll enjoy the story

Any one of these bits of information will help get to the other. If you can pick out the arguments, this will focus you on the relevant participants, which will draw your attention to the event in which they are participating. So if you are the child in the following scene:

and you hear an utterance containing the familiar words

Granny . . . ball . . . you

this will focus you on the event which currently involves you, granny and the ball. You can then identify the event focused by the verb, in this case, a change of possession event. However, this information will not be enough to distinguish between different change of possession events. If you also notice the order of the arguments, this will lead you to a 'give' rather than a 'take' event. But even this will not narrow your focus down to that of a single verb – for example 'give' as opposed to 'hand'.

Alternatively, if you know exactly what is being focused in the scene, you will be in a position to make a good guess at the meaning of the verb. For example, suppose you are in the above scene, and you know granny's current focus is not just the exchange, but her role in bringing about that exchange. This will enable you to narrow the likely reference of her verb from just any change of possession event to one in which the source of the exchange is the agent – to a 'giving' rather than 'taking' sort of verb.

Best of all, if you know the verb – as adults do – this immediately directs you to the relevant event in the scene. The moment the verb is heard and recognised as 'give' or 'take' or 'hand' or 'listen' or 'tell' or 'enjoy' or whatever, you know exactly which event is focused.

The problem is that children set out without any of this information. To all appearances, they are caught in a vicious circle. To know what is being focused in even the simplest scene, you need to know the verb and its argument roles. But the child's task is precisely to discover the verb and its argument roles. And to discover the verb and its argument roles, you need to know what is being focused. Children somehow break this apparently vicious circle. The evidence is their successful acquisition of verb–argument structures. How do they crack the connection between scenes and sound to get at the specific meanings and the specific forms of verbs and their arguments?

Bootstrapping

The answer, according to current theories, is that children are equipped with 'bootstraps' which give them a leg-up from one type of information to another. Bootstrapping might start from any of the information which children receive from scenes or utterances, and lead them to new information about the way the two are connected.

Suppose that children are extremely sensitive to what speakers are focusing on at any moment in time. They notice whether the speaker is focused on something moving, or moving in a certain manner, or changing its state, or changing possession, and so on. If they share the speaker's focus on the scene, this will provide a leg-up to the meaning of the verb used by the speaker. Once they know what that verb picks out in the scene, they can work out which participants are involved, and how they are involved. And once they know the role of different participants, they can work out where those roles go in relation to the verb. For example, the child sees an adult pouring water into a glass. If the child shares the adult's focus on the moving water, he will expect the adult to use a verb referring to movement, and focusing more on the thing moving than the thing it moves into. He can then deduce that the thing moving, which is most affected by the event, will be most directly connected to the verb – 'pour' will be followed by 'the water' rather than 'the glass'. If, on the other hand, the adult's focus is on the state of the glass and the child shares that focus, he will expect the adult to use a verb referring to the change of state, and focusing more on what changes state. In this case, he will expect 'the glass' to be closest to the verb – 'fill' will be followed by 'the glass'.

These are examples of **semantic bootstrapping** (Pinker 1989). The child is using information about the scene to get to the argument structure of the verb describing the scene. It appears that children do this from an early age. The evidence comes from experiments in which children are shown events they have never seen before, to find out if the particular focus of the event influences the structure they use to describe the event.

In one experiment (see Pinker 1989 and Gropen, Pinker, Hollander & Goldberg 1991), children were introduced to the following two events: a sponge being moved in a zigzag path towards a cloth, the salient aspect of the event being the particular manner in which the cloth moves; a sponge being moved towards a cloth which then changes colour, the salient aspect of the event being the change of state of the cloth. In each case, the children were taught a novel verb for the event using a form which does not require arguments: 'This is pilking'. Children were then asked 'Can you tell me what I'm doing?'. Where children did not provide a clear direct object, they were given a further prompt 'Can you tell me what I'm pilking?'. The question was whether the different focus of each event would affect their response. Apparently it did. Even a group of 3-year-olds were more likely to make 'the sponge' the object ('pilking the sponge') when its movement was salient, and more likely to make 'the cloth' the object ('pilking the cloth') when its change of state was salient. This shows that they were sensitive to which of the two objects was most affected in the event, and knew that affected objects are linked to the slot directly following the verb. It seems that even 3-year-olds can use semantic information about the verb to get to its syntax.

This points to one possible way out of the vicious circle. If children can find the relevant focus in a scene when they hear a new verb, and if they know where focused argument roles go, they will be able to work out the argument structure of that verb. But these are two big 'ifs'. The experimental situation confronting the child is a long shot from the real-life situation in which children meet new verbs. In the experiment, children were shown a single event, and one which involved an eye-catching effect – either a change of colour or a peculiar movement. The child's attention was therefore easily caught and focused. In real life, events are not usually isolated. And even when they are, the aspect of the event focused by the verb is not spotlit. When children hear verbs such as 'pour' and 'fill' in real scenes, the event is likely to be one in a sequence in which the movement of the liquid or fullness of the container will not stand out in any way. If children notice differences in the speaker's focus within such real events, their sensitivity to the speaker's focus must be extremely acute.

Alternatively, they may turn to some other source of information about the focus of the event. Perhaps they have other bootstraps under their belts. Rather than using semantics to get at syntax, how about using syntax to get at semantics? Enter the theory of **syntactic bootstrapping** (Fisher, Hall, Rakowitz & Gleitman 1994). According to this theory, if children can identify the verb and its arguments, this will tell them which participants play key roles in an event, and this will in turn tell them the focus of the verb. Returning to our pouring/filling scenario, we now have children observing the event while they hear the utterance which contains 'pour' or 'fill'. When it's 'pour', they notice that the verb is followed by the argument 'the water'. This focuses them on the water rather than the container, they notice what is happening to the water, and they deduce that 'pour' refers to movement. When the utterance contains 'fill', they notice that 'fill' is followed by 'the cup', which focuses them on what is happening to the cup, and they deduce that 'fill' refers to the state of the cup.

Evidence suggests that children can use syntactic bootstrapping. This emerges from another experiment presenting children with novel verbs (Fisher et al. 1994). Here, children were shown a video of a familiar event which could be seen from two perspectives. The video might show a rabbit feeding an elephant with a spoon, an event roughly captured in the following still picture:

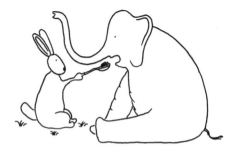

This could be seen as a rabbit feeding an elephant, but it could also be seen as an elephant eating. Children heard the event described in one of two ways:

> The rabbit is ziking the elephant

or

> The elephant is ziking

Children as young as 3 to 4 were influenced by the argument structure in which they heard the nonsense verbs. If they heard 'The elephant is ziking', they were more likely to translate the nonsense verb with a real verb fitting the elephant's perspective – 'eating' or 'licking the spoon'. If they heard 'The rabbit is ziking the elephant', they were more likely to come up with a verb fitting the rabbit's perspective – 'feeding' or 'giving him medicine'.

Here, then, is another break in the vicious circle. As long as they can pick out the verb form, notice the order of arguments around it, and know what the arguments refer to, they can deduce something about the verb's meaning. In particular, they can work out what angle the verb takes on the event.

Again, the child has a lot of processing to do before syntactic bootstrapping can come into play. Picking out the verb and arguments in the stream of speech is no small feat. This is where **phonological bootstrapping** enters the scene. Perhaps the sound pattern of utterances gives children a leg-up to what they contain, in particular, to the verb form and its arguments.

We know that verb–argument structures have a characteristic

rhythm in which certain word categories are more prominent than others. In particular, nouns typically receive more stress than verbs. Suppose children are acutely sensitive to these rhythmic structures. This could help them separate out the verbs and nouns within the stream of speech. It could also draw their attention to the order of nouns in the rhythm, which is crucial to establishing the verb–argument structure. The techniques of **preferential listening** and **preferential looking** have begun to reveal just how sensitive infants are to the rhythm and structure of utterances. Through these techniques, we have seen infants under a year recognising the way words are grouped into larger units (chapter 2). We have also seen how early they connect units in a particular order to participants in events (this chapter). We have reason to suspect that infants' sensitivity is even finer, enabling them to register the detailed rhythmic characteristics of verbs and their arguments. Unearthing the evidence to support this suspicion will, however, depend on refining still further our techniques for penetrating the hidden depths of infants' rhythmic processing.

Tying the bootstraps together

Research into bootstrapping has shown that children are sensitive to fine differences in scenes, in sound patterns, and in the organisation of words within sound patterns. Furthermore, they know something about how each of these relates to the other. This means they can use information they have about one to glean information about the other.

It seems that children are equipped with a number of bootstraps which are anchored in one type of information and extend this into new information, and that new information may be reached by more than one of the bootstraps. The focus in a scene can cue the child to the verb's focus, but so can the presence and order of arguments in the utterance describing the scene. The rhythm of the utterance can cue the child to the presence and order of arguments, but so can the focus within the scene. Perhaps it is this convergence of bootstraps which gets children out of the vicious circle they appeared to be caught in. By *putting together*

- the speaker's perspective on the scene
- the rhythm of the speaker's utterance
- the order of words within the rhythm

they can arrive at the meaning of the verb and the structure it takes. It is the 'union' or 'coalition' of cues in the input (Hirsh-Pasek & Golinkoff 1996), rather than any one of these cues, that gets children to this destination.

The implications for the skills children bring to the sentence-processing task are profound. They must be ready to notice subtle features of events and of sound patterns. More than this, they must be ready to notice when particular features of events co-occur with particular features of sound patterns, and make connections between these.

Tuning into the child's tune

We have come some way in understanding how children solve the apparently insoluble problem of mapping events onto verb–argument structures. Our conclusion is that children are attuned to the rhythm of speech, the highlights of scenes and, most significantly, to the connection between the two. Only such a finely tuned mind could steer children to the sort of verb–argument structures they typically use by around 4 years old.

The input the child receives could not on its own account for this. But it could make a difference. If the input harmonises with the tuning of the child's mind, it could make the child's task easier. Given our conclusions about the tuning of the child, we can see how adults might adapt their utterances to suit it.

First, they might help the child identify the *focus* of verbs by using them at just the moment when the relevant event is most salient to the child. Depending on the way the event happens over time, this moment may be before, during or after the event. With events such as 'fill', 'open', 'melt', or 'break', which have an observable effect after the event has occurred, it may be best to hear the verb *after* the event when its focus is most obvious. Events such as 'move', 'pour', 'push', 'spin', on the other hand, may be quite brief, and leave no conspicuous effect. With such events, it may be more useful to hear the verb just before the event, alerting the child to the dynamic change which the verb focuses (see Tomasello & Kruger 1992, Ambalu, Chiat & Pring 1997). Notice, though, that such manipulation of adult input can only help the child to work out the connection between scene and sound. No matter how effectively adults focus the child's attention on the event, the child *still* has to deduce just what the verb is getting at.

Adults might also help the child identify the verb's *form and argument structure* by exaggerating the rhythm of the utterance. This is something adults typically do when they are talking to children, suggesting they are intuitively aware that it helps. Such exaggerated rhythm will highlight the nouns acting as participants in the event. This will help the child zoom in on the relevant participants, and hence on the event in which they are involved. It will also highlight the position of those nouns within the rhythm, which will help the child make the link between argument positions and argument roles in events.

Such adult cues may be most effective if they work in unison to push the child's attention in the same direction. By making certain components of the scene *and* certain components of the utterance more salient, adults may help children find the connections between scene and utterance and pull out the verb and its argument structure.

9 Shortfalls with verbs

When children have problems with words, their problems may hit some types of words harder than others. A number of studies of language-impaired children have exposed verbs as an area of particular difficulty.

One study involved an extensive comparison of the words and structures used by a group of language-impaired children and a group of normally developing children (Fletcher & Peters 1984). The two groups were of similar age and non-verbal intelligence. Each child's language was sampled in four different activities: free play with toys, talking about pictures in a book, playing a board game, and re-telling a story about a set of pictures. Each sample consisted of 200 utterances, 50 from each activity. The samples from the two groups of children were then compared in terms of a wide range of lexical and grammatical categories. This revealed that the vocabulary of the language-impaired children was generally more restricted than the vocabulary of the normally developing children, and significantly, the *verb range* of the language-impaired children was especially limited.

Similarly, in a study focusing on verb use, it was found that a group of fourteen language-impaired children had a narrower range of verbs than normally developing children matched in age (Watkins, Rice & Moltz 1993). Even more striking, though, was the comparison between these language-impaired children and a group of normally developing children who were *nearly two years younger* than them, but at the same general language level. The verb range of the language-impaired group was still more limited than that of the control group, even though their vocabularies as a whole did not differ significantly. This finding was echoed in yet another study, which compared three language-impaired children with normally developing children whose mean length of utterance had reached the same level: the language-impaired children used a smaller number and variety of verbs (Conti-Ramsden & Jones 1997). When compared with a younger brother or sister at the same language level as them, the three children were also found to make less use of the verbs they had available (Jones & Conti-Ramsden 1997). The implication is clear, and the evidence solid: verbs are more of an obstacle for language-impaired children than other aspects of language.

Verbs go hand in hand with **arguments** – the participants involved in the event. We might therefore expect children who have problems with verbs to have problems with arguments as well. And so they do. Rice and Bode (1993) analysed the verb usage of three language-impaired children. Again they found the children relying on a limited set of verbs, and sometimes substituting one verb for another. But they also found that the children omitted verbs or arguments on some occasions.

How do these difficulties with verbs and arguments manifest themselves? In the most extreme disruptions, children may produce just a verb or just an argument, as 10-year-old Richard sometimes does:

My dad's boss – house. Down lane. Not farm. Walk up.

With no explicit relationship between verbs and arguments, we are left in the dark about the states of affairs Richard is trying to get across. In some cases, we might observe a verb accompanied by an argument but in a rather disjointed structure, as in Richard's comment about the fate of lambs on his farm:

Girls, keep, boys, not keep.

In other cases, verb–argument structures may be incomplete, as in Eamonn's repeated stabs at explaining who is going to call who about what:

. . . my mum gonna call – Mary gonna call me – Anna gonna call m – [ɪgədə] call my mummy I sick . . . I'm getting sick in [ə] school – Anna gonna t – phone – my mum out – phone my mummy out.

Or they may be mixed up, as in Eamonn's further attempts to explain the situation:

> . . . phone my mummy out . . . Because he write my mum – because my mum write in my book.

Evidence of problems in the production of verb–argument structure may be matched by problems in comprehension. This was checked out in an experiment where language-impaired children were asked to act out sentences such as:

The boy pushes the girl	The girl is pushed by the boy
The cup is in the box	In the box is the cup
Give the boy to the girl	Give the boy the girl

(Van der Lely and Harris 1990)

These children had more difficulty than a group of younger, language-matched controls, who themselves had more difficulty than a group of age-matched controls. In a second experiment, the children had to demonstrate their understanding by selecting one of four pictures to match the sentence. Again, the language-impaired children's scores fell below those of younger but normally developing controls.

Some experiments have probed children's comprehension in more detail. For example, they have investigated whether children can make connections between syntactic roles of arguments and the semantic roles these are most likely to play (Van der Lely 1993, O'Hara & Johnston 1997). The children are presented with a syntactic structure containing a nonsense word in place of a verb, for example:

> The woman *soogs* the bunny
> The man *keeds* the clown to the monkey

(O'Hara & Johnston 1997)

The children are then asked to make the toys do the 'little stories', or 'to make something up'. The question is whether they know which argument is acting as the **agent** which brings about the event, the **theme** which undergoes the event, or the **goal** with which the theme ends up. In the above examples we would expect the woman and the man to be carrying out an action; the bunny and the clown to be acted on; and the monkey to be the goal of a transfer action. Yet again, language-impaired children fared less well than younger normally developing children. They were less likely to act out events with each participant playing the role we would expect from the syntax.

Studies of language-impaired children therefore provide evidence enough that verbs and their argument structures pose special problems for some children. Where might their problems arise?

Locating the problem

Verbs have particular characteristics which could make every component of word processing more challenging:

- Verbs rarely occur in isolation, and when they occur in a stream of words, they are typically less stressed than the nouns around them. So, if children have problems picking out the sound patterns of words, this may particularly affect their **identification and storage of verb phonology**.
- Verbs refer to events from certain perspectives which focus on certain participants. They are typically dynamic, and may be very brief. So, if children have problems picking out relevant aspects of scenes, these may be particularly acute when they have to pick out an event from a certain perspective, and may markedly affect their **identification and storage of verb semantics**.

Where children have difficulties with verbs, these could arise at any point in the processing of verbs:

Figure 9.1 Processes in acquiring verbs

However, this view of verb processing is still only part of the story. The special phonological and semantic properties of verbs flow from their inherently relational nature: they express relations between arguments. The acquisition of verbs therefore goes beyond the acquisition of single words. It also entails the acquisition of argument structures. To acquire argument structures, the child must pick out the **participants** involved in the event, pick out the **arguments** which accompany the verb, and relate the two. Problems could arise in any of these processes:

Figure 9.2 Processes in acquiring argument structure

The acquisition of verbs and the acquisition of argument structures are not independent: the argument structure of a verb provides information about the perspective the verb takes on the participants. This in turn provides information about the verb's meaning. These connections lie behind **syntactic bootstrapping** – the possibility of using argument structure to work out a verb's focus. If children have difficulties picking out the arguments, they

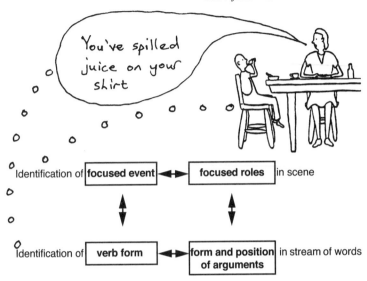

Figure 9.3 Processes in acquiring verb–argument structure

will be less able to use arguments as a cue to the meaning of the verb. Conversely, the meaning of the verb provides information about which participants are focused and how they will be organised around the verb. These connections lie behind **semantic bootstrapping**, where knowledge of a verb's meaning is used to predict the structures it will or will not take. If children have limited knowledge of a verb's meaning, this may limit the predictions they can make about the verb's structure.

Putting together the processes involved in connecting sentences and events, we see where problems may arise and how a problem in one process may impact on another (see figure 9.3).

Even if children make good headway with these processes in **input**, they may falter in **output**. When they come to talk about scenes, they may have difficulty homing in on a particular event which would lead them to a particular verb. Or they may know exactly what event they are going for, but have trouble accessing the phonological form of the verb, or accessing information about where the participants go in relation to it. Or they may successfully select a verb and arguments but struggle to hold these in mind in order to articulate them.

How can we begin to track down the source of a child's difficulties within the complex web of verb processing?

Exploring the problem

Psycholinguistic tasks used to investigate single word processing (see chapter 4) can be adapted to investigate verbs in particular. For example, we may want to check whether the child recognises verb forms regardless of whether she knows their meaning. This would require a **lexical decision** task, but one in which the stimuli were verbs together with similar-sounding non-words:

Real verbs	*Matched non-words*	
run	[lʌn]	lun
sing	[ʃɪŋ]	shing
break	[pleɪk]	plake
spin	[stɪn]	stin
think	[vɪŋk]	vink

More likely, though, we will want to home in on connections between verb forms and verb meanings. This could be done using a **picture-pointing** task such as the one shown opposite:

Place each of the following pictures in front of the child and ask:

'Which one is spinning?'

'Which one is cutting?'

'Which one is giving?'

To pick the right picture in the pairs, the child must appreciate particular aspects of the verb's meaning, such as direction of movement, or manner of movement, or change of state, or direction of change of possession. Alternatively, an **acting-out** task can be used. Here the child is given a set of appropriate props and asked 'Can you show me spinning?', 'Can you show me giving?', and so on. We can then see if the child includes crucial features such as manner or direction of movement in the acting out.

If the child appears to have verb forms, but interprets them in odd ways, or produces them in odd contexts, we may want to explore the child's perception of events independently of verbs themselves. For this, we might use an **event copying** task which involves no use of language at all. Here, the child watches a particular sort of event such as spinning, or giving, or breaking, and is asked to 'do the same thing'. The child might also be invited to demonstrate events for the adult to 'copy'. Through the child's actions, we will gain some insight into what the child notices in events, and most importantly, whether she notices aspects of events which are relevant to particular verbs of the language.

These tasks can throw light on the child's processing of verb semantics and phonology. To investigate the processing of **arguments** in relation to the verb, we must move beyond single word tasks. The tasks we use may involve similar procedures, but the input or output required will be sentences rather than words.

From events to verb–argument structures: event description tasks

The surest entry point to the child's verb–argument processing is what she has to say about events. As a first step, it would be helpful if we could pin down more precisely what the child does and doesn't do with verbs. Samples of **everyday talk** may give us some clues, but they are unlikely to provide a comprehensive picture. To sample a wide range of events, we need to devise scenarios which will communicate different sorts of events to the child, and find out how the child translates these into words.

Events are dynamic, so they are more clearly captured using dynamic representations such as videos or real-life actions than static pictures. To elicit responses, we need to maintain the child's interest in the events, and provide some motivation to describe them. The use of *novel* events can do the trick. Events can be made novel by casting things or people in roles which they do not normally play – a boy kissing a key, a book hitting a bus, a girl tickling a flower, an animal pushing a car, a tree pulling a bike, a man biting a dog, a baby pushing a pram . . . The more novel the events, the more likely they are to hold the child's attention and elicit a response, and the more sure we can be that the response reflects the child's ability to create verb–argument structures she has not met before. To make the task more meaningful to the child, we can give it a communicative purpose:

(Set-up: child sits behind a screen with Sam, a friend, sitting on the other side)

I'm going to show you something funny. Sam can't see what's happening. So watch carefully, and see if you can tell Sam what happened.

This technique can be extended by giving the same set of props to the child and to the party on the other side of the screen, and saying:

Let's see if Sam can make the same thing happen. You tell him what happened, and then we'll take the screen down and see if he does it right.

Sampling a range of events in this way may reveal particular areas of difficulty. We will need to scan the child's responses for descriptions which match the event and are complete, and descriptions which are incompatible with the event or contain errors or omissions. We can then compare these to see whether difficulties occur more with verbs conveying certain sorts of events, or requiring certain sorts of argument structure. In searching out the roots of those difficulties, we will want to check whether parallel difficulties crop up at other points in processing.

From verb–argument structures to events: acting out tasks

The most robust method for tapping the child's *understanding* of verb–argument structures is to ask the child to act them out. We might, for example, offer the child a number of miniature figures and say

Can you show me 'The boy gives the shoe to the granny'

A correct response would involve putting the shoe with the boy and then making the boy move it such that it ended up with the granny. In contrast,

'The boy takes the shoe from the granny'

would have the shoe starting with the granny and ending up with the boy. What is crucial about such sentences is that understanding of the words and knowledge of the world are not enough to interpret them correctly. This is because grandmothers are as likely to take shoes from boys as boys are to take shoes from grandmothers. Correct interpretation can only be achieved if the child recognises that 'the boy' is in the subject position, and that the subject is the source with 'give' but the goal with 'take'. Such sentences are said to be **reversible** because both characters can plausibly occupy both roles. Contrast a sentence such as

'The boy gives the carrot to the rabbit'

Since boys are much more likely to give carrots to rabbits than rabbits are to give carrots to boys, the child could get by if she knew what 'boy', 'carrot' and 'rabbit' mean, and had experience of feeding rabbits. The advantage of using reversible sentences is that they truly test the child's mapping between syntax and semantics and push it to the limit. However, interpreting sentences without support from context or world knowledge is much more demanding than interpreting sentences in everyday contexts in real life.

Recognising the argument structure of verbs: judgement tasks

Some children clearly have connections between verb–argument structures and events. They show understanding of these in everyday life, and their understanding is confirmed by, say, an acting-out task. They also use verbs with arguments to talk about events. Yet their production is unreliable. They sometimes struggle to recount events, or leave out verbs, or leave out arguments, or put arguments in the wrong place. If they have connections between structures and meanings, why do they not use structures consistently to express meanings? It looks as if the structures themselves are the problem. That is, they have not established patterns of sentences, which are to some extent independent of the meaning we want to convey. They have not established that sentences require at least a verb and the arguments entailed by that verb even if these elements are not all crucial to their 'message'.

Trying to tap a child's knowledge of **sentence structure** is akin to trying to tap knowledge of **word phonology**. In both cases, our target is linguistic knowledge which is *independent of meaning*. If we are to probe this knowledge, we must devise tasks which require processing of word and sentence form, but do not require connections to meaning. Judgement tasks allow us to do this. **Lexical decision tasks**, for example, asked the child to judge whether something sounded like a word or not, a judgement which requires knowledge of word phonology but makes no demands on word meaning. At the sentence level, **sentence judgement** tasks offer a similar opportunity. If we are checking knowledge of verb–argument structure, we need to create sentences which are correct, and sentences which violate verb–argument structure, and ask the child to judge these. Presentation might run along the following lines:

> Remember this puppet? She's the puppet who sometimes says things right and sometimes says funny things. When she says something right, you can give her a tick. And when she says something wrong, you can give her a cross. Then at the end we can see how many she got right. Let's try this one: 'Broke the vase the boy.' How does that sound? Are you going to give her a tick or a cross? And now how about this one: 'The boy cleaned the plate.' How does that sound?

In this example, the non-sentence violated the *order of arguments* in

English. The expected order would be 'The boy broke the vase.' Other examples might *leave out an argument* which the verb demands:

'The man found'

where 'find' requires a direct object. Or they might *include an argument which the verb does not take*:

'The woman disappeared the hat'

where 'disappear' cannot take a direct object. If the child is able to distinguish the 'good' and 'bad' sentences, we might conclude that she does know which arguments occur where in relation to the verbs used. In this case, any errors she makes in talking about similar events could not be attributed to ignorance of the verb–argument structures.

What about a child who makes no response at all, or responds 'yes' to every example, or responds at random? In such cases, no immediate conclusions can be drawn. First of all, she may have problems with the task. Making judgements about words is a hard enough task; making judgements about sentences is even harder. But the sentence-judgement task is problematic in other ways. Although its aim is to elicit *syntactic* judgements about sentences, the child may go about judging the sentences on some other grounds. The sentences and non-sentences used contain real words which have meaning for the child. It is highly likely that some children will judge the examples according to whether they can make sense from the words, ignoring how they 'sound'. For example, on hearing 'Broke the vase the boy', the child may conjure up an image of a boy breaking a vase, decide this is a plausible scenario, ignore the wording she actually heard, and accept the sentence. The task has then tapped the child's word semantics and world knowledge, and her responses do not reflect her syntactic knowledge. One way round this might be to make *all* the sentences nonsensical:

Syntactically okay: 'The boy broke the milk'
Syntactically out: 'Broke the boy the milk'

and see if the child can make any distinction between these

semantically odd examples. Very obviously, this makes the task even more abstract and obscure. We would only contemplate attempting such a high-level task in an older language-impaired child who had shown sufficient ability and motivation to undertake the linguistic challenge.

Sentence judgement tasks, then, are not at all straightforward. They must be handled with caution. As with any psycholinguistic task, they can be practical and informative provided they are used discriminatingly and as a tool for exploration, rather than mechanically. We can try out the task just to see how the child reacts, look out for any evidence that the child notices differences between the examples, and invite the child to say how she might like to change the sentences. The results of such exploration may not be definitive, but may still yield some evidence that the child notices when something is wrong.

From verb–argument input to verb–argument output: repetition tasks

Sentence judgement relies on *conscious* reflection about sentences to tap the child's *unconscious* awareness of how sentences should sound. A rather different way of coming at this is via a **repetition task** asking the child to reproduce verb–argument structures such as

The boy gives the shoe to the granny

To do this, the child must at least register the *phonology* of the sentence – its rhythm, and the sound patterns of the individual words within that rhythm. She must hold onto these rhythmically organised word forms. And she must plan their production. She may well take in their meaning as well, but repetition does not require this. Nor does it require *conscious* reflection, concentration or effort. Children are therefore unlikely to struggle with the general demands of the task, so that their responses will provide a clear window onto processing skills. If the child has the *capacity* to recognise, hold and produce the sentences in a task, we can be pretty sure this will show up in correct repetition.

Conversely, if repetition falls short of the target, we can be pretty sure the child does have problems with phonology. Since repetition involves input, storage, and output of phonology, the problems could be arising in any or all of these processes. In order to distinguish these possibilities, we must make comparisons with other tasks:

- **event description**: involves semantics and phonological output but not phonological input
- **acting out events**: involves phonological input and semantics but not phonological output

As well as revealing problems at one or more stages of phonological processing, repetition offers a key to the nature of those problems. The key will be the pattern of errors. Does the child omit words, or does she distort them? Which words are most likely to be affected? Are nouns preserved better than verbs? Is word order preserved? The answers to these questions will indicate which aspects of sentence phonology are strongest for the child, and which are vulnerable.

Making the mapping: semantic and syntactic bootstrapping tasks

The tasks we have surveyed so far all draw on verbs the child *has already met*. The child's response to these is a product of all the components of verb processing which she has at her disposal. Components of verb processing are, as we have seen, highly interdependent. It may therefore be difficult to sort out which components of verb processing are chickens and which are eggs when we look at verbs about which the child has already received information. We can get round this by providing the eggs ourselves, and seeing what chickens they hatch. If we introduce *new* verbs, we can control the information the child receives about those verbs, and see what the child can do with that information. Experiments on **bootstrapping** in normally developing children offer us the tools we need (see chapter 8).

In these experiments, children are introduced to *nonsense* verbs in contexts which give them limited information about those verbs. They may be given just semantic information, using a

semantic bootstrapping task (Gropen et al. 1991). Here, the adult introduces a novel verb in a context which provides no syntactic information about it:

let me show you what *keating* is . . .

The adult then demonstrates the event, in this case, moving a packet of marbles onto a square of cloth causing the cloth to sag. The child's attention is drawn to what is important in the event:

when I do this [moving a packet directly towards an unsupported square] . . . and it ends up like that [placing the packet onto the square, causing it to sag] . . . it's called *keating*.

This is reinforced by showing an event in which the marbles move onto the cloth *without* causing the cloth to sag:

now let me show you something that's *not keating* . . . when I do this [moving a packet towards a *supported* square] . . . and it ends up like that [placing the packet onto the square, without it changing its shape] . . . it's *not* called *keating*.

(Gropen et al. 1991: 168)

After demonstrations of 'keating' by the adult and the child, the action is performed again and the child is asked a question designed to elicit a structure with the novel verb:

Can you tell me what I'm doing?

If this does not elicit a structure with the verb, further prompts may be used:

Can you tell me what I'm keating?

or

Keating what?

(based on Pinker 1989: 346)

The question is whether the child will select the cloth or the marbles for the direct object slot. If she uses semantic bootstraps, she will note that the verb focuses on the sagging state of the *cloth* and will make this the direct object of the verb, in which case she will come out with 'Keating the cloth' or 'The cloth'. We would expect a different response if the focus of the verb were different.

This is tested with a second type of event. In this case, the marbles are moved onto the cloth in a zig-zagging manner. This event is demonstrated in a similar way to the previous one, with the adult saying:

> when I do this . . . and it ends up over there . . . it's called *pilking*.
>
> (Gropen et al. 1991: 169)

To exemplify an event which is *not pilking*, the marbles are moved in a bouncing manner. The focus of the verb is now the zig-zagging movement of the *marbles*. Semantic bootstraps will therefore lead the child to select the marbles for the direct object slot, and produce 'Pilking the marbles' or 'The marbles' in response to the prompt questions.

Investigation of **syntactic bootstrapping** requires input which gives syntactic information about the verb, but limited semantic information. One example of this starts with the following introduction:

> Mac [a puppet] doesn't speak English very well, so sometimes he uses puppet words. Can you help us figure out what the puppet words mean?
>
> (Fisher, Hall, Rakowitz & Gleitman 1994: 344)

The child then hears a sentence such as 'The bunny is nading the ball from the elephant', and watches a video of a scene, captured here in a still picture:

In this case, the child is watching an elephant handing a ball to a bunny who takes the ball. After seeing the video and hearing the sentence, she is asked:

What does 'nading' mean?

She may be probed further with the prompts:

What's happening? What's going on?

Any change of possession verb such as 'give', or 'hand', or 'take', or 'get' would be compatible with the scene. But only verbs such as 'take' or 'get' are compatible with the argument structure accompanying the nonsense verb and the focus implied by this. Will the child come up with a verb such as 'taking' or 'getting'? If so, she has 'translated' the nonsense verb with a real verb sharing the same argument structure as the nonsense verb and therefore the same focus. This would suggest that she has recognised the position of the arguments and has established the links between positions in argument structure and the way roles are focused in events. If she has, she should make a different response when she meets the arguments in a different order, as in 'The elephant is nading the ball to the bunny.' Here, the argument structure and the implied focus should elicit real-verb 'translations' such as 'give' or 'hand'.

We might think about using these experimental techniques to tap bootstrapping processes in language-impaired children, but with some important reservations and adaptations. In the case of language-impaired children, the use of nonsense verbs might be considered unethical and inappropriate. But it would not be difficult to find real verbs which, like nonsense verbs, would be new for the child. These could be verbs which the child had shown difficulty understanding or producing. Or they could be verbs which a child of the same age would not be expected to know anyway. Unlike nonsense verbs, these verbs would be potentially useful to the child. This would overcome ethical objections to teaching the child nonsense words.

However, we may have concerns about other aspects of these experimental techniques, such as the high demands they impose. A semantic bootstrapping task would seem quite feasible with language-impaired children who are at least at the stage of producing two-word utterances. The syntactic bootstrapping task described above, however, requires a more sophisticated type of response. In order to succeed, the child must have the notion of using one word to explain the meaning of another. Only children who have shown that they have this notion will be able to undertake syntactic bootstrapping tasks of this nature. If they do succeed in these tasks, we know for sure that they have links between argument positions and roles focused in events.

Any pursuit of verb–argument processing in a child will require careful selection of tasks which are not only relevant to the child's problems, but are appropriate to the child's general level of development and interests. The following case study of 6-year-old Travis illustrates the use of various tasks to investigate a child's processing of verb–argument structures. By the end of this exploration, we arrive at some understanding of the ways in which a child's 'bootstraps' might fall short, and so limit his ability to talk about events.

10 'Thing out. Tip in there': problems with verb processing

Travis has much in common with the children we followed up in chapter 6. He too comes across as a bright, responsive child who interacts well with other people. He takes turns in conversations, and his contributions befit the context. Pragmatically, he is on the ball. But when we home in on the specific content of his utterances, we start to notice problems. These problems also show up in formal tests of his language. At 6, he performs at the level of a 4- to $4\frac{1}{2}$-year-old in tests of word and sentence comprehension:

> British Picture Vocabulary Scales (BPVS): scored at age level 4;1
> Test for the Reception of Grammar (TROG): scored at age level 4;6

In contrast, his score on a test of non-verbal intelligence is average for his age. Like the children presented in chapter 6, Travis shows particular difficulties when it comes to dealing with words and combinations of words. In presenting Travis's case, however, the spotlight will move from words in general to the particular words needed to express events, namely verbs and their arguments. Our purpose will be to find out where, in the connections between events and verb–argument structures, Travis's difficulties arise.

Our starting-point is an **event-description** task which established that Travis did have particular difficulties in talking about events. In this task, Travis watched his therapist act out 127 different events. These events represented thirty verbs, which were enacted in different contexts and with different participants. The verbs spanned a variety of event categories, including:

- something moving in a particular manner or direction,
  e.g. a ball rolling, a penny sliding, books or cards falling
  down
- something changing state, e.g. a spider dying, a door
  opening
- the therapist causing something to move in a particular
  manner or direction, e.g. rolling a ball, rocking a doll,
  pushing a pram or a box
- the therapist causing something to change state, e.g.
  opening a card or box or mouth, cutting bread or paper

After he had watched each event, Travis was asked 'What is
happening?' or 'What am I doing?'.

In order to see whether the description of these events posed
unusual problems for Travis, they were also presented to three
normally developing children. These children were matched with
Travis on vocabulary age, which put them well below his chronological age – they were two to two and a half years his junior. We
have already observed that normal 4-year-olds have very good
control of verb–argument structures in the output they produce
spontaneously (see chapter 8). But how would they fare in an
elicitation task calling for them to produce 127 verb–argument
structures on command? Just fine, as it turns out. They co-oper-
ated in the activity quite happily, and were virtually spot-on in
their descriptions. For at least 90 per cent of the 127 events, these
children used a verb which was consistent with the event, and
combined it with any arguments it required to depict that event.
Between them they produced 363 such descriptions. Typical
examples are their descriptions of pouring sugar into a bowl:

    Hazel: Pouring something into the bowl
    Rosie: Pouring it into there
    Ross: Tipping it all into there

or dropping apples:

    Hazel: They all comed out
    Rosie: You dropped them
    Ross: They dropped out

or a top spinning:

Hazel: Spinning
Rosie: It's twirling round
Ross: The top is spinning

These results confirm that normally developing 4-year-olds are extremely adept at seeing an event in an appropriate way and representing this with an appropriate verb or verb–argument combination.

How about Travis? He too provided appropriate event descriptions. His description of dropping straws as

Travis: Straw [ə] fall on carpet

and breaking a pencil as

Travis: Pencil broke

contain adequate verb–argument structures to characterise what he had observed. But such descriptions account for just over 50 per cent of his responses, showing that he is far less consistent than the control children. The majority of his inappropriate descriptions fall short in the following two ways:

Verb omission
Twenty-two of Travis's descriptions contained no verb, as in his versions of:

Pouring sugar into the bowl: 'Sugar in the pot'
Dropping apples: 'Fruit on floor'
Shaking the fist: 'Strong'
A top spinning: 'Round'

In contrast, the one and only example of verb omission from the control children was Ross's description of shaking the head as 'Nos'.

Use of a 'bare' verb
Thirty-three of Travis's descriptions consisted of a 'bare' verb with no arguments and no verb ending, as in his versions of:

Breaking an egg: 'Break'.
Tractor pushing mud: 'Dig, dig, dig'
Shaking a bottle: 'Shake'

The controls produced only five examples of 'bare' verbs between them.

Evidently Travis is not able to describe events as reliably as these much younger children. This suggests that the event-description task posed special problems for him.

What is the source of those problems? Our initial hunch might be that events themselves are not the obstacle. If they were – if Travis understood events differently from other people – we would surely expect his behaviour to be odd in ways which it is not. His generally appropriate interactions with the world, both non-verbal and verbal, argue for a normal orientation towards things and people and the events in which they participate. If the problem is not with events, it must be somewhere in the connection between events and verb–argument structures.

Questions arising from Travis's event description

Our investigation so far has revealed limitations in Travis's output. Those limitations could, though, have their origins in input. To be able to produce his own verb–argument structures, Travis must first process verb–argument structures which he hears. At first sight, Travis seems able to do this. His comprehension in context is good, which suggests that he is interpreting events appropriately. But such evidence is loose. Comprehension in context can be aided by all sorts of non-linguistic cues – from the situation, the direction of the speaker's gaze, the speaker's gestures. It may be that Travis is able to use these sort of cues very effectively and so mask difficulties with precise processing of verb–argument structures. One hint that he does have such input difficulties comes from his performance on formal tests. Recall that his score on a test of sentence comprehension, the TROG, had found him nearly two years behind his peers. This does not prove that Travis is behind in interpreting events, since the TROG is too wide-ranging to identify such specific deficits, but it does indicate that all is not well in input.

It is therefore possible that the problems observed in Travis's output do have their origins in input. Perhaps he omits verbs in his output because he has failed to identify verb forms in the stream of speech, or to connect these verb forms to corresponding events, or to recognise that they are obligatory. Perhaps he uses 'bare' verbs because he has failed to identify the way arguments are organised around verbs, or to connect arguments to participant roles, or to recognise that they are sometimes obligatory.

A closer look at Travis's description of events throws up some relevant evidence. If omissions were due to ignorance of verb forms and structures, we would expect these omissions to be consistent. But they are not. On some occasions *Travis succeeds in using the very forms which he could have used on other occasions where he used no verb at all.* Of his twenty-two verb omissions, sixteen were in response to an event which could have been described with a verb he did use for other events. For example, he used the verb 'tip' for:

Emptying a jar: 'Tip in there'

which would have served him perfectly well for describing all the other emptying events where he omitted the verb:

Emptying bottle: 'Drink in there'
Emptying glass: 'Water – and drink in there'
Emptying pocket: 'Thing out'
Emptying box: 'Thing out'

Similarly, compare his descriptions of different rocking events with the verb 'rock':

Rocking side to side: 'Rocking'

and without it:

Rocking arms: 'Wobbly jelly'
Rocking forwards and backwards: 'I don't know'

In the same way, Travis's use of 'bare' verbs cannot have been due to ignorance of argument roles and positions, *because on some occasions he uses the very same verbs with arguments.* For example, he used just 'shake' for:

Shaking a bottle: 'Shake'

yet combined it with the direct object argument for

Shaking the head: 'Shake [ə] head'
Shaking hands: 'Shake [ə] hand'

There was only one case of a verb being used without arguments in all instances.

These inconsistencies provide evidence that Travis has recognised and stored verb forms and argument structures which he does not always use. When he does use them, they are generally appropriate. On only a handful of occasions does he use a verb unsuited to the context, as was the case in:

Pushing a pram: 'Drive [ə] baby chair'

where 'drive' is wrong for the movement of a pram. But he was not alone in doing this. Ross, one of the control children, also made a handful of verb selections which were slightly odd for the event:

Wetting the brush: 'Twisting it in there'

This shows that Travis, like the control children, has verb forms and argument structures associated with appropriate events and event roles.

The inconsistencies we have observed in Travis's event description rule out a total blockage in his recognition of verb form or meaning. What they do not rule out is some sort of limitation in the connections he has made between form and meaning. It may be that he has acquired certain verb forms and their argument structures, has established some of the events they can refer to, but has not established their full semantic range. For example, he may have the verb 'tip' associated with movement from a jar, but not from a bottle, glass, pocket or box. Or he may have adequate semantic information about many verbs including 'tip', but fail to realise that verbs are essential in sentence structure leading him to treat 'tip' or any other verb as optional in the sentence.

Assuming Travis's output is constrained by some such *limitations* in verb information, these might stem from limitations in input processing which have repercussions for output, or they might arise only in output.

These possibilities were followed up by designing a variety of input and output tasks. All the tasks used the same set of verbs in the same structures, so that any differences in Travis's responses could be attributed to the task rather than the linguistic items. The verbs used were:

Change of possession: 'give', 'take', 'offer', 'accept', 'buy', 'sell'
Change of location: 'put', 'throw', 'drop', 'chase', 'follow'
Psychological state: 'like', 'hate'
Possession: 'have'

The tasks were again carried out with three normally developing children matched to Travis's vocabulary age.

Input investigations

Two tasks tested Travis's comprehension of verb–argument structures.

In an **acting out task**, the therapist presented Travis with an appropriate set of toys to act out sentences such as the following:

The girl gives the apple to the boy
The pig buys the orange from the sheep
The boy puts the box on the ladder
The balloon has a picture on it

She introduced the task by saying:

I want you to make the toys do what I say

and then gave him each sentence to act out. To show correct comprehension, he had to use all the participants mentioned in the sentence, and put them in their appropriate role in the event. For 'The boy puts the box on the ladder', for example, he would have to make the boy the agent causing movement; the box the theme, undergoing movement; and the ladder the goal, where the theme ends up. Responses which overlooked a participant or put it in the wrong role were scored as incorrect.

Travis's performance on this task was not significantly different from the control children's, though it did fall at the bottom end of the group. Travis also made the same sort of errors as the controls. Over half of these involved the reversal of arguments in acting out the sentence. For example, he acted out

The pig buys the orange from the sheep

with the pig, who should end up with the orange, as the starting-point (source) and the sheep, who should start out with the orange, as the end-point (goal). Travis made at least twice as many reversal errors as any of the controls. However, the verbs which were most troublesome for Travis were also those which gave most trouble to the controls. These verbs were 'take', 'accept', 'buy' and 'sell'.

In a **picture-pointing task**, the therapist presented Travis with two pictures, one representing a sentence such as

The boy takes the apple from the girl

and the other representing the same event but with the roles reversed as in

The girl takes the apple from the boy

The therapist then said:

I want you to point to the picture that goes with what I say.

Again, Travis made some errors, but he performed above chance level, and just as well as the control children. Again, he had most difficulty with possession verbs such as 'give'/'take', 'buy'/'sell', 'offer'/'accept'.

What do these two tasks tell us about Travis's comprehension of argument roles? First, since his performance was not significantly worse than the vocabulary-matched controls, the tasks do not expose any problems in identifying argument roles beyond those which occur in normal development. But nor do they expose just how much Travis or the controls understand from verb–argument structures. While Travis shows some success with these tasks, he could be succeeding with many of the items on the basis of a rather broad understanding of the verbs and the argument structures. Suppose he knew roughly what sort of event the verb expressed, for example whether it referred to state or location or possession. Suppose he also knew the most typical mapping relationship between syntactic and thematic roles around the verb, that is

subject NP = agent
direct object NP = theme
PP = goal

Such broad knowledge would get Travis a long way. He would only come unstuck where the sentences contained verbs which go against these generalisations. 'Take', 'buy' and 'accept' are just such verbs: all map their goal onto the subject NP, contrary to the expectation that the goal will map onto the PP. And it was with just these verbs that Travis, and some of the controls, came most unstuck. Thus, Travis's relatively good performance on this task does not rule out *limitations* on his understanding of verbs or verb–argument structure.

On the other hand, it is also possible that his understanding is *better* than it appears in these tasks. It may be that the demands of remembering the sentence, picking out the characters and their role, and then having to perform the actions or select one of two almost identical pictures to match his interpretation are just too much, and he loses track of who was doing what. In this case, difficulties with the task would be masking a perfectly good understanding of the sentence. This is an unavoidable hazard of input tasks, which can only tap language processing indirectly.

The upshot is that these tasks have left us little the wiser about the precise nature of Travis's input processing. We can be sure that Travis is able to discriminate the order of arguments in the sentence, and knows something about the relationship between the position of an argument and its role in the event. But this much was already evident from his output: he might omit arguments, but when he does include them, he does not mis-order them. Input tasks have not revealed just how much he knows about the event roles which different verbs impose on their arguments.

To make more headway, we might turn to **output** tasks, which tap the child's language much more directly, to see whether these allow us to make more precise and reliable inferences about input.

Output investigations

Three output tasks were carried out. These were description of a picture, repetition of a sentence, and repetition of a sentence with the support of a picture. These tasks give us further evidence of Travis's output. But they could also yield evidence of his input, since the tasks use different sorts of input – a picture or a heard sentence or both – in order to elicit the same output.

In the **picture-description task**, the children were shown a picture and given a verb to see if they could put that verb into a sentence matching the picture. The pictures were the same as those used in the picture-pointing task. The lead-in went like this:

This picture shows pushing. Tell me all about this picture.

As in the original event-description task, Travis's performance was way below the control children's: the lowest of their scores was almost double Travis's. His picture descriptions were sometimes reminiscent of the event descriptions we have already seen, for example those containing no verb:

(Picture shows boy putting ladder on box; the verb *put* is supplied)

Travis: Train track on the box

But on this task, where he was given a verb to use, his errors more often involved substitution of a different verb and sometimes multiple verbs for the target:

(Picture shows cat accepting cake from dog; the verb *accept* is supplied)

Travis: Cat – dog *get* the cake [ə] cat.

(Picture shows panda buying pear from monkey; the verb *buy* is supplied)

Travis: Monkey – panda *want* a pear – monkey *want* money.

(Picture shows man offering biscuit to lady; the verb *offer* is supplied)

Travis: The man *make* pizza – *give* a man – lady

(Picture shows sheep selling pear to pig; the verb *sell* is supplied)

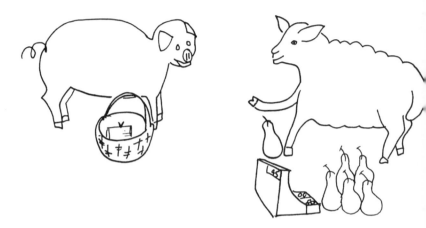

Travis: Pig *want* – *want* pear in basket – sheep *give* it pig – pig *want*
pear – um basket and sheep and he *give* it and lot – lot of 5p

Such examples provide evidence that Travis is trying to convey all aspects of the event entailed by the target verb. Though he never uses *buy* or *sell* he covers their meaning pretty exhaustively with *want*, *give*, *money* and *lot of 5p*. But he has separated these elements out rather than integrating them into a single verb. The controls made no such responses.

In the **repetition task**, Travis's performance sank to its lowest and moved furthest from that of the control children. Here, the children were required to repeat the sentences used in the acting-out and picture-pointing tasks. The controls did this effortlessly and almost without error. In contrast, three-quarters of Travis's responses showed omission of a verb or argument, or substitution with weak, unintelligible forms consisting largely of [ə]:

Target: The pig chases the sheep
Travis: [ə] pig [əhə ə] sheep
Target: The cow gives the banana to the horse
Travis: [ə] cow [hə həə] horse

Again, Travis was inconsistent, producing the same target verb correctly in some instances:

Target: The boy chases the girl
Travis: [ə] boy chase [ə] girl
Target: The boy gives the apple to the girl
Travis: [ə] apple [ə] give [ə] girl

Following Travis's very poor performance on pure repetition, the task was repeated with the support of pictures. In the **repetition with pictures task**, the therapist showed Travis a picture, produced the corresponding sentence, and asked him to say that sentence. Travis now made fewer omissions, but more often substituted a different verb for the original one:

Target: The monkey chases the panda
Travis: [ə] monkey ['fɒlə ə] panda
Target: The boy gives the apple to the girl
Travis: Boy [hæ] apple [ə] girl

His responses on this task were therefore more like his picture descriptions, suggesting he was using the picture input to generate a sentence rather than simply repeating what he heard.

It seems that repetition is the greatest stumbling block for Travis and even harder than picture description (hence the improvement when repetition was supported by a picture). This reverses the response patterns of the control children. For them, repetition is no problem, yielding even higher scores than picture description, where they already surpassed Travis by a long shot.

The difference between these tasks lies in input – one starts from pictures, the other from heard sentences. Travis's response to them tells us something about his processing of these different inputs. His overriding difficulty with pure repetition points a finger at phonology. Suppose Travis has particular difficulty registering the phonological forms in the input utterance. This would certainly stymie his attempts at repetition. It would explain the occurrence of those weak unintelligible forms such as [ə] and [əhə] and partial forms such as [hæ] where verb forms should occur. It looks as if Travis registers the overall rhythm of the utterance. He also registers the phonological form of two or three key words. But he does not register the phonology of all the words, and in the absence of any other cues, he can only fill the rhythmic slots with some sort of phonological padding. When repetition is supported by pictures, on the other hand, he can supplement the information from the heard utterance with the information from the picture. Having missed the form *chase* in the input utterance, he can observe the chasing/following in the picture and go from semantics to a form he has stored.

If phonology is the culprit for Travis, the gulf between his pattern of response and the control children's falls into place. For the control children, input phonology is no challenge at all. Hearing each sentence, they can register the word forms and their order and can produce the verb and its arguments even more reliably than when they generate these from meaning. It could be that they are repeating the sentences without accessing their meaning fully or at all. What lies in the gulf between Travis and these children, it seems, is their rock-solid capacity for processing input phonology.

If a child's phonological processing is shaky, we might expect problems with verbs and verb structure as fall-out. The *verb form* will be vulnerable because of its typical position within the sentence. Recall that verbs, because they often take arguments, rarely occur in the final position which carries the greatest stress. Verbs are typically surrounded by words which are more stressed than they are. So Travis is likely to have more difficulty with verb forms than, say, nouns. This could account for his less reliable production of verbs, both in repeating sentences and in describing events.

Argument structure will also be vulnerable. Though the nouns in the arguments will be more stressed, more salient, and more strongly represented, this will not protect their relationship to the verb. In order to represent the verb–argument structure stably, the child must hold the verb unit *together with* the arguments. A constraint on phonological input may prevent Travis from registering the verb unit and all accompanying argument units simultaneously. Unstable representation of elements in the rhythmic structure will undermine the **phonological bootstraps** by which children reach for verb structure and will prevent them establishing a secure relationship between verbs and arguments. This could explain why, even when Travis knows and can use verbs with their arguments, he does not do so reliably.

The insecurity of verb structure will in turn affect **syntactic**

bootstrapping. Only by noticing that 'pour' is followed by a NP referring to a moving substance while 'fill' is followed by a NP referring to a container can the child use their arguments to work out the different events focused by each verb. If Travis's information about what follows the verb is precarious, his access to the verb's focus will be precarious too. He will have to rely much more on information from the scene he is observing to work out what the focused event is likely to be.

Such information should allow him to use **semantic bootstrapping,** which involves working out the syntactic position of participants in the sentence from their role in the scene. However, even semantic bootstrapping may be undermined. Semantic bootstrapping relies on the child having secure knowledge of the way participant roles link to argument positions around the verb. If the child's access to verb structures is haphazard, it may take longer to identify and consolidate these links. He may have specific examples of verbs which focus on different thematic roles, such as 'fill' and 'pour', but these may be too few or too insecure for him to establish the ways in which focused participants connect to syntactic positions. We saw above (chapter 8) that the different bootstraps – semantic, syntactic and phonological – are mutually dependent. It seems likely that the potential of semantic bootstraps may be curtailed where it it not supported by other bootstraps.

On our interpretation of Travis's difficulties with verb structure, we would not expect either semantic or syntactic bootstraps to be totally lacking, but we would expect both to be affected to some degree. An in-depth investigation of bootstrapping in a child like Travis would throw more light on what information he can and cannot use in learning verbs. It would also indicate what kind of information can best help the child get on top of verbs and their structure.

The journey we have taken through Travis's processing has landed us in a rather unexpected place. We started off from an observed problem with verbs and verb–argument structure, which would seem to suggest difficulties with syntax and semantics. Yet we have concluded that Travis's difficulties lie in his processing of phonological input, which is crucial for acquiring and using verb–

argument structures to convey events. The implication is that any children whose phonological processing is similarly limited – as evidenced by their particular difficulties in repeating sentences – will struggle to establish and produce verbs and verb structures. Another implication is that these children will have even more problem with words which are even more phonologically challenging than verbs. It is to such words that we now turn.

Note: This chapter is based on research carried out by Mary Evelyn, Speech and Language Therapist, Mid Anglia Community Health NHS Trust, at City University, London (Evelyn 1996).

Part III
Missing function morphemes

11   Filling out sentences

When we hear Ruth say:

> Stay under water long time, that hurt my eyes

and Richard say:

> Girls, keep, boys, not keep

we automatically fill in certain missing 'bits'. These 'bits' will depend on our interpretation of the utterances and knowledge of their context. In the light of this information, we might expand Ruth's and Richard's utterances into:

> *When I* stay under water *for a* long time, that hurt*s* my eyes
> *The* girls *we* keep, *the* boys *we don't* keep

The missing bits are a well-known stumbling block for children with language impairment, a classic sign of their difficulties. Collectively known as **function morphemes**, these 'bits' are distinguished by their minor status relative to the **content words** – such as nouns and verbs – on which they depend.

Phonologically, they are weak. Their phonological 'bittiness' shows up in different ways. In English, they are typically **unstressed words** or **inflections**.

Unstressed words take up the weakest beats in the rhythm of a sentence. Examples are **auxiliary verbs** such as *can, has/have, was/were*. When these occur in context, they typically **reduce**, with the vowel of their full form shortening:

he can dance	he [kən] dance
they have danced	they [əv] danced
we were dancing	we [wə] dancing

or they lose their vowel altogether, **contracting** onto a previous word:

they've   (they have)
he'll   (he will)

Inflections are part of a word. Examples are the sound segments *-s, -ed* and the syllable *-ing*, which attach to verbs:

walk*s*,walk*ed*, walk*ing*

These unstressed words and inflections contrast with content words which always consist of at least a syllable with an irreducible vowel. So, we cannot do to the content words *pan* and *fur* what we can do to the function words *can* and *were*: we cannot reduce them to [pən] and [fə].

Semantically, function morphemes typically do not refer to things or events in the outside world. They depend on the references which are made by the content words to which they attach.

Some specify a dimension of that content word, such as the **number** of a noun (*book_s_*) or the **timing** of a verb (*walk_s_, walk_ed_*). Function morphemes in different languages pick out different dimensions, and cut them up to different degrees. For example, the marking of number on nouns may be obligatory, or confined to certain classes of nouns, or optional, or absent. It may divide into just the categories singular and plural, or it may include a further category, dual, which distinguishes two items from more than two. Time, too, is divided in different ways. Some languages make a two-way distinction between past and non-past, or future and non-future; some make a three-way distinction between past, present and future. Some mark other dimensions of time, such as the time course or completeness of an event.

Other function morphemes contribute nothing to the meaning of the content word. They are determined by a syntactically related content word, and act as a marker of **agreement** between these content words, indicating their *syntactic* relation to each other. Many languages, for example, mark *verbs* according to features of their subject or object, such as its number or gender. In English, this accounts for the difference between

you walk

and

he walk*s*

where the inflection -*s* is determined by the 3rd-person-singular subject. Many languages mark *adjectives* and *determiners* according to particular dimensions of the noun they modify, for example its number, gender or animateness.

Syntactically, the hallmark of function morphemes is that they are obligatory. Languages vary widely in the dimensions and relations of content words which they choose to mark, but within any one language those distinctions are sacrosanct. That is precisely why we can fill in the 'bits' which Ruth and Richard omit. Given the context and the content words they have used, English speakers know which aspects of content words have to be spelled out.

Somehow, children must discover these phonologically meagre, semantically abstract items on which their language insists. This does not happen overnight. Function morphemes unfold gradually, even in the language of normally developing children.

Output: the normal road

The clearest evidence comes from their own utterances. As we have seen, children's early words are typically content words identifying things, people, and events or relationships in which these participate. When children start producing word combinations, these are also largely confined to content words. The predominance of content words was apparent in the sample of utterances produced by Alison (chapter 8):

Utterances produced by Alison, aged 2;3

Drop (after penny dropped)	Wash teddy
Fall out (after money falls out of purse)	Open it
Hiding (when teddy is in cupboard)	Push me
Open (trying to open purse)	Got some
Off (taking socks off doll)	Go in there
Ali do it (= open door)	Teddy wake up
My daddy go home	I [wanə] money

Phonologically, almost all her words are those which carry stress and cannot reduce. Semantically, they are words which convey events and participants in those events. The only exceptions are the pronouns 'it', 'I' and 'me', the possessive determiner 'my', the preposition 'in', and the verb inflection '-ing'. These are usually amongst the earliest function morphemes to emerge.

These first signs of function morphemes are often unreliable. Some children will use a particular item in just one or two phrases to start with. For example, 'it' may appear only in 'Do it' and 'Get it'. This suggests that the child is using each of these phrases as a whole, frozen chunk, and does not yet have 'it' as a form in its own right. For other children, the earliest signs of function morphemes are more prolific. They turn up in a wide range of contexts, but take a very rudimentary form. They consist of weak, unintelligible syllables which occur in positions where function morphemes would be expected – like Claire's [ɳən], [əs], [əə], [amə], [mə]:

Claire, aged 2;2
SC: Shall we look at these?
C: [ɳən] in there? (looking at bag of toys)
SC: I'll show you.
C: [u] got?
SC: Huh?
C: [əs] in [ɛə]? [əə] slide . . . Get out (tries to get swing out of bag) . . . Can't. Can't . . . Done it! . . . Go . . . Swing . . . [amə] head. [mə] bang [ə] head.

In the wake of these first glimmers, it is not long before function morphemes take off. Their forms become distinct and recognisable, and they are used more extensively and consistently. These developments are gradual and to a certain extent predictable within any one language (Berko 1958, Brown 1973, de Villiers & de Villiers 1973, Slobin 1985, and see Owens 1996 for a very useful overview).

As Alison's utterances illustrated, the earliest examples in English are:

- certain pronouns (*I/me, you, it*)
- the odd possessive determiner and pronoun (*my/mine*)
- the verb inflection *-ing*

These emerge between 12 and 24 months. Later, around 27 to 33 months, *nouns* will be elaborated with

- the plural marker *-s*

and a little later still, with

- determiners *a/the*

The emergence of *verb* markers is a drawn-out affair. The inflection *-ing*, which is well in the lead, is followed by sporadic uses of

- certain irregular past forms such as *came*, *went*, *broke*.

These are followed by the use of

- the regular past form *-ed*
- 3rd-person-present form *-s*
- auxiliaries *have*, *be*, *do*, *can*, *will*

The auxiliary verbs first appear in contexts where they must take their full form, for example, in **elliptical** responses such as *I am*, *He is*, and in negatives *can't*, *don't*. This precedes their use in contexts where they can **contract**, as in *I'm*, *he's*. From about 30 months, the range of auxiliaries grows, with the use of

- other modal verbs such as *shall* and *could*

(See Brown 1973, Owens 1996, Fletcher & Garman 1979, 1986 for further details.)

By this stage, the child is producing most obligatory function morphemes in most contexts which require them, and we perceive the child as having pretty well reached adult language. Some children get there as early as $2\frac{1}{2}$ to 3 years; others are closer to 4. So we see that Shel, just four months older than Claire, deploys a far wider range of function morphemes in her utterances which sound almost complete and adult:

Shel, aged 2;6
S: Can't shut that (miniature box, in which she has tried to put playpeople). Oh yes I can . . . Them get out and she – little baby's can go in there. Can't get she in.
SC: Huh?
S: Can't get her in.

SC: There. Where do they go?
S: On swing. Push him. Should I push him? Oh.
SC: What happened?
S: Oh, poor little girl! Don' let them fall . . . Where's [ə] other girls
        . . . Look, I found two. Can you bend her legs?

Shel's output is still not entirely in line with the English of those around her. She makes odd errors which are characteristic of emerging function morphemes. These errors do not usually affect meaning. Take Shel's incorrect use of pronouns:

Them get out . . . Can't get *she* in.

She puts these pronouns in the right position, so their role in the sentence is perfectly clear. It's just that the form of the pronouns is at odds with their position and role. When Shel eventually sorts out which pronoun goes where and uses each correctly, this will have no effect whatsoever on the meaning she communicates.

The same applies to overgeneralisations where children use the regular form of an inflection on a word which is exceptional. This gives rise to child-typical plurals – *mans, womans, sheeps, tooths* or *teeths*; and pasts – *maked, breaked* or *broked, falled* or *felled, comed* or *camed*; and possessives – *him's, she's, them's*.

When children do use a form which is semantically not quite right, it is likely to be just off target. A good example is the use of preposition 'by' in place of 'with':

Can I pick it up by my hands?
Cover me up by my silk

(Tomasello 1987)

Such are the fine-grained errors which dot the slow but predictable path to function morphemes which most children follow.

Output when the road is blocked

For children identified as language-impaired, the path is a rocky one and may stop short of its destination. Time and again, these children's use of function morphemes has been found to be limited compared with normally developing children, even when the comparison is with younger children matched on some other measure of language such as their **mean length of utterance (MLU)**. For example, a large-scale study of 287 language-impaired children ranging in age from 3;0 to 16;2 (Johnston & Schery 1976) found that their acquisition of function morphemes was not only way behind normally developing children *of the same age*. It was also behind younger normally developing children *of the same language level*. The language-impaired children were not only older but tended to be *at a higher MLU level* when they achieved reliable use of function morphemes. Yet the stage at which they *first* used each morpheme, and the *order* in which different morphemes emerged, were much the same as those observed in normally developing children.

Such disproportionate delays have been observed in studies of individuals and groups, and of different function morphemes. These studies have highlighted persistant omission of articles *a/ the*, plural *-s*, possessive *-s*, auxiliary verbs *be* and *have*, past tense *-ed*, 3rd-person-singular *-s* (Ingram 1972, Leonard, Bortolini, Caselli, McGregor & Sabbadini 1992, Leonard, Eyer, Bedore & Grela 1997, Oetting & Horohov 1997).

Difficulties may be life-long. This is evident from a study of three generations of a family, about half of whom were language-impaired (Gopnik & Crago 1991). The study focused on six of the older language-impaired members of the family who could be assumed to have completed their language development. They ranged from a grandchild of 16 to a grandmother of 74. Together with six unimpaired relatives, aged 8–17, they participated in a variety of language tasks. On many, the language-impaired members of the family did not differ from their unimpaired relatives. The tasks on which they did differ involved function morphemes. Presented with the following sort of input:

This is a zoop (pointing to an imaginary animal)
These are – ? (pointing to two or three of these animals)

the language-impaired members were less able to create a plural form for the word they had not met before. Similarly, they were less able to generate auxiliary verbs and inflections in response to lead-ins such as

Table 11.1. *Difficulties with function morphemes reported for languages other than English*

	Noun-related	Verb-related
German[a]	Omission of articles Errors in case marking of nouns Errors in marking of articles and adjectives to agree with nouns	Errors in marking of verbs to agree with subject (through use of verbs in an uninflected, infinitive, or incorrectly inflected form) Omission of auxiliaries
Italian[b]	Omission of articles	Errors in marking of verbs to agree with 3rd-person-plural subject
Hebrew[c]	Omission of marker of direct object	

[a]Clahsen 1989
[b]Leonard et al. 1992, Bortolini, Caselli & Leonard 1997
[c]Rom & Leonard 1990, Dromi, Leonard & Shteiman 1993

Every day he walks eight miles
Yesterday he – ?

The boy always cries
Right now he – ?

Yet function morphemes are not all equally problematic. Comparison *between languages* reveals that while function morphemes are commonly affected, the marker for a particular function may be more affected in one language than another. Table 11.1 draws together some of the cross-linguistic evidence.

It turns out that English-speaking children have greater difficulty with plural and 3rd-person-singular markers than their Italian- or Hebrew-speaking counterparts (Leonard 1992). Italian-speaking children struggle more with articles than Hebrew-speaking children. Hebrew-speaking children, it seems, have an easier time all round with function morphemes. When compared with MLU matches, they show no special difficulty with present and past tense inflections on verbs, number inflections on nouns, or gender inflections on adjectives; the only function morpheme which gives them more trouble is the marker which Hebrew requires before a definite direct object (Dromi, Leonard & Shteiman 1993).

Comparison *within* languages also reveals variable levels of difficulty. *In English*, the 3rd-person-singular marker *-s* on verbs is more affected than the plural marker *-s* on nouns. For example, a group of 4- to 6-year-old language-impaired children showed some delay in their use of plural *-s* compared with 2- to 4-year-old normally developing children matched on MLU, but the discrepancy was greater for the 3rd-person *-s* (Rice & Oetting 1993). *In Italian*, a language-impaired group produced plurals as reliably as their language matches, but not determiners (Leonard et al. 1992). *In German*, children were observed to inflect verbs correctly for past participles, but not for agreement with the person and number of the subject (Clahsen 1989).

Whether they are more or less acutely affected, it is striking that function morphemes are not entirely absent. What is notable is the *unreliability* of their use. Children may, for example, use plural *-s* or past tense *-ed* in some or even many of the contexts requiring them, yet still not attain the reliable use of the normal 3 to 4-year-old. They may even be inconsistent within a single lexical context, producing the same word both with and without a required function morpheme. An analysis of spontaneous speech samples produced by nine language-impaired children revealed that 50 per cent of the words they produced in two or more contexts requiring an inflection were produced at least once *with* that inflection and at least once *without* it (Leonard et al. 1997). Every one of these children exhibited inconsistency with at least some words.

This finding is important. It rules out the possibility that the children have acquired individual inflected items as wholes, for example *balloons* for a group of balloons or *walked* for a past occurrence of walking, without separating out the inflections and their plural or past function. If they had done this, they would use those specific inflected forms consistently, but would not use other similarly inflected forms.

Even stronger evidence that they *have* separated out the inflection rather than acquiring it as a fixed part of a word is that they produce inflected forms which they have not met. They sometimes use **overregularised** forms which they cannot have heard. They produce past tense forms such as *throwed* and *catched*, and plural forms such as *peoples* and *mans* (Rice & Oetting 1993, Oetting & Horohov 1997, Leonard et al. 1997). They also show novel use of function morphemes when they add them to nonsense words. Such inflected forms are elicited by introducing children to a nonsense word and then asking them to complete a sentence containing that word:

> Here is a boy and here is a nep. See, a boy and a nep. This is the boy's food and here is the . . .

> (Leonard et al. 1997)

Nine language-impaired children did produce the required function morpheme with a nonsense word on at least some occasions. These novel uses are evidence that the child's acquisition of function morphemes is not piecemeal or frozen. It is just slow and unreliable, trailing even further behind their acquisition of content words.

Input

Considering the spotlight that has fallen on function morphemes in *output*, surprisingly little has been said about what children do with function morphemes in *input*. This is probably because it is much harder to track children's recognition and understanding of function morphemes than their production. The problem is that most function morphemes do not make reference, as noted above, so they are largely redundant to communication in context. This means that children could make good headway in understanding everyday utterances even if they didn't understand the function morphemes. We may try to get round this problem by testing comprehension of function morphemes outside of context – only to encounter other problems. How do we design a comprehension test for items which cannot be represented by pictures or actions?

A minority of function morphemes do convey referential meaning. Prepositions such as 'in', 'on', 'under', 'behind', for instance, may be used to make reference to spatial relations which are observable in the outside world. In the case of these items, experiments can easily be designed to test children's understanding. We can ask children to 'put the doll in/on/under/behind the box' and see if the child does this. Judging from this sort of evidence, normally developing children's comprehension of spatial prepositions – extending from 'in' and 'on' through to 'above', 'below', 'in front of', 'behind' – unfolds between around 18 months and 4 years. (See Owens 1996 for an overview.)

The majority of function morphemes are less easy to test. The time relations expressed by -s, -ed and -ing cannot be depicted by an action or picture, nor can the specificity of reference expressed by *the*. To find out whether children recognise and understand these forms, we have to find ways of probing children's reactions to function morphemes indirectly. Techniques which do this have produced gems of evidence indicating that normally developing and language-impaired children may be more sensitive to function morphemes in *input* than their output would have us believe.

These techniques do not elicit conscious judgement or full interpretation of the function morpheme. Instead, they check children's responses to sentences with and without correct function morphemes to see if they react to these differently. If they do, they must be registering the function morphemes. In one study, children were presented with sentences which included obligatory function morphemes:

Throw me the ball!

and sentences which, like their own, were 'telegraphic':

Throw ball!

or

Ball!

(Shipley, Smith & Gleitman 1969)

Children whose own utterances were mostly a single word obeyed the shorter child-like commands more frequently than the longer, well-formed commands. However, children whose own utterances were just a bit more advanced – mostly two words or less – obeyed the longer, well-formed commands more often than the shorter, telegraphic commands. This shows that children who are not yet using certain function words may nevertheless distinguish and 'prefer' sentences which include them.

More refined probing reveals children's sensitivity not only to whether a function word occurs, but to which function word occurs where. Children are presented with sentences containing an appropriate function word and sentences containing a different and inappropriate one:

> Find the dog for me (appropriate: determiner *the* before noun)
> Find was dog for me (inappropriate: auxiliary *was* before noun)

(Gerken 1996)

Children of 21–28 months did show a different response to these different inputs. Some of the children – those whose own utterances had a mean length of over 1.5 morphemes – were better able to point to the correct picture for the noun following a determiner (appropriate) than following an auxiliary (inappropriate).

What about language-impaired children whose own production of function morphemes is unreliable? Will they respond differently to correct and incorrect use of those function morphemes? To follow up this question, a group of language-impaired children were presented with instructions containing appropriate or inappropriate use of function morphemes:

> Find <u>the</u> bird for me (appropriate)
> Find – bird for me (omitted)
> Find <u>was</u> bird for me (inappropriate)
> Find <u>gub</u> bird for me (nonsense)

(McNamara, Carter, McIntosh & Gerken 1998)

The children were significantly better at selecting the correct picture when they heard correct *the* than incorrect *was*. They were less affected by the omission of the function morpheme and its substitution with *gub*. These findings show that the children were at least sensitive to the form *the* and its context. If they were not, they would respond to the appropriate and inappropriate instructions in the same way.

Where children react differently to the determiner and the auxiliary, they clearly know the *form* of the function word which goes with the noun. They don't necessarily know the *meaning*. This brings us back to the difficulty of tapping children's knowledge of abstract meanings. We can overcome this only by devising situations where that abstract meaning has repercussions for the concrete interpretation of a sentence. This can happen with determiners, whose function is to identify which 'thing' a noun refers to in a particular context. Names such as 'Susan' or 'Fred' or 'Fido' inherently refer to a particular individual rather than a class of individuals, so do not normally occur with a determiner:

*The Susan
*A Fido

The presence or absence of a determiner can therefore indicate whether an unknown word is a name or a common noun:

This is dax (taken to be a name)
This is a dax (taken to be a common noun)

Do children interpret these differently?

This has been checked out experimentally (Katz, Baker & Macnamara 1974). Two-year-old normally developing children were introduced to toys they had not met before – either small plastic dolls or large plastic blocks. Some children received the lead-in:

This is dax

and were subsequently asked to 'point to dax'. Others received the lead-in

This is a dax

and were asked to 'point to a dax'. Girls as young as 17–24 months distinguished the name from the noun when it referred to a doll. Those who met 'dax' were more likely to point to the *same* doll they had been introduced to, rather than a different doll. Those who met 'a dax' were as likely to point to a different doll. This shows they already know that dolls can be labelled as individuals or as a class. More than this, they must know that the determiner signals the class of dolls rather than the name of the doll. They did not show this distinction with blocks, presumably because they do not expect blocks to be identified as unique individuals. (Two-year-old boys showed no difference with dolls or blocks. Either they were insensitive to the possibility of dolls being individualised like people – reflecting a quite plausible gender bias! Or they were less linguistically sophisticated than girls and did not appreciate the contribution of the determiner.)

Such experiments have not yet been tried with language-impaired children. Evidence of their comprehension of function morphemes remains sparse. Anecdotal reports of their misunderstandings often involve confusion over matters such as time which can crucially depend on function morphemes. When they fall down on clinical tests of comprehension, it may well be that items which rely on function morphemes are amongst those which trip them up. Limited data from the Italian group of language-impaired children (Leonard et al. 1992) suggest that their difficulties in output may indeed be parallelled in input. When these children's comprehension of function morphemes was tested, they performed poorly on the same two morphemes which they produced less reliably than their language-matches. Poor comprehension, though, does not imply no comprehension. On the contrary, the Italian language-impaired children scored above chance on all but one of the function morphemes tested. This suggests that the children could recognise their form and function.

It is possible that a speaker may recognise and understand function morphemes, but not realise that they are obligatory. This aspect of function morphemes is picked up in the study of three generations mentioned above (Gopnik & Crago 1991). The language-impaired members of the family *understood* plural *-s* in instructions such as:

> Please touch the balloons
> Put the crayon on the balloons

Here, their scores were on a par with their unimpaired relatives. But they were much less able when it came to *making judgements* about sentences such as

The boy eats three cookie_
The little girl is play_ with her doll

where the judgement hinges on the plural marker or a verb inflection. They were also less able to correct the errors in such sentences. They often left the error unaltered and changed something that was already correct, for example turning

The boy eats three cookie

into

The boy eats four cookie

While the language-impaired individuals clearly recognised and understood the plural form, they did not recognise that its marking is obligatory, in contrast to their intact relatives who did.

Stretched and overstretched

Unlike most children who progress to full and reliable use of function morphemes, some children do not make it all the way. The processes by which children normally acquire function morphemes are somehow falling short. To find out more, we need to consider what is involved in those processes.

Consider their starting-point. Children are not handed function morphemes on a plate. On the contrary, function morphemes come welded to content words, in whole utterances relating to whole scenes. Children must discover these morphemes using their own resources for unpicking the complex information they receive. The patterns of emergence of function morphemes within a single language, and across widely different languages, are beginning to throw light on the nuts and bolts of this process.

Cues from phonology

Young children have acute antennae for the complex rhythms of the speech they hear, as we have seen. Early on, they pick out the rhythmic peaks which highlight the key content words. They rarely make errors of word segmentation. They rarely use a content word together with a function morpheme but with the meaning of just the content word, an error which would suggest they had not separated out the function morpheme. Function morphemes are more likely missing from their early speech, or reduced to some neutral and unrecognisable form. When they have consolidated a good number of content words, they move on to the phonological forms which embellish those now familiar content word forms. What prompts this move?

The ball probably starts rolling with children beginning to notice the phonological snippets whose detail they have previously ignored or skimmed over. Their increasing sensitivity to the phonological forms may trigger their 'search' for the function which these subsidiary forms fulfill. This possibility is in keeping with evidence of the ways in which phonology influences children's acquisition of function morphemes.

Studies of language development in English have indicated that children tune into unstressed forms which *follow* the stress in a rhythmic unit more than those which precede the stress. As we saw in chapter 2, this is true within words, where children are much more likely to leave out an unstressed syllable which precedes stress than one which follows it. Hence, the typical

'raffe, 'mato, 'tato, 'jamas

for

gi'raffe, to'mato, po'tato, py'jamas

As further evidence, when 2-year-olds are introduced to novel four-syllable forms such as

zam pa ka sis

they reproduce these forms differently according to where the stress occurs (Gerken 1996). Where a weak syllable *precedes* the stress, for example *pa* in

pa ZAM ka SIS

children omit that syllable. Where it *follows* the stress as in

ZAM pa ka SIS

it is preserved, at the cost of the subsequent weak syllable.

Likewise, when children produce word combinations, they are more likely to omit or collapse an unstressed word which *precedes* a stressed word than one which follows. They are very likely to miss or blur a **preposition** such as *on* in:

Draw paper

or

Draw [ə] paper

yet produce it clearly in:

Shoe on
Light on

The repercussions of this phonological bias on the acquisition of function morphemes are evident. We find that function morphemes which have the *same function* appear at different stages depending on their *position*. This emerges from comparisons between children acquiring different languages. Take the case of **determiners** which precede the noun in English:

Determiner – Noun, as in *a table, the table*

but follow it in Bulgarian:

Noun – Determiner

Children acquiring Bulgarian use determiners earlier than their English-learning counterparts. An even more striking contrast has been cited from the speech of bilingual children acquiring Hungarian and Serbo-Croatian. Serbo-Croatian marks spatial relations like 'in' and 'on' with **prepositions** which precede the noun (as does English):

Spatial marker – Noun

In Hungarian, on the other hand, such spatial relations are marked by **suffixes**, word endings which follow the noun:

Noun – Spatial marker

Though these children are acquiring Serbo-Croatian and Hungarian simultaneously, they use the spatial suffixes of Hungarian in advance of the spatial prepositions of Serbo-Croatian. They have clearly grasped the notion of spatial relations, since they mark these in Hungarian. The hold-up in Serbo-Croatian must therefore reflect the children's greater difficulty in getting hold of the *form*. It seems that the form following the content word is easier for them to get hold of. (Examples taken from Slobin 1973.)

The greater salience of phonological forms which follow the stress can to some extent account for the road to function morphemes which we have observed in children acquiring English. The plural marker, a suffix following the noun, emerges before determiners, which precede it. Verb inflections *-ing* and *-ed*, which follow the verb, are acquired earlier than the accompanying auxiliaries *be* and *have* which precede the verb.

But such phonological biases cannot be the whole story. We can, after all, find examples of unstressed words which precede the stress, and so should be harder for the child, emerging earlier than others which follow the stress and should be easier. *In* and *on*, which are prepositions, emerge relatively early, and before some of the inflections which follow the verb.

The use of cues from phonology, commonly known as 'phonological bootstrapping', may launch the child on the road to function morphemes. But other forces will influence the direction that road takes.

Cues from meaning

Children are initially focused on things and people, and their actions, states, location and possession in the here-and-now, as we have seen. We might expect their sensitivity to relations in the world to be a launching pad for discovering what function morphemes contribute to the meaning of sentences. Is this what happens?

Consider the morphemes which take the lead in English: '-ing', 'in/on', 'I/me', 'my', 'mine'. Each of these relates to one of the salient aspects of the here-and-now scene. '-ing' identifies events as on-going, so when it is used in the present, it applies to events which are directly available to the child in the here-and-now. Early uses of 'in/on' represent the rare case of function morphemes with referential meaning: they refer to salient spatial relations between things. In contrast, prepositions which apply to less salient space relations, time relations and relations of an even more abstract nature are not yet used. 'I/me/my/mine' identify the speaker, the most salient role in the communication event, who of course coincides with the child herself when she is speaking. 'My/mine' also identify possession which is in itself a salient relation, but especially so when the possessor or would-be possessor is the child!

Turning to later acquired function morphemes, these identify less salient aspects of scenes, or relations which have no direct reflection in the scene. Determiners 'a/the' limit the reference of a noun by indicating whether or not it is a specific entity already focused in the context. Tenses '-ed/-s' and auxiliary verbs such as 'will/can/could/would' mark an event as outside the here-and-now – past, habitual, future, hypothetical, and more.

The slowest-to-be-acquired function morphemes not only mark notions which are less accessible. They **conflate** two or more such notions, as in the case of auxiliary verbs which convey complex information about timing of the event *and* mark agreement of the verb with the subject:

He *is* eating	present tense + 3rd person singular
They *are* eating	present tense + 3rd person plural
He *was* eating	past tense + 3rd person singular

On top of all this, these auxiliary verbs play a role in marking questions and negation:

Is he eating?
He *isn't* eating

Phonological cues first

Function morphemes, it seems, are more or less accessible to the child depending

- how closely they fit the child's phonological biases
- how closely they fit the child's semantic biases

The most easily accessible and earliest acquired are those which

have consistent phonological forms, occur in phonologically salient positions, and pick out a single salient aspect of here-and-now
scenes. The effect of both phonological and semantic factors indicates that the child draws on both semantic and phonological
'bootstraps'. This is very much in line with our conclusion about
children's acquisition of verb structure: that it must result from a
coalition of 'bootstraps'. However, when it comes to function morphemes, the partners in this coalition appear far from equal.

This is not surprising. After all, function morphemes of different
languages pick on different aspects of entities and events. Children
cannot know in advance which aspects will be obligatorily marked
in their particular language. They cannot know, for example, that
English insists on distinguishing past events according to whether
their occurrence at a specific time in the past ('fell') or their effect at
a later time ('has fallen') is being pinpointed. The only evidence
available to children at the outset is the different linguistic *forms*
they encounter. The English-acquiring child encounters verbs
with *have* and verbs without, both referring to events in the past.
This can alert the child to look for a difference between the two
forms for past reference, and notice that *has fallen* occurs in scenes
where the focus is on the effect following from the event. At this
point, semantic bootstrapping comes into play: children's sensitivity to different aspects of the scene will influence their discovery of
the feature which goes hand in hand with the form.

Where function morphemes have no direct relation to the
context, the argument for phonological bootstrapping is even
stronger. Take the case of **agreement markers**. These have no
significance in themselves, so they cannot be reached by semantic
bootstrapping. The only cue to agreement children receive is the
phonological variation which occurs in the word which 'agrees'.
For example, where verbs are marked for number, the distinction
between one and more than one does not arise from the event to
which the verb refers. It is the subject of the verb which is one or
more than one, and the marker on the verb does no more than
echo this property of its subject. Only the phonological variation in
the verb form can cue the child to this subject–verb agreement.

Logically, phonology must drive the search for the function of
these forms. Actual evidence of the way they emerge supports the

case. Children easily pick up phonological patterns which have no semantic correlate. For example, where gender carries no meaning, as is the case with nouns which are inanimate and do not come in male or female guise, children readily negotiate the phonological patterns associated with it. In languages as diverse as Hebrew, French and Polish, they acquire gender between the ages of 2 and 3, appropriately matching the phonology of determiners or noun inflections to the noun. In some languages, such as Russian, gender marking is slower to emerge. The difference is that gender marking is less distinctive and less consistent in Russian, making it harder for children to sort out the phonological patterns (Slobin 1985).

The strength of children's phonological bootstraps is such that phonological cues to gender can take priority even when semantic cues are available. This is illustrated by an experiment carried out with French-speaking children which pitted phonological and semantic cues against each other (Karmiloff-Smith 1978). Children were presented with pictures of martian-like persons of female or male appearance. These characters were given novel names with typically masculine or typically feminine endings. How would children react when the gender of the character in the picture and the gender marking of the word were in conflict: when males were given feminine-sounding names, and vice versa? They might use the semantic information from the picture, and assign masculine gender to males. Or they might use the phonological information from the word ending, and take the name for the males to be feminine. The finding was that phonology won out over semantics. Children as young as 3 to 4 determined gender from the name. The mismatch between their gender marking and the gender in the picture apparently did not trouble them.

If phonology is the first cue to function morphemes, we might expect these be a problem for children to whom phonology does not come so naturally. A special difficulty with items of relatively short duration has been put forward as a possible explanation for the vulnerability of function morphemes in language-impaired children (see, for example, Leonard & Eyer 1996). According to this explanation, function morphemes which take the form of syllables which are unstressed or precede the stress, or of single consonants, should be most affected. This is consistent with the differences between language-impaired children acquiring different languages which were noted above. We saw, for example, that language-impaired children acquiring Italian showed much less problem with verb and noun inflections than their English counterparts. The inflections which the Italian-speaking children produce as reliably as children matched on MLU are precisely those which are phonologically more robust. They are phonologically stronger than the inflections which so challenge English-speaking children.

The interaction between phonological and semantic/syntactic bootstrapping

Phonological bootstrapping is clearly a necessary and powerful force in the acquisition of function morphemes, driving the process of discovering the semantic and syntactic contexts which determine their occurrence. But noticing the phonological left-overs of content words is not enough to see this process through. Children must also have some idea of the sorts of functions these forms fulfill. If they were not pre-set to notice the co-occurrence of these phonological forms with certain sorts of semantic or syntactic context, it is hard to see how they would ever hit on their specific function and know when they are required. Phonological bootstraps may kick-start the process, but semantic and syntactic bootstraps must kick in. The ease with which children acquire a function morpheme depends on the salience of its semantic/syntactic function and the salience of its phonology, but also on the *connection* between these.

Phonological forms or patterns which are *distinct* and *consistent* for a particular function are picked up more easily than those which are less distinct or vary. This accounts for the observation that children acquiring Russian take much longer to establish gender than those acquiring Polish who, as we saw in the previous section, achieve this at an early age. In Russian, the phonological marking of gender is notably less distinct and consistent than in Polish.

The leap from phonological form to function is easier where

phonological links *mirror* semantic links than where they are mismatched. Function morphemes which are attached to the relevant content word are established earlier than those which are syntactically remote from the relevant content word. Take forms which mark definiteness. Definiteness is the notion conveyed by the English determiner *the* (as opposed to *a*). Its function is to identify the reference of the noun. The determiner marking definiteness is separate from but closely connected to the noun. In Hungarian, *verbs* are marked according to the definiteness of their object. Here, the marker of definiteness is attached to a verb, but is not semantically relevant to the verb. This marker of definiteness on the verb poses a much greater problem for children than markers for definiteness which are connected to nouns, including the determiners of English, German, Romance languages, the noun prefix of Hebrew and the noun suffix of Turkish. (See Slobin 1985 for extensive examples and discussion.)

The connection between the phonology and semantics of function morphemes, as well as their phonological and semantic salience, determines how far they stretch the child's bootstraps.

Working through the complex processes which go into the acquisition of function morphemes, it becomes clear that limitations on the use of function morphemes which we observe in some children could have many different sources. To illustrate how we may explore such limitations, we turn to the case of Ruth.

12 'That one not working, see': problems with auxiliary verb processing

Ruth is a spirited 10-year-old who loves horse riding and wants to work in a stable when she grows up. She has lively exchanges with her class mates and teacher, chats enthusiastically about school and home activities, jokes, fantasises, gets embarrassed, has fun putting down friends or family, throws side-long glances at adults when she knows they are discussing her, is both keen and shy to take the stage. She is observant and sensitive and initiates conversation in just the ways you would expect of a girl approaching adolescence:

> (Ruth has just come into the room)
> R: I know, your hair cut.
> SC: I'm going to have one? Or I have had one?
> R: You *have* one.
> SC: Yeah. I did have one. It's too short, isn't it? But it will grow.
> R: Like me.

Ruth's open and interested demeanour only clouds over and closes up when her difficulties with language come into focus. At this point, she is likely to fire angry and conversation-closing words:

> SC: Yeah, your hair's getting long. Who cuts your hair?
> R: Tressers (rather distorted).
> SC: Tracy's?
> R: Nothing!! [ʌn] your business.
> SC: (catching on, but too late) Oh, hairdressers! Like me.

Once her difficulties are touched on, and especially if they become apparent in public, she is likely either to withdraw or to lash out

with expressions of rejection. These negative feelings also surface
in role-play games which are in her control. She often acts out
aggressive fantasies through the roles she creates:

> (Ruth has SC working for her, and after ordering her about, finds ways
> of ensuring that her employee cannot get away)
>
> R: There – is – ['bʌzə] bar.
>
> SC: Huh?
>
> R: ['mʌzə] bar there.
>
> SC: Bar?
>
> R: Yeah me-tal bar.
>
> SC: Oh, a metal bar.
>
> R: Yeah [sdæn] there. And there too. [du] can't get out . . . [zu]
> 'scape, [ðə] f – we find you. You come back here, no food.
>
> SC: Oh no! Will I get food now?
>
> R: No.
>
> SC: If I don't escape, can I have food?
>
> R: Think about that.
>
> SC: What will happen if I have no food?
>
> R: Dead. No sweat . . .

Such negative or aggressive reactions are hardly surprising. The
gulf between what Ruth *wants to express* and what she *is able to
express intelligibly* would be enough to drive a person to distraction.

Ruth's language is severely impaired. She produces a flow of
speech which, at a distance, might sound like normal English.
Closer up, the impression changes dramatically. Many utterances
are partially or entirely unintelligible. Many are fragmented. In
contrast to her very disrupted output, Ruth seems to understand
language well, at least in context. Up to the age of 5, her performance on a comprehension test (the Reynell Developmental Language Scales) was normal. At 5, her comprehension dipped relative to her peers, and appeared to plateau at this point. At 10 her
comprehension, as assessed on the Test for the Reception of Grammar, is at the level of a 6-year-old. It looks as if Ruth's input skills
are in some way limited, but they see her through everyday life
quite well and outstrip her output skills by a long shot.

Focusing on Ruth's output, the more detailed impression is of
easily recognisable words interspersed with phonological chunks

which are unrecognisable but sound like English. Where Ruth produces enough recognisable words, we observe that she *orders* them appropriately for her intended meaning. She also assigns them their appropriate *stress*, producing a rhythmically appropriate utterance:

I 'kafter you, you 'kafter me (= 'look after')
Told you I got lots
Pretend you don' know me
Stay under water long time, that hurt my eyes

To this extent, Ruth's utterances appear to be syntactically and phonologically on track.

Because Ruth produces so much unintelligible speech, calculating her **mean length of utterance (MLU)** (following Brown 1973) is not at all straightforward. Do we include in our count every form we judge to be an attempt at a word? Or do we count only those which are recognisable? Alternatively, do we avoid such decisions by using only utterances in which every word is recognisable? For the purposes of rough comparison with normally developing children, Ruth's MLU was calculated counting *only* the recognisable words in the usual sample of 100 consecutive utterances. Using this rather ungenerous measure, Ruth's MLU came out at 3.7, with utterances ranging from one to nine morphemes. This MLU is normally characteristic of a 3- to $3\frac{1}{2}$-year-old. It is obvious that Ruth's output is very different from a typical child of either her age or her MLU. She has a profound problem with words.

Sometimes, the intended target of her unintelligible forms can be worked out from the context:

No inerbrup [nəʊʔ ɪnəˈbrʌp]

– uttered when Ruth is in the full flow of a story and the listener cuts in to seek clarification – is surely an attempt at

Don't interrupt

Sometimes Ruth's unintelligible form sounds very like a word which has just been used and which we can assume to be her target:

SC: Nobody can see it. It's invisible (referring to an imaginary aeroplane).

R: Yeah, [ˈvɪgzɪɪl kleɪn]
SC: Huh?
R: [ˈvɪvɪbɪl] plane.

Sometimes, with repeated attempts, Ruth arrives at a recognisable target. This happened in the conversation cited above: from '[ˈbʌzə] bar' she progressed to '[ˈmʌzə] bar' and then hit the target with 'metal bar'.

Since we can sometimes identify specific targets for Ruth's unrecognisable forms, we can be sure that at least some of the time Ruth is aiming for particular English words even when what we are hearing is a stream of unintelligible phonology. In so doing, we discover that *words of all sorts* are a problem for Ruth. Her distorted forms include nouns, verbs and adjectives *(plane, interrupt, invisible)*. And when we compare these with their known targets, we discover that Ruth distorts content words in particular ways:

1. While they usually preserve stress and number of syllables, unstressed syllables are sometimes omitted or reduced, especially where they precede stress:

disgusting → [ˈgʌstɪn]
invisible → [ˈvɪgzɪɪl], [ˈvɪvɪbɪl], [ˈvidəbəl], [ˈvizəbəl]
injection → [prəˈʒɛʔʃən], [ˈdʒɛʔʃəns], [ˈsdʒɛʔʃən], [ˈdʒɛgʃən]

2. Consonant clusters are often reduced:

problem → [ˈpɒbləm]
next → [nɛʔ]

3. Within syllables, individual vowels or consonants are often omitted, added or replaced with a closely related sound:

stay → [səʔ]
luggage → [ˈlʌgwɪz]
festival → [ˈfɛsəbəl]

In all these cases, Ruth has a specific word *meaning* in mind. Only the *phonology* of the word is obscured – often out of all recognition.

If content words are so affected, we would certainly expect function morphemes to suffer. First impressions of Ruth's speech indicate that they do. Function morphemes are obligatory in certain contexts and where the context is clear enough from the scene or from the words Ruth has used, omissions and distortions of function morphemes are apparent:

Ruth	*Likely intention*
Me borrow mum camera us go out	*I'll* borrow mum*'s* camera *when we* go out
I ring you last time	I *rang* you last time
We walk up	We walk*ed* up
You and me getting married	You and me *are* getting married
[wɪnwə] finished, we play the game	*When we've* finished, we*'ll* play the game
[təzə] got my telephone number?	*Have you* got my telephone number?

These examples illustrate problems with pronouns, possessive *-s*, tense and auxiliaries, most of which would be well established in a normally developing child with Ruth's MLU.

Where do Ruth's problems with function morphemes lie? Does she have problems recognising or producing the *form* of function morphemes? Or is their *function* the problem?

We will set about exploring these questions through the particular case of *tense and auxiliaries*. We will start by looking at Ruth's spontaneous output.

Ruth's production of auxiliary verbs and inflections is inconsistent, but some patterns emerge within the inconsistency. On some occasions, Ruth produces recognisable auxiliary verbs and inflections, including those listed in table 12.1.

Where Ruth does not produce obligatory auxiliary elements, these are either entirely absent, or some unintelligible form appears where the auxiliary would be expected (see table 12.2).

In **questions** and **negatives**, whose structure depends on auxiliaries, Ruth very rarely produces auxiliaries correctly. In questions, an auxiliary should precede the subject Noun Phrase. This is sometimes omitted:

You go [ə] church?

More commonly, an unintelligible weak form turns up just where the auxiliary and a subject pronoun are called for:

Table 12.1. *Ruth's correct use of auxiliaries: some examples*

be + present participle	*have* + past participle	*can/will*	Past tense
Pretend you're tickling me	I've been on television before	She can eat sweets	[mɪə] hated food on [ə] plane
		You can see me	
These are hurting me	I've grown up		You said no!
		He'll help with me	
I am – dreaming		She will like it	

Table 12.2. *Ruth's omission of auxiliaries: some examples*

be	*have*	*be gonna* or modal such as *can/will*	Past tense
You and me getting married	Oh no you 'gotten	Her come in some time	I ring you last time
	This is my – Ian what borrowed		We walk up
Us going on Friday		Your baby come out soon	
		Here I do it for you	

[də] go home now? (= 'shall we')
[də] type that for me please (= 'will you')
[ʒ] got a husband (= 'have you')

In negatives, an auxiliary should precede the negative particle *n't* or *not*. Again, the auxiliary is often lost:

That one not working, see (= 'isn't/'s not')
She no coming back in (= 'isn't/'s not')

Strangely, the negative particle is sometimes lost as well:

Andrew got any telephone number yet (= 'hasn't')
Nanny got any teeth up [ə] top got any teeth down [ə] bottom
(= 'hasn't')

Unintelligible substitutions which 'squash' a subject pronoun, auxiliary and negative particle are also common:

[amə] ask her yet (= 'I haven't')
[anə] telling you (= 'I'm not')
[amnə] steal things, no (= 'I don't')

Ruth's only reliable use of auxiliaries is in **elliptical responses**, where the auxiliary 'stands for' a previous Verb Phrase and occurs at the end of the utterance:

Oh yes you are
She tickling me, I not go on [ə] floor. She can!

But here, where an auxiliary is always included, it is not always the correct one for the context. The auxiliary in the elliptical response should match the utterance to which it is a response, and sometimes does not:

(Shall we go out now?) → Course we are
(I do like you really) → No you won't
(Is she at home?) → Yeah, in the mornings she's does

In summary, the pattern which emerges is:

1. inconsistent use of *be*, *have*, a limited range of modals, and tense/participle inflections
2. unintelligible substitutions, especially in questions and negatives
3. auxiliary substitutions in elliptical responses

What is stopping Ruth from achieving consistent use of the full range of auxiliaries?

One possibility is that she struggles with the sort of concepts that auxiliaries convey – the situating of events in relation to time and reality. Ruth gives us strong reason to think that she *does* have these concepts and attempts to convey them.

First, when she does use auxiliary markers, they are almost always appropriate for the context, suggesting she does understand them.

Second, she sometimes conveys time relations of just the sort that tense and auxiliaries convey, but using time adverbials (see Moore & Johnston 1993 for experimental evidence that adverbials may be less taxing than tense for some language-impaired children). Ruth uses 'last time' referring to a past event:

> I ring you last time

and 'yet' referring to a past event relevant to the present:

> [amə] ask her yet

Third, the context and content of certain utterances provide evidence that she has understood just the sort of timing and contingency relations between events which auxiliaries capture. Take her impressive attempt at time reference in the following interchange:

> (Will you still know me when you're 15?) → Forgotten you by now

The verb with which Ruth responds to the question, 'forgotten', clearly signals an event *after* the present time, when Ruth *does* know the questioner. The past participle form *forgotten* clearly signals an event prior to another event, that of being 15. This adds up to a reference to a future event which is past relative to a later future:

> — Time of utterance — Time of forgetting — Time of Ruth being 15 →

It is true that Ruth uses 'by now' rather than 'by then'. But the implications of her response indicate that neither this confusion, nor the omission of the auxiliaries 'I'*ll have* . . .' are due to confusion about the time relations between the events.

We find similar evidence that Ruth talks knowingly about hypothetical and possible events:

> SC: If we leave our bags here, what might happen? If we leave our money?

R: The people come up – [ðət] – [tə] ladder – [ðə] come in there – that window down – that window down – to come and pinch your money. [kətə] take it with us. [ðə] case. [tə] money with us. [ðə] case.

Here, Ruth conveys two events which are clearly related in her and our experience of the world – someone breaking in, and not leaving money around. Her linking of these events and her use of '[ðə] case' (= 'in case') imply the contingency of one event on another: one event is a possible one and its possibility is the motivation for the other event. But she does not use any of the modal verbs, such as '*might* break in' and '*should* take our money', which would normally make explicit the status of these events and their interrelations. If she has a grasp of these notions and is trying to convey them, why does she not do so with the modal verbs which make them explicit? The implication is that she has problems not with their semantic function, but with their form or with the connection between their form and function.

We already have solid evidence that Ruth struggles with the phonological form of words: even when she is targeting a particular content word semantically, she is liable to distort its phonology. It may be that she has a similar problem with the phonology of function morphemes such as auxiliaries. The phonology of auxiliaries is particularly challenging. They are typically unstressed, and have weak forms which reduce and contract, though only in certain contexts (see chapter 11). We would expect auxiliaries to be especially affected by difficulties with phonological forms.

The pattern which has emerged from Ruth's spontaneous output points to phonology as a prime suspect. The fact that we frequently find unintelligible phonological forms where auxiliaries should occur – often alongside other weak forms – suggests Ruth knows *something* is required at these points in the rhythm. But she doesn't know quite what.

A second reason for suspecting phonology is the way that Ruth's use of auxiliaries varies. Her distorted forms occur only in positions where auxiliaries are unstressed, liable to reduction, and even merge with other weak forms. For example, the auxiliary and subject pronoun which are normally subject to reduction or merger as in

> shall we → [ʃwɪ]
> have you → [vju]

are liable to be inappropriately squeezed in Ruth's speech:

> [ðə] go home now? (= 'shall we')
> [ʒ] got a husband? (= 'have you')

In contrast, Ruth's clearest use of auxiliaries is in elliptical responses, where the auxiliary either carries the sentence stress or follows it. Both are phonologically salient positions. In these positions, the auxiliary cannot take its reduced form.

Curiously, in just these contexts where Ruth produces a fully intelligible auxiliary, we find her sometimes selecting the wrong one:

> (I do like you really) → No you won't

In this case, the phonological form is correct and cannot be the problem. Ruth's confusion between auxiliaries must stem from some other difficulty. This looks like evidence against our suspicion that phonology is the primary culprit. But it may not be. Consider the function of auxiliaries in elliptical responses: to affirm or deny a state of affairs referred to previously. Semantically, the auxiliary carries no new information. It simply echoes the auxiliary in the utterance to which it responds. This matching of auxiliaries appears to be the sticking point for Ruth. At first sight, this looks like a syntactic problem: Ruth doesn't realise that the auxiliary in the response must agree with the original. The identification of this syntactic connection, however, relies on phonological bootstrapping. If the child is to extract the pattern of auxiliary matching, she must register the phonological form of the two separate auxiliaries which match. Any difficulty with phonological forms will surely be an obstacle to discovering connections between phonological forms which are separated. Such a problem could therefore account for Ruth's errors in elliptical responses.

So, the patterns of auxiliary use in Ruth's spontaneous output are in keeping with our hunch that their phonological forms may be at the root of her problems. If they are, we should find that she has the same problems producing auxiliaries when she does not have to deal with their function. We can check this by seeing what she does with auxiliaries when she is repeating rather than generating utterances.

Repetition

Ruth was asked to 'make her puppet say sentences', with no pressure to achieve correct repetition, and no correction of what she said. Under these conditions, Ruth responds to repetition tasks readily, and her responses are interesting.

Her repetition is certainly impaired. She was given sentences of two, three, or four words. With two-word sentences, she has little problem. No words are omitted, and 90 per cent are reproduced correctly. As sentence length increases, her repetition deteriorates. The percentage of correctly repeated words reduces to 80 per cent in three-word sentences, and 60 per cent in four-word sentences. These correct words are interspersed with word omissions or with Ruth's by now familiar unintelligible forms. The net effect is that the utterances Ruth produces in repetition sound very like her own spontaneously produced utterances. With spontaneous output, we cannot be sure what the target words are. With repetition, we know exactly what the targets are. Her responses to repetition therefore offer a clear window onto what she is doing with words.

Looking through that window, we find that Ruth's repetition is selective. Her response to an utterance which is 'too long' is not simply to reduce the number of words by, say, repeating only the first two or the last two or just any two. This becomes apparent when we focus on different types of words and see what happens to them in different positions in the sentence and in sentences of different lengths. What happens to auxiliary verbs compared with content words like nouns and verbs?

The repetition stimuli included nouns, verbs and auxiliaries in varying positions. The position of auxiliaries was varied by placing them in questions, statements and elliptical structures (see table 12.3).

Ruth's responses to these stimuli show that she is not simply parroting the stimulus sentence, without recourse to her knowl-

Table 12.3. *Examples of repetition stimuli*

	Initial	Medial	Final
Two-word	Is John? Can she? Won't Mary? Doesn't he?		John is She can Sue can't He hasn't
Three-word	Is John driving? Can she go?	Mary will cry They have left	Soon John will Old men do
Four-word	Can boys read books? Will Jane leave soon?	John will be coming They must have left Mary will not cry He was not driving	John knows he is She says she can

Table 12.4. *Percentage of words repeated correctly*

Position in sentence	Category of target		
	Noun	Verb	Auxiliary
Final	99	94	92
Medial	87	53	30
Initial	84	73	44

edge of words. The final word in a sentence is the one most reliably repeated, whatever its category. In other positions, nouns are better preserved than verbs, which are in turn preserved better than auxiliaries. A summary of all the repetition data shown in table 12.4 illustrates this.

Focusing on auxiliaries, it is apparent that Ruth can recognise and reproduce these reliably in two positions. One is in two-word sentences, where her only problem is with negative auxiliary targets:

Target	Ruth
Won't Mary	Not Mary
Mary *won't*	Mary not
Doesn't she	[dən] she

The other is the final position of all stimuli, whatever their length. In this position, auxiliaries even outstrip preceding nouns and verbs: see table 12.5. But as soon as they lose this privileged

Table 12.5. *Repetition of auxiliaries in sentence-final position*

	Target	Ruth
Three-word	Old men *do*	The old man do
	Soon John *will*	John John can
	There Jane *is*	Jane is
Four-word	John knows he *is*	Knows he is
	Paul thinks he *will*	[bɪl ɪz wɪ]
	Anne knows she *mustn't*	[ɪsɪ] mustn't

position, they are extremely vulnerable: see table 12.6. Here, we find Ruth replacing them with the same sort of form she would use in her spontaneous output, for example

auxiliary + pronoun → [də]

This suggests that she has separated out and recognised the auxiliary or the chunk in which it occurs. She occasionally substitutes a quite distinct form with a related function:

won't → not
will/was → is

This suggests that she has processed the word further still, accessing at least some aspect of its semantic/syntactic function. These findings reinforce the evidence that the difficulty with auxiliaries stems from difficulties with their phonology rather than their semantic or syntactic function.

Is the problem in *recognising* their phonology or *producing* it?

Table 12.6. *Repetition of auxiliaries in sentence-medial and sentence-initial position*

Position of auxiliary	Target	Ruth
Medial	Mary *will* cry	Mary [zə] cry
	She *will* cry	She is cry
	They *have* left	[hæðə] left
	John *is* feeling sick	John feel sick
	She *can* go now	She go now
	Mary *has been* crying	[ðə] Mary's is crying
	They *must have* left	[mʌz əv] left
Initial	*Will* Mary cry	Mary [nəʔ] cry
	Will she cry	She [əzə] cry
	Was Bill driving	[də] Bill driving
	Have they left	[dædə] left
	Is John feeling sick	John is feel sick
	Can Mary go now	[ðə] Mary go now
	Has he eaten late	[də] eaten late
	Will she leave soon	[zɪ] leave [ə] soon

Judgement

In order to check out Ruth's ability to *recognise* auxiliaries, she was asked to judge sentences. These sentences consisted of either Noun–Verb–Noun, or Noun–Auxiliary–Verb. For each correct sentence, three incorrect sentences were created by replacing each word in turn with a nonsense word: see table 12.7.

These sentences were presented to Ruth in blocks, each containing the correct sentences mixed up with one set of the 'nonsense' sentences.

Ruth's responses were not random. She said 'yes' in response to 115 out of 120 correct sentences. In response to the 'nonsense' sentences, she said 'no' as often as she said 'yes' – 62 'yes' to 58 'no'. Nor were these 'yeses' and 'nos' randomly spread. When a nonsense word occurred in the middle or at the end of the sentence, she was quite likely to say 'no' (56 out of 80). When the

Table 12.7. *Examples of judgement stimuli*

Correct	Nonsense substitutes		
Cats drink milk	[ri] drink milk	Cats [rʊg] milk	Cats drink [və]
Birds can fly	[və] can fly	Birds [fɛn] fly	Birds can [ri]
Bill is eating	[kɪg] is eating	Bill [kɪ] eating	Bill is [fɛnɪŋ]

nonsense word occurred at the beginning of the sentence, on the other hand, she almost never said 'no' (2 out of 40 times), even though these nonsense words occupied a *noun* position. In fact she made more errors judging a nonsense word occupying a noun slot at the beginning of the sentence:

[kɪg] is eating

than a nonsense word occupying an auxiliary slot in the middle of the sentence:

Bill [kɪ] eating

These responses show clearly that Ruth can distinguish a correct auxiliary form from a nonsense form, even in the medial position. They also show that she has greatest difficulty noticing unfamiliar material at the beginning of an utterance.

It looks as if Ruth's recognition of auxiliary forms, reflected in her judgement, is better than her production of those forms, reflected in her repetition and spontaneous output. However, our conclusions must remain tentative, as we do not know whether Ruth recognises *which* auxiliary is the correct one, since she was not asked to judge sentences where an *incorrect auxiliary* – as opposed to a nonsense word – was inserted.

Putting the pieces together

Our final source of evidence, the judgement tasks, reveals two things. One, Ruth can recognise auxiliary forms in input. Two, her capacity for input is limited. She has difficulty noticing the beginning of an utterance when it exceeds two words. Both findings are in keeping with her output.

The previous source of evidence, the repetition tasks, reveals three things. One, Ruth's capacity for repetition is also limited. Beyond two words, she comes into problems. Two, Ruth can recognise and can produce auxiliary forms, since she does so when they occur at the end of an utterance. Three, Ruth has great difficulty holding onto or reproducing auxiliaries when these are outside her focus on the end of a sentence. In contrast, she preserves nouns quite well even when they are at the beginning of a three- or four-word utterance. This difference indicates that Ruth is gleaning at least some semantic and syntactic information from the words in the utterance she is to repeat – something she cannot do with the nonsense words in the judgement tasks. It must be this further information which strengthens her repetition of nouns even when they occur in a position on which she is weak in the judgement task.

Putting the evidence from repetition together with the evidence from judgement, the picture begins to take shape. The results of the judgement tasks show that her difficulties are not confined to output. She also has difficulties registering forms in input. These difficulties will affect her repetition, since repetition involves input as well as output. The results of repetition further show that she registers forms selectively, depending on their position and their function. These factors influence which words she produces best, and which she skips or blurs in her production.

How do these pieces fit together with Ruth's everyday under-standing and use of language? Ruth's difficulties with registering forms, particularly when they fall outside her focus on the last word or two of an utterance, have massive implications for her acquisition of words. The more words occur in positions which pass her by, the harder it will be for her to notice their phonology, and the harder it will be for her to work out their meaning and their syntactic relation to the words with which they combine. We would predict particular difficulties with words such as auxiliaries which typically occupy weak phonological positions *and* whose function is dependent on other words. It should be hard for Ruth to establish their phonology *and* to establish the contexts in which they occur. In contrast, she should have less difficulty with the phonology of words which frequently occur in prominent positions. She should also have less difficulty with words whose meaning is not so dependent on the words with which they combine. Nouns are most favoured on both these scores. Verbs are less so, as we saw in our analysis of Travis's difficulties with verbs (chapter 10), and the consequences for Ruth would be apparent if we turned the spotlight onto her verbs.

The disruption in registering phonology and the consequent disruption in connecting phonology to semantic/syntactic function will have some impact on Ruth's comprehension. However, she should get quite far with the words which are more accessible to her, these being the information-carrying ones. And she does. Her comprehension in context is generally good. Even so, everyday conversation must often stretch Ruth, and it is not surprising that misunderstandings and frustration do occur. But only the high-level demands of comprehension tests reveal clearly that something is amiss. We don't know exactly where comprehension falls down, but we might expect it to happen when the interpretation of an utterance depends on those forms or syntactic relations we know to be vulnerable.

The impact on production will be much more damaging. To produce an utterance, Ruth must map her meaning onto the word forms and structures she has picked up from the input. These include the markers of meanings or syntactic relations which are obligatory in English, for example auxiliaries. The difficulties Ruth has had in *getting to* the functions of these forms will affect the planning of her own utterances. She will be less predisposed to pick out features of the context which are obligatorily marked, such as the timing of an event. This may lead her to mark a time distinction sporadically but unreliably. Her unstable phonological representations of these forms will compound the problem. Even when she has established a function and plans to mark it, she is likely to have difficulty accessing the correct form. Take the form of her questions. We can tell Ruth is asking a question thanks to her questioning intonation and the context of her utterance. She also appears to know that something at the beginning of a question differentiates it from a statement. But her phonological representation of that something is rough, and she comes out with one of her fillers:

[təzə] got my telephone number? (= have you)

In contrast, she has been able to establish solid phonological representations of the required forms when they occur in strong positions, in elliptical structures. Here she produces the identical forms clearly:

You have now

Her difficulties with phonology will be highly disruptive for longer-distance syntactic relations, where the form of one word depends on the form of another. If it is difficult for Ruth to discover these interdependencies, it will be even more difficult for her to reproduce them. This may account for her odd errors in elliptical responses, where her auxiliary fails to match the auxiliary on which it depends:

(I've got to start?) → Oh yes you are

The picture may be incomplete, but the pieces appear to fit together. Even with severe limitations on her processing of phonological forms, Ruth can make headway with words – particularly words which are phonologically strong. This takes her a long way in understanding language in context which does not depend on recognition and comprehension of every function morpheme. The repercussions are much more evident in Ruth's production of language. Just to get by in production, the speaker must preserve at least enough phonological information for words to be intelligible to the listener. To sound 'normal', much more is required: the speaker must have precise information about meanings and about syntactic relations which are marked in the language. And she must have precise information about the phonological forms which mark these. If the speaker has not secured this information, it will either be missing or it will be insecurely represented in her output. It may be that different speakers deal with insecure information differently, some tending to skip it altogether, others to fill in partial information. Ruth appears to do both. Her general uncertainty about the phonological form of words shows up in her variable and sometimes unintelligible pronunciation of words. Her particular difficulty with phonologically weak forms shows up in her omission and distortion of unstressed syllables and unstressed words, especially those which precede stress, such as auxiliary verbs. Her difficulties in discovering which meanings or relations must be marked in English show up in her unreliable use of forms such as auxiliaries.

It seems that Ruth's difficulties with phonological forms cascade through her language processing. The relatively minor ruffles in her comprehension become tidal waves in her production of utterances, which can end up as a stream of unintelligible speech. Hence the yawning and for Ruth painful gap between the rich meanings she has in mind and the blocks she faces in getting them out.

Part IV
Hidden meanings, baffling meanings

13 The roots of meaning

Some children use plenty of words. Yet their utterances are in some way bizarre. Take this conversation with 9-year-old Sally:

SC: What languages do you speak?
S: I speak with Oxford Junior.
SC: You speak with Oxford Junior?
S: Oxford Junior English.
SC: Do you speak Chinese?
S: Yeah I speak Chinese. But English – but I can't speak Chinese.
SC: You *can't* speak Chinese? Or you *can*?
S: I can speak Chinese but my mum can't speak English. But he can speak English because – but he can't speak Chinese. And she can speak Chinese too.

Every one of Sally's words is clear enough. The way she combines these words into sentences is, in certain respects, fine. But taken together within this dialogue, they leave the listener reeling. What *does* Sally mean? Information about her linguistic background – that her parents speak Cantonese while her six brothers and sisters all speak English – does not answer that question.

Meaning: the packaging of experience

Any exploration of a child's problems with meaning in language must set out with some handle on what language can mean. In previous chapters, we have grappled with the meanings conveyed by different types of words and their integration into sentences. We have seen that sentences relate to scenes which we

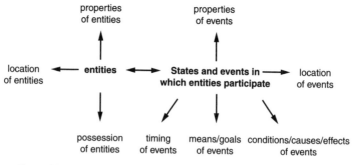

Figure 13.1 Core components of scenes

observe in the world or evoke in our minds. Words focus particular components of those scenes, from particular perspectives. They fall into different categories which reflect the way we structure scenes in terms of certain core components, including those shown in figure 13.1.

But what is the content of these abstract components of scenes? In what do word meanings consist?

Word meanings are cut from the vast and intricately woven material of human experience. That material comes in different qualities which we might conceive of as different **tiers of experience**:

- perceptual experience: experience of the senses (seeing, hearing, feeling, smelling, tasting)
- affective experience: experience of emotions/moods
- mental experience: experience of having something in mind

These tiers of experience are distinct: no one tier of experience is the same as, nor can it be reduced to, another. We may be predisposed to associate experience on one tier with experience on another. For example, something we experience perceptually:

may be associated with something we experience affectively: happiness. The perceptual experience may therefore trigger the affective experience. But registering the perceptual features of the face above is not the same as registering the affective state of happiness. Experience on one tier may also provide the content for experience on another. We can, for example, have an image in our mind, in which case we have a mental experience of a perceptual experience. Here, the perceptual experience is embedded in, but still distinct from, the mental experience.

The points are well illustrated by our everyday experience of an **utterance scene**, depicted below:

Imagine you are Y. What do you experience? *Perceptually*, you see the configuration of X's face, including the moving mouth. You also hear the sounds emanating from X's mouth. *Mentally*, you take X to have something in mind and to be conveying that something to your mind. *Affectively*, you take X to be wanting to convey something to you and also to be feeling anxious. Based on these core experiences, you are likely to make further connections. You may, for example, take X's anxiety state to be the trigger for X's intention in speaking (this would of course be influenced by what X is saying, which we are ignoring). But however automatic and intricate the interconnections we make, they stem from tiers of experience which are ultimately distinct.

Children's packaging of experience

If words are a packaging of experience, the words children use can provide a window onto the experiences they have packaged and the way they have packaged them. Looking through the window of children's earliest words, we have seen that from the earliest stage children take a range of perspectives on the world around them (chapter 2). It is true that the majority of their earliest words identify entities, and do so at what is known as the **basic level**. They typically come out with nouns such as 'dog', rather than 'poodle' or 'animal'; 'chair' rather than 'armchair' or 'furniture'. But they are not confined to labelling at the basic level, nor to using only one label for one entity (Clark 1997), nor to labelling only entities:

- They refer to entities at different levels and from different perspectives. They may refer to one woman with a specific term 'mummy' and another woman with the basic-level term 'lady'. They may refer to a flower with the basic-level term 'flower' or may use the term 'that' which simply points it out.
- They sometimes refer to a single entity at different levels and from different perspectives. They may refer to the family pet as 'Fido' and 'doggie', or to the plate in front of them as 'dinner' or 'food'.
- They sometimes pretend that one thing is another thing and refer to it by its 'pretend' label as well as its usual label. They may use a banana as a telephone and call it a 'telephone'.
- They focus on an entity but refer to its state, location or possession. They may say 'hot' in relation to food, 'broken' or 'mine' in relation to a toy.
- They refer to actions, events and relations in which entities are involved. They may express these with prepositions such as 'in', 'on', 'off', or verbs such as 'look', 'come', 'push'.

The semantic variety already evident in children's early words is a seedbed for the breadth and complexity of meaning in language which they will soon attain. The number of items at this stage may be small. What is significant is their range. They span different components of experience, such as entities, locations, states and events. They also span different tiers of experience, with some drawing more on perceptual experience (hot, broken) and some drawing more on affective interpersonal experience (mummy, mine, yours).

In order to use such words in appropriate contexts, children must have picked out the particular experience on which they focus *and* must have registered that other speakers were focusing on that experience when they used that word. Children's appropriate use of words proves not only their own differentiation of experiences, but also their sensitivity to *others'* experiences. Their use of 'mine' illustrates the point particularly clearly. Take the scenario of a child handing out cups, then pointing to the cup in front of her and saying 'Mine'. In order to arrive at her appropriate use of 'mine', the child must have recognised the experience of attachment between people and entities about which they say 'mine', and this must have resonated with her own experience of attachment. If she had not *identified with* this experience of attachment of the speaker to the entity, she would come up with the wrong meaning for 'mine'. She might incorrectly take 'mine' to refer to *other people's* connection to an entity, but not her own. In this case, she would use 'mine' to mark possession by her addressee, but not her own possession. She might say 'mine' when pointing to something belonging to a child she is talking to. Alternatively, she may take 'mine' to mark possession by a particular individual she has heard using it, say her mother. In this case, she might focus on her mother's nose or coat and say 'mine'. She may be even further off the mark, and take 'mine' to be a label for the entity itself rather than a person's relationship to it. She could then use 'mine' to indicate an entity or all entities which she has heard other people claim as 'mine'. Children's normally correct use of 'mine', as well as 'yours', indicates how easily they recognise that the speaker is focusing on the attachment of speaker/listener to an entity.

It is true that certain sorts of experience are not represented among children's earliest words. While some words may have an affective dimension (dirty, mine, mummy), children are unlikely to use words which *focus* on affective or mental experience. Their *use* of words, though, is proof of their sensitivity to affective and mental experience in themselves and others. They do not utter words aimlessly and to an empty space (though they may play games with words when they are on their own). They use utterances intentionally and direct them towards an addressee. They request and reject:

Biscuit!   Down!   No!

and react negatively if they don't get the response they are looking for. They point out:

Bus!

and check to see that their addressee takes notice of what they are pointing out. They question:

Dirty?   [wɒsæt]?   [huzæt]?

and expect a response. You can only seek to draw a person's attention to something if you experience that person as having attention to draw. You can only seek to question a person if you experience the person as having in mind something which you do not have in mind. Likewise, if you comprehend these intentions in what other people say, you must be assuming that they experience you as having attention and a mind that they can put things into or take things out of. (See Tomasello 1995 for more extensive discussion.)

This appreciation of affective and mental perspectives is *implicit* in children's appropriate use of utterances and responses to other people's utterances. It is not long before it surfaces *explicitly* in their words. By $2\frac{1}{2}$ to 3, children start using mental state verbs such as 'know', 'think', 'remember', 'pretend', 'guess' (Shatz, Wellman & Silber 1983). They use them in some cases to indicate discrepancies between a person's mental state and reality:

Before I thought this was a crocodile; now I know it's an alligator

or between one person's mental state and another's:

I was teasing you; I was pretending 'cept you didn't know that
(Shatz et al. 1983: 309)

Such uses prove conclusively that the child distinguishes between direct experience of the world and mental experience.

Over this period, around ages 2–4, children's meanings also become wonderfully diverse. They have words which make fine differentiations in entities and events, from different types of animals through different manners of speaking (whispering, shouting) and different types of mental/affective experience (hoping, dreaming, imagining, guessing) and different affective/mental goals of speaking (telling, persuading, promising, lying). At the same time, words extend to components of experience which were previously unrepresented – times, causes, effects and conditions. Their range of time modifiers and auxiliaries grows, and they use connectors such as 'when', 'while', 'to', 'because', 'so', 'if' to indicate the ways one event may depend on another.

By 4, most children have in some sense acquired all the *qualities* of adult meaning. They have the breadth of adult meanings, in that all the core tiers of experience are represented in their language. They have the depth of adult meanings, in that they embed experiences within experiences. Obviously they do not control the *same range and complexity* of meaning as older children and adults. But later developments involve the elaboration of these core structures, affecting the variety and subtlety of their packages of meaning, and the scale of embedding of experiences within one another.

What are children doing as they make their way to the vocabulary of the average 4-year-old? We must assume that they can only package into words what they themselves can experience. They can only acquire the meaning of 'look' if they understand the experience of vision, and that human beings each have a visual perspective. They can only acquire the meaning of 'happy' if they can separate out the experience of positive affect both for themselves and other people. The fact that their earliest words span different tiers of experience and different components of experience is evidence that they have registered different sorts of experience and organised these in ways which are suited to the meanings of words. That organisation of experience is the starting-point for the earliest **semantic bootstrapping** (see chapter 2): it is the impetus for children to find words – phonological forms – for the experiences to which they are sensitive.

At this point, **phonological bootstrapping** necessarily comes into play. Only by registering phonological forms which consistently occur with certain experiences can children discover the *particular* ways experience is packaged into words in their language. Phonological bootstrapping, then, shapes children's initial organisations of experience. It will play a more minor role with words whose meanings most closely match their initial organisations of experience. Its role becomes increasingly important as they tackle words which go beyond the sorts of experience on which they first focus. Only by noticing the wealth of phonological forms which occur with similar experiences will the child be alerted to look for the subtle differences in those experiences which serve to differentiate the meanings of the words. When it comes to the packaging of non-perceptual experiences such as time, whose packaging varies dramatically between languages, phonological bootstrapping will be crucial (as we saw when we considered the acquisition of tense and auxiliaries in English).

Once phonological bootstrapping comes into its own, it is a powerful force in driving the child's extraction of increasingly differentiated and abstract aspects of experience. In the extreme, phonological bootstrapping can be used to create meanings when children have no access to the experience on which their meaning relies.

Children with 'experience disabilities'

Take the case of blind children. They lack the perceptual experience which is the focus of words such as the verbs 'see', 'look' and 'show'. Yet they come to understand the meanings of such words. How do they get there? They cannot start from the normally salient experience of vision and use semantic bootstrapping to zoom in on words which refer to categories of visual experience. Instead, when they meet the phonological forms *see, look, show*, these must provide the impetus to find a meaning for visual terms. The child can then discover what in *her* experience is focused whenever she hears these words. The common experience for her will be in the domain of touch rather than vision, and so the meaning of these words will be a packaging of experience in this domain. For her, 'look' will mean 'explore by hand', even if she comes to understand that for others it means 'explore with the eyes' and relates to an experience which her eyes cannot give her. (See Landau & Gleitman 1985 for much more extensive evidence and discussion.)

Blindness blocks visual experience. It leaves the child's potential for other types of experience unaffected. These readily fill in the gaps in her experience in ways which allow her to deduce the meanings of vision-focused words.

Suppose it is not the perceptual tiers but the affective and mental tiers of experience which are disrupted. This will have dramatic effects on the sense the child makes of any words whose reference is to things experienced affectively or mentally. If the child can only approach these words through other tiers of experience – for example, perceptual experience – the child will come up with a partial and oddly orientated meaning for them, or will find them meaningless.

But the effects of deficits in these core tiers of human experience may be expected to spread beyond just the meanings of words which depend on these tiers. Such deficits are liable to affect word meaning more generally. Recall that all words *take a perspective* on experience, whatever the tier of that experience. A child can therefore only discover the meaning of a word if its meaning coincides with the child's own perspective on experience, referring to what is most salient to the child at the moment of hearing the word *and/or* the child is able to identify the speaker's perspective on experience at the moment of using the word.

This second possibility – using the speaker's perspective as a cue to meaning – is only open to children *if they appreciate that people have a perspective* (see also Tomasello 1995). This is precisely the issue for children whose difficulties lie in the tier of affective/ mental experience. The more limited their ability to recognise other people's perspectives, the less they will be able to use other people's perspectives as a cue to the meaning of their words, and the more they will equate words with whatever is salient for *them* when they hear a word. They may then come up with partial or oddly orientated meanings even for words which are not focused on affective or mental experience.

The effects of deficits in these tiers of experience may run even deeper, striking at the very essence of language. As we saw in our analysis of the **utterance scene** above, the use of language is itself an event drawing on affective and mental experience. It involves 'a speaker', who has something *in mind* and *an intention* to convey that something *to the mind* of 'a listener'. If a child's capacity for affective and mental tiers of experience is disrupted, this will strike at language as a tool for communication – for putting something into someone's mind or taking something out of it.

The difficulties of children diagnosed as **autistic** are widely attributed to deficits in affective and mental experience. We find autistic children described as 'profoundly limited in their capacity for and experience of personal relatedness . . . Their sense of psychological connectedness to and affective engagement with other people is seriously impoverished' (Hobson 1993: 194). 'It is as if their capacity to experience desire for another . . . is either absent or distorted', and their difficulties 'set limits on the building of an inner fantasy life' (Mayes, Cohen & Klin 1993: 460–1). Their difficulties have also been construed as the consequence of 'mind-blindness': an unawareness that people have minds and an inability to read minds (Baron-Cohen 1995).

Consistent with deficits in the experience of emotion and mind are the oddities which autistic children display in aspects of language and uses of language which rest on affective/mental experience. Commonly recorded observations are:

- Reduced use of terms referring to mental states (Tager-Flusberg 1993)
- Difficulty picking out which words refer to emotion and to 'what the mind can do' (Hobson 1993, Baron-Cohen, Ring, Moriarty & Schmitz 1994)
- Confusion of 1st- and 2nd-person pronouns (*I/me* vs *you*):

  > You want candy (for 'I')
  > I write (for 'you')

  (Tager-Flusberg 1993)

- Use of a question for a statement/request:

  > Did we say bye?
  > Want a cracker?

  (Tager-Flusberg 1993)

- Use of language primarily to satisfy a need or desire, with little use of language to request information or comment (Hobson 1993)

All of these oddities point to problems in distinguishing the affective and mental orientation of different individuals. Children may use terms which normally refer to these experiences, and their use may even be appropriate to the context. But it may stem from *partial* understanding, based on tiers of experience which are intact. For example, in the absence of affective experience, words such as 'happy' and 'sad' could be understood by their association with different visual configurations of the face; 'enjoy' and 'hate' could be understood by their association with positive or negative perceptual experiences such as tasting chocolate as opposed to medicine. Similarly, 'I' and 'you' could be understood as referring to the one physically speaking, and the one at whom the speech is directed, without appreciating the sense of 'own self' and 'other self'.

Some individuals are able to become aware of their difficulties in understanding certain kinds of experience. For example, a 20-year-old man who cannot grasp what a friend is keeps trying to find out, and repeatedly asks 'Are you a friend? Is he a friend?' (Hobson 1993). A 16-year-old describes a character in a story as 'distraught' and promptly asks 'What does distraught mean'? (L. Rosen, personal communication). A young autistic man describes his experience of people:

> I really didn't know there were people until I was seven years old. I then suddenly realised that there were people. But not like you do. I still have to remind myself that there are people . . . I never could have a friend.

> (Cohen 1980, cited in Hobson 1993)

Difficulties with meaning and use of language are not confined to children diagnosed as autistic. Some children convey bizarre meanings and use utterances in odd ways, but do not fit the general profile of autism. Clinically, these children have been grouped under the umbrella term **semantic–pragmatic disorder** (Rapin & Allen 1987, Bishop & Rosenbloom 1987, McTear 1991, Mogford-Bevan & Sadler 1991, Boucher 1998), though more recently the term **pragmatic language impairment** has been proposed as more appropriate (Bishop in press). Typical features of their language are:

- odd associations and reasoning
- tangential or inappropriate remarks
- undue attention to literal rather than underlying meaning
- problems in understanding normal conversation, for example, descriptions of sequences of everyday events which are related temporally or causally
- lack of awareness of what knowledge is shared between speaker and hearer

(as specified by McTear 1991: 22, with reference to Bishop & Rosenbloom 1987)

A profile of this sort may emerge from informal observation of conversations, or from more systematic assessment using a tool such as the Children's Communication Checklist (Bishop in press).

Samples of conversation taken from a group of 8 to 12-year-olds who fitted this clinical picture illustrate the inappropriacy of their language (Bishop & Adams 1989). To generate conversation, they were shown pictures of a doctor examining a sick boy; a girl having a birthday party; and a man and girl with a broken down car. Their responses to these pictures were characterised by certain oddities which did not occur in the samples of normal children, even those who were considerably younger. These oddities were classified as:

Too much information:
Adult: Is that a good place to break down?
Child: The answer whether it's a good place to break down is no, because if see if anybody broke down, cos there's no telephone to telephone, there's no telephone for the breakdown.

Too little information:
Adult: So what did you do when you were sick?
Child: I can't remember. I did though when I was run over by a car.

[What does 'did' refer to?]

Unusual or socially inappropriate content or style:
Adult: What's going on there?
Child: It's someone's birthday. Something could be dangerous you
        know like a fire from the candles.

(Bishop & Adams 1989: 250–4)

These children, it seems, have perspectives on the content of the conversation and on their conversational partners which are different from those which we would expect and which other children take. Their experience of the situations which are the focus in the conversation and of the conversation situation itself must in some way be different. But while it is obvious to conversational partners that these children have an odd perspective, it is not at all obvious just how their perspectives differ from those we would expect. Nor is it obvious just what differences in their way of experiencing the world are responsible for their odd perspectives. To approach these questions, we need to find ways of tapping the sorts of experiences to which the children do and do not have access.

Exploring a child's capacity for experience through language

How can we establish the quality of another person's experience which we cannot observe directly? One way is for the person to tell us about her experience. But this depends on her ability to reflect on her experience and express it in words, and is ruled out when reflection on experience is the experience under suspicion and in question. In this case, we can only find out about the person's experience by making inferences based on what she does and says. Her language may offer the tightest source of evidence, provided our probes are sensitive enough to pick it up.

We know that words convey highly specific and quite precise aspects of experience. They can only be acquired and used appropriately to the extent that the child is able to identify the experience relevant to them. Suppose the child can identify some but not all tiers of experience relevant to a word. This will enable her to use the word appropriately in contexts which fall within her experience. But where a context involves tiers of experience which are unavailable to her, her understanding and use of the word will be inappropriate. A careful comparison of a child's appropriate and inappropriate use of words can therefore cast light on the tiers of experience which are or are not available to her. Does the child deal with words differently depending which experiential tier they draw on? Does the child deal with a word differently depending on the context in which it occurs, and the experiential aspects of the word which are pertinent to that context?

The obvious way to investigate this is to test the child's understanding and use of different sorts of words in different sorts of contexts. But *experimental* investigation is in some ways unsuited to the purpose. The experimental method lends itself best to testing words whose meaning can be demonstrated. Demonstration depends on the *perceptual* dimensions of words. Even when the meaning of words is not essentially perceptual, we are likely to test them through the perceptible aspects of their meaning. We test understanding by asking the child to point to a picture matching the word or to act out the word; we test production by providing a picture or demonstration of the word and asking the child to describe it. Pictures and actions: the perceivable faces of words. We focus on these not because the perceptual dimension of words is the most significant aspect of word meaning in general, and not even because it is the most significant aspect of word meaning for children, but because the perceptual dimension is the one which, by its very nature, can be demonstrated in a way that *the experimenter can see*. It is much harder to elicit demonstrations of affective and mental aspects of meaning.

The point is well illustrated by a set of experiments carried out with a group of autistic youngsters (Lee, Hobson & Chiat 1994). The purpose of the experiments was to investigate their understanding and use of pronouns. The experiments presented them with photographs of people, including themselves and the experimenter. In order to elicit pronouns, they were asked questions about the photographs:

Who is this a picture of?
Who is wearing the hat/scarf?
Tell me who they are

The probes for testing comprehension were:

Point to the picture of me/you
What am I wearing? What are you wearing?

According to their teachers, the majority of these youngsters had difficulties with pronouns. By way of example one teacher reported that, on her return from sick leave, she was met with the comment 'I'm better now'. Yet in the 'photograph' experiments these same youngsters did not make a single pronoun reversal of this sort. Bafflingly, one 19-year-old performed perfectly on the tasks – and then left the room saying 'Thank you for seeing you Tony', reversing the pronoun in an idiomatic construction where we might least expect it. How can we make sense of these apparently contradictory responses? It looks as if some people may actually perform better in a highly structured experimental situation which focuses on pictures and action, than in everyday interaction where identifying the focus is precisely the problem. This is the reverse of the more common finding that children's performance is poorer in experiments, which remove the contextual support offered by everyday situations.

A similar observation was made about a group of 8–10-year-old children who fitted the clinical picture of semantic–pragmatic disorder (Bishop & Adams 1991). These children fell well outside normal limits on measures of conversational inappropriacy, obtaining high scores for the categories 'too much information' and, in some cases, 'too little information' in the conversational analysis procedure described above (Adams & Bishop 1989). Yet these children were well within normal limits in a structured communication task. This task presented them with an array of eight pictures which differed from each other in one of a set of three features, for example, colour, size or shape of an item. The children were required to describe one of these pictures to an adult who had to find the card within the array. Under these conditions, the information the children provided was no less appropriate than age-matched controls. Again, we find that communication of *visual* information in a *structured* setting does not bring out problems which are evident in open-ended conversation.

It is striking that **non-verbal tests of IQ** typically rely on *perceptual* material which is presented in a *highly structured* context. This may explain why some children who go off the rails in quite basic everyday communication can come out as 'average' or 'above average' in an intelligence test.

If we are to probe these children's access to different aspects of word meaning, we may do better to probe this in more everyday contexts which vary in respects which cannot be picked up through purely perceptual cues. It is not easy to do this within a tight experimental format. Within a more informal setting, though, it is possible to manipulate contexts systematically and explore how changes in context influence a child's understanding or use of words. If we are sufficiently ingenious in deciding which sorts of experience may be critically involved, and in devising scenarios which probe for these, we should gain valuable insights into the invisible tiers of the child's experience.

For a flavour of how research in this vein might be pursued and what it may reveal, we turn to selective observations of children which point to important differences in what they can experience. We start with Eamonn and Ruth, whose difficulties were followed up in chapters 6 and 12. When we explore their sensitivity to different types of experience, we find strengths which are in striking contrast to their difficulties. We then move onto children whose difficulties appear to lie in their ability to experience the world as other people do.

14 '[æ] you don't tell nobody this?': strengths in pragmatic processing

Eamonn, at 6, and Ruth, at 10, are sometimes hard to understand, as we saw when we met them in previous chapters (see chapters 6 and 12). They often produce words which the listener doesn't recognise. In full flow, they can leave the listener completely at sea with their meaning. On other occasions, their utterances are quite clear, but fragmented and lacking some of the forms that sentences demand. Where enough words can be recognised, the listener gets the gist of what they are saying, but may still be in the dark about certain details which we expect in language. The listener might gather who the children are talking about, what happened to them, but be confused about whether it has happened, may happen, or will happen. The listener may know they are asking something about an event, but not be sure whether they are asking who was involved, where it occurred, or when. Consequently, conversations with Eamonn and Ruth are not as smooth as with other children of their age: their conversational partners often find themselves confused or at cross purposes, and the conversation has to backtrack to get back on course. *And yet* these children are perceived as bright, on the ball, responsive and participating appropriately in conversations. Despite the considerable obstacles to communication, the gut feeling of the listener is that the meanings they have in mind are normal. What is the basis for that feeling? What is the evidence that they have access to the normal range and complexity of experience on which meaning is built, even if these are not reliably encoded in their language?

The evidence emerges when we scrutinise the meanings they convey through their use of words in context. We necessarily rely on utterances which contain recognisable words. These allow us to identify the word meanings which the child has selected. By considering these word meanings in relation to the context of their utterance, we can make inferences about the meaning the child is trying to convey. This in turn reveals the quality of experience which underpins that meaning.

Of special interest are the more abstract, non-perceptual tiers of experience. These are not directly observable through children's visible responses to objects, actions or pictures. But they can be inferred from the contributions children make in scenarios which are defined by non-perceptual states, events and relations. Children may themselves conjure up such scenarios. They may initiate references to a state of affairs which is not perceivable. Or they may string together references to states of affairs which are themselves perceivable but whose connection to each other is not. Their initiation of such scenarios can provide powerful evidence of experience which we cannot observe. This can also be tapped by presenting children with similar sorts of scenarios, and exploring their responses to these.

In the context of such scenarios, both Eamonn and Ruth prove their sensitivity to invisible events, and to invisible relations between events.

Sensitivity to mental and affective events

Eamonn and Ruth both refer to invisible events which are in the mind of one person, and not in the mind of another.

Forbidden fruits kept secret   Eamonn initiates a scenario in which an event he desires must be kept secret, that is, outside the minds of others:

SC: So what do you want for next week?
E: Ribena (= a blackcurrant drink).
SC: Are you allowed to have Ribena at school?
E: No. You can put it – You can put it [ɲə] bag and the' eibody know you –
SC: Huh?
E: You put it in [ə] bag and edibody know [jun] taking Ribena.

SC: You mean nobody would know I was taking it?
E: You put the Ribena the big bag – and then edibody know you taking Ribena.
SC: And then nobody would know?
E: No.
SC: It would be a secret . . . You would tell somebody!
E: I not!
SC: You would say Anna, S. brought me some Ribena.
E: I not. I not tell him.

Some of Eamonn's contributions to this interchange are quite hard to decipher. In one of his more intelligible utterances, he appears to omit a crucial element of meaning: the negative element needed to indicate that if the Ribena is in the bag *nobody* will know about it. This could be a sign that Eamonn is confused as to whether other people will or won't know about the Ribena. However, the context strongly suggests that Eamonn is seeking to *prevent* other people knowing about the Ribena, and that he *does* intend the negative. It is he who comes up with the suggestion of putting the Ribena in the bag which, in the context of Ribena not being allowed, carries the implication that he wants to stop other people knowing about it. It is also he who initiates reference to people knowing about the Ribena. Given the coherent relation between the events he selects to talk about and the state of affairs posed in the question, we can infer that the meaning he intends is 'nobody knowing', and that his confusion is between the words *everybody* and *nobody*. Despite this confusion, he is quite clear in his mind about the discrepancies between the contents of different minds.

A touchy matter in the family   Eamonn has started recounting a family saga when he realises he's got himself in emotionally deep water. Well into his tale, he suddenly says:

E: Oh, I can' tell you this. Oh! Can you keep this a ['swikwɪʔ]?
SC: Can I keep it what?
E: Keep it a ['swikwɪʔ] becau' my mum said don't tell this t– . . .

and Eamonn launches back into the story. After he reports:

E: M's little bit upset

he returns to the secrecy:

E: [æ] you don't tell nobody this?
SC: Of course not.
E: Because my mum said don't tell nobody . . .

In this lengthy exchange, Eamonn conveys a complex layering of affective and mental experiences. Some of these are expressed explicitly, and some are implicit in the sequence of utterances. He has understood M's affective state (explicit in *upset*). He has understood that M's state and the events leading up to it are a sensitive matter: this sensitivity is implicit in his understanding that the matter should be kept from other people's minds (explicit in *can't tell, secret, don't tell*). Apart from the affective and mental experiences which he conveys within his account, he reveals his own conflicting feelings about giving the account. He is bursting to go on with it, but this desire battles with the guilt of divulging matters which he knows he should not. His way out of the conflict is to commit the account to secrecy.

Eamonn's understanding of mental experience goes a step further when he initiates a scenario of *pretence about mental experience*. After receiving a robot for his birthday, he conjures up an impressive fantasy:

Mental telepathy with a robot

E: You put the two wires on them and then you push this button and [ə] wire goes to my – the wire come to the robot [unintelligible word] and [ə] robot come to [ə] my brain so I talk like him. And he talk like me. So that's clever.

Although it is not absolutely clear what Eamonn has in mind, this much is clear: he is playing with his knowledge that one person's 'brain' is not normally available to another; his pretence is that a wire connected to a robot can overcome this reality.

Ruth's engagement in fantasy shows a similar understanding of mental states.

Monkey business   In this case, I have initiated a fantasy, the fantasy being that we each have a secret pet monkey. Ruth's response shows a full understanding of the content of the fantasy, and that it is a fantasy. Ruth has named her secret monkey

'Aeroplane', while mine is named 'Coconut':

> SC: Did you bring Aeroplane with you?
> R: Yeah, [ɪmə] head. [də] got – Coconut with you?
> SC: Yeah. Where?
> R: In your – head! . . . Monkeys in ours head. Nobody know us got
>   monkeys in our head.

When Ruth situates the monkeys 'in ours head', she shows she
has them firmly established as characters in a fantasy and not in
the real world. When she says 'nobody knows', she proves her
understanding that the contents of one mind are not available to
other minds.

Ruth's understanding of 'secrets' comes in handy as a way of
deflecting the discomfort she feels when her difficulties with language are exposed:

The right to silence

> R: I know my phone number is.
> SC: What?
> R: I'm not telling you. Secret.

Here again Ruth refers to information which she has in her mind
(or claims to), and the withholding of that information from
another mind.

Sensitivity to conditions and consequences of events

Eamonn and Ruth not only refer to the abstract events of
knowing, hiding of knowledge and communicating of knowledge.
They also refer to abstract relations between events. This is evident
in their linking of two events within a single utterance. The events
which they link may themselves be abstract.

The precise nature of the relation between events is not always
made explicit. Where it is not, it can usually be inferred from the
content of the combined events, because these hold a particularly
plausible relation to each other.

Eamonn volunteers many examples of one event embedded

within another:

Utterance	*Gloss of utterance identifying events*
I tell off I get Ribena so I not tell anybody	I'll get told off *if* I get Ribena *so* I won't tell anybody
[æ] you don't tell nobody this	Can you not tell anybody this.
. . . Because my mum said don't tell nobody	*Because* my mum said don't tell anybody

Where he uses 'because' and 'so', the specific link between the events is clear. In some cases, the link is less clear. He appears to use the form [æ] to introduce a hypothetical or anticipated event as a *condition* for another event, where the link should be 'if':

Utterance	*Gloss of utterance*
[æwi stɪp] it, it be die	*If* we step on it, it will die
. . . we can take them home	We can take them home *if* we
[æ] we be [fi fi] good	are very very good

Eamonn does not stop at one embedding. He produces utterances which embed already linked events within a further event:

> E: We gonna be good because [æ] we good we 'llowed to take our flowers home.

Here, one event, being good, is the condition for another event, being allowed to take flowers home; these linked events, being allowed to take the flowers home on condition of being good, are the cause of another event, being good.

Ruth's linking of events is less explicitly marked than Eamonn's. The links she intends can be inferred, though, because the events she has chosen to link hold a clear relation to each other. In some cases, one event is appropriate as a condition for the other:

Utterance	*Gloss of utterance*
Talking about communication between sessions	
You can ring up [əθə] want to	You can ring up *if* you want to

Playing the role of boss talking to secretary

[tədə] someone call, [tədə] put a note down, right	*If* someone calls, you put a note down

Playing the role of prison guard, talking to prisoner

[zu] 'scape, we find you	*If* you escape, we'll find you

In some, one event is appropriate as the consequence of another:

I do I want to, s'you shut up right	I do I want to, *so* you shut up

On occasion, Ruth layers events. This happens when she explains why, after unlocking the door, she has kept one key separate from the rest of the bunch:

SC: Why do you need to know which key?
R: Because [ə] wrong key, [tə] can't do it.
SC: Yeah, but we've already opened the door. We don't need it now.
R: Yes, lock it!
SC: When?
R: After us.

Here, Ruth's reason for one event (keeping the key separate) is the event which would follow from the hypothetical situation of having the wrong key ('can't do it').

Use and content of utterances as evidence of invisible experience

When we comb through conversations with Eamonn and Ruth, we find strong evidence of the breadth and depth of the experiences to which they are sensitive. The fact that they initiate and respond to communication appropriately already implies an understanding that language can convey what is in one person's mind to another person's mind. When they communicate, they provide further evidence of this understanding, by referring to affective and mental experiences, and responding to other people's references to these. They also refer and respond to dependencies between events, and they can do this with events which tap different tiers of experience. Their language may be severely limited and limiting (see chapters 6 and 12), but it shows that their ability to experience is not.

Not so with some children. We turn now to three children whose language may be quite intelligible, but whose meanings are elusive or bizarre.

15 'I can speak Chinese. But I can't speak Chinese': problems in pragmatic processing

The children presented in this chapter come out with language which is odd. But the oddness of these children's behaviours is not confined to language. They are all reported to have shown certain obsessive behaviours. All are observed to react to situations in unusual ways. Their play is very limited: when offered toy miniatures, they are likely only to reproduce scenarios they have seen, rather than constructing novel scenarios with the toys. When they talk, they commonly echo another person's utterance.

All of these behaviours suggest that their experience of the world and of other people is unusual. Since shared perspectives are fundamental to establishing meaning in language, we would expect them to attach unusual meanings to the language they hear, and to express odd meanings when they talk. It is not surprising, then, that they have all been found to perform well below their age level on tests of comprehension. They have also been very slow to produce language. When we home in on the language they produce, it proves quite odd.

Tony, who was observed between the ages of 3 and 7 in a study by Conti-Ramsden and Gunn (1986), showed all of these characteristics. Alongside these, he showed certain strengths. He was very good at tasks using visual materials. He successfully sorted, matched and sequenced items by size; recognised and matched numbers and symbols; copied patterns; and was able to do puzzles. Throughout the period of observation, his score on a test of non-verbal intelligence was consistently *above average*. Yet his use of language remained odd.

He reversed pronouns such as *I/you*, and he was still having difficulties with these at the age of 6. This confusion points to problems with perspective. His language revealed other evidence that he had difficulty taking and maintaining perspectives. At 5, when he played the game 'What am I?', Tony took it upon himself both to ask and to answer the question, thereby defeating the purpose of the game:

> T: I have long ears and a short tail, what am I? A rabbit.
>
> (Conti-Ramsden & Gunn 1986: 345)

At 6, his responses to questions about various scenarios showed that he had picked up some aspects of each scenario. But he did not maintain perspectives on individuals, times of events, and relations between events in the scenario:

> Teacher: What might happen if you didn't look and listen before you crossed the road?
>
> T: She's falling in the road. She went to the hospital.
>
> (Ibid.: 346)

The references to 'road' and 'hospital' are potentially relevant to the scenario in the question. But Tony has not maintained the perspective on person ('you' shifts to 'she') or time ('would' shifts to 'is falling', 'went'). Nor has he maintained the perspective on events: he leaps from 'not looking when you cross the road' to the unconnected event of 'falling'.

> Teacher: Why do you have to be quiet when there's a baby in the room?
>
> T: 'Cos she's crying.
>
> (Ibid.: 347)

This response illustrates clearly Tony's failure to appreciate the perspective on events which is presented to him. His response refers to 'crying', which is certainly not a reason for the event in the question, nor is it a likely effect, condition, or goal of that event. It looks as if Tony has simply found an event which is loosely connected to various references in the question, 'crying' being associated with 'quiet', and 'baby'.

Similar shifts in perspective occur in his response to a play scene in which Carl, a doll, has fallen:

> Teacher: Is Carl frightened?

T: Yes.
Teacher: Why is he frightened?
T: He is falling down, he cried, he is sore mouth. (. . .)
Teacher: Why has he got a sore mouth?
T: Because you are falling (to doll). Why are you getting on the
          floor?   (Ibid.: 347)

Tony's utterances again refer to events which are plausibly associated with each other and with the question ('frightened' → 'falling down', 'cried', 'sore') and this time, the sequence of events is
more coherent. But relations between the events are still by no
means clear: he's frightened because he fell down and he cried
because he got a sore mouth? he fell down and got a sore mouth
and so he cried? In addition, Tony has confused time reference ('is
falling', 'cried'). He also appears to have shifted person reference
('he' to 'you'), though if he has turned away from the teacher to
address the doll this shift of person reference is appropriate.

Tony has clear *forms* of reference to people, times and events,
yet his use of these shows considerable confusion. A 10-year-old
observed by McTear (1985) shows similar peculiarities. Unlike
Tony, this child's non-verbal as well as his verbal abilities are
depressed: he comes out as low average/borderline on a test of
non-verbal intelligence. However, by 10 he makes substantial
contributions to conversations. And he produces intelligible utterances of some complexity, albeit with odd voice quality and
intonation.

This child appears to sustain references better than Tony. But
he still shows evidence of difficulties with perspective. For example,
he makes assertions which assume a perspective at odds with the
context in which they are made:

Adult: Now do you want to see if you can play some games with me?
Child: Yes
Adult: They're very easy games um
Child: They are indeed   (McTear 1985: 133)

As he did not yet know what the games were, he could not have
known that they were easy. The perspectives he takes on individuals and events can also be at odds with each other:

Adult: Which race would you like to be in?

Child: I like to be in X (= place) at the Sports Day
Adult: In X?
Child: Yes
Adult: What do you mean?
Child: I mean something
Adult: Is there a Sports Day in X?
Child: There is not, there is a Sports Day in Y (= child's school)
Adult: Then what's X got to do with it?
Child: Nothing
Adult: Then why did you mention it?
Child: Indeed I did mention it
                                                      (Ibid.: 135–6)

Here, the child makes clear enough references to events and places, but he shifts his perspective on these to the point of contradicting his own assumptions: he refers to a Sports Day in X and then states that there is no Sports Day in X. Sometimes, he flatly contradicts himself:

(referring to a boy in a picture)
Adult: Does he have to pay for his dinner?
Child: Yes
Adult: Why?
Child: Because he wants to eat it
Adult: Do you have to pay for your dinner?
Child: Yes
Adult: Do you?
Child: No I don't pay for my dinner.
                                                      (Ibid.: 138)

Similar contradictions crop up in conversations with Sally. At 9, Sally appears to relate well to her conversational partner. She makes good eye contact. She initiates and responds to talk, and her talk is generally fluent and delivered with normal-sounding voice quality and intonation. Yet it can be very difficult to follow who or what she is talking about, or what she is saying about them. This is illustrated by the conversation with her which was quoted at the outset of chapter 13:

SC: What languages do you speak?
S: I speak with Oxford Junior.
SC: You speak with Oxford Junior?
S: Oxford Junior English.
SC: Do you speak Chinese?

S: Yeah I speak Chinese. But English – but I can't speak Chinese.

SC: You *can't* speak Chinese? Or you *can*?

S: I can speak Chinese but my mum can't speak English. But he can speak English because – but he can't speak Chinese. And she can speak Chinese too.

In this conversation, Sally uses words which clearly hold some connection to each other and to the questions she is answering: 'English', 'Chinese', 'Oxford Junior English', 'speak' all relate to 'language speaking', which was the focus of the opening question. The problem is the reference of the words. Her shifts from 'my mum' to 'he' to 'she' are confusing, because we can't tell whether these refer to the same person or not. If we take her to be maintaining reference to one person, she is directly contradicting what she says about that person without turning a hair. If we take her to be referring to different people, she is shifting reference haphazardly, making it impossible to identify who she is talking about. Alternatively, it may be that she loses track of which language she is focusing on. Whichever way we play it, we find ourselves in the appropriate ballpark – language-speaking in Sally's family – but none the wiser as to who speaks what.

The impression is that Sally cannot hold a perspective on a person or a state of affairs. The same thing appears to be happening in the following exchange:

(Sally has spontaneously made reference to a teacher who has had a baby; seeing the baby in her tummy; and the teacher having eaten too much)

SC: You haven't got any babies in your family have you? (S is the youngest)

S: I have a aunty.

SC: Has she got a baby?

S: Yeah.

SC: Who's the baby in your family?

S: Um. Ellen. My sister. And a baby name called Sophie. Sophie called mummy. And she called daddy. I mean – and she called mummy and she called papa.

SC: Who's called mummy?

S: Sophie.

SC: And who's papa?

S: Sophie. Sophie called papa. I heard that.

SC: Oh, is Sophie the baby?

S: Yeah.

SC: And she can say words? (no response). Is she a little baby?

S: No, er, then she was a zero years old. And when she grown up and she was one years old and when she grown up again she was two years old.

Sally again uses a number of related words: aunty, sister, mummy, daddy; Ellen, Sophie, name, called; baby, grown up, years old. But again, her references appear to float, unmoored, in an uncharted sea. She refers to people in her family, but we have no idea who is who. She refers to ages, but we are still in the dark about the age of the baby in question. Her reference to events is similarly unanchored. It looks as if she is sliding between two meanings of 'called', so that her talk about what the baby is named (called) suddenly flips into talk about what the baby said (called). A similar slipperiness in her event reference may account for her initial response 'I have a aunty'. With some inside information about her family – that she has an older sister who has a baby – it seems likely that the reference in the question to 'having a baby in the family' has slipped into the related event of being an aunty to a baby in her response.

Sally's confusion of perspectives is exposed most dramatically when she plays a game called 'Guess who?'. In this game, each player picks out a picture card from a set representing different characters. These characters have names, and are distinguished from each other by sex, age and a variety of features such as hair colour, having a beard or moustache, wearing glasses or a hat (see

(GUESS WHO? © 1999 Hasbro International Inc.).

illustration). Players can look at their own card, but not at anyone else's, the aim of the game being to guess the identity of other players' characters. They do this by asking questions such as

> Has this person got white hair?
> Has this person got a beard?

which enable them to identify the character by a process of elimination. Look at Sally's explanation of the game:

(We have each taken our picture card)
SC: So, what do we have to do?
S: Don't look the card. That's what Jane said.
SC: Don't look at the card?
S: Yeah. Guess what it is. If Jane and could – is it – or is it a Peter or is it a – or is it a Joe.
SC: Can I look now?
S: No. Don't look at it and trying to guess (S points to *my* card as she speaks).
SC: Right . . . You looked at yours.
S: U-huh.
SC: Is that all right?
S: Don't look for it otherwise it's just cheating.
SC: But you did look at yours. Can I look at mine?
S: Er – no. Jane say you can't and then you have to guess.
SC: Which must I guess? Must I guess this one (pointing to my card)? Or that one (pointing to her card)?
S: This one (S points to *my* card).
SC: So I mustn't look at it.
S: No. Um. Put over here. Put over here (S points to the slot for my card, which is facing me).
SC: But then I'll see it. Can I look at *this* one (my own, which she is telling me to put in the slot)?
S: No. You – Can you tell Jane?
SC: Huh?
S: Will you tell Jane. I dunno what [əzə'baʊdɪz].
SC: You're not sure what – I think you look at yours and I look at mine.
S: Yeah.

Sally knows that 'not looking at' is important in this game. She has clearly heard this many times, and heard that it is cheating. But she seems unable to sort out who is allowed to look at which card. When she is directly confronted with the contradictions in the set-up as she presents it, she cannot resolve these contradictions, and she appeals to the higher authority of her therapist (Jane). Interestingly, she uses the verb *tell* when her object is in fact to *ask* Jane.

Once her confusion is set aside, Sally proceeds to play the game appropriately, with no confusion about which picture each of us looks at. She asks appropriate questions which enable her to narrow down and ultimately identify my picture. In the course of the game, she makes just one slip in response to one of my questions:

SC: Has the person got white hair?
S: (mistakenly looking at the set of pictures in front of her rather than her own picture) One has, two has . . . What did you say?
SC: Has the person got white hair?
S: No. No. Sorry I made a mistake.

Sally's responses to the scenario of this game are bafflingly inconsistent. They are worth working through in some detail to see whether we can bring any coherence to their seeming incoherence. On the one hand, she can play the game. She can select features appropriately as the focus for questions such as 'Has this person got a big nose?'. She can also use responses appropriately. If the response is 'yes', she throws out all those characters who have not got a big nose; if 'no', she throws out those who have. Here, her logic is impeccable. Yet in explaining the game, she cannot hold onto its simple logic: that you must look at the picture you are answering questions about. How can we make sense of this apparent paradox?

The paradox may be resolved in terms of the different tiers of experience tapped by the different activities. Suppose the *perceptual tier* of Sally's experience is normal. She observes and holds onto what things and people look like, and what they are seen to be doing. This would enable her to recognise the way players in the game are visually oriented towards their picture cards. Equally, she would be able to recognise the visual features which distinguish the characters on the cards. When the material is visual, her logic is intact: she recognises that having a beard is mutually exclusive with not having a beard. This would account for her ability to work through the process of elimination systematically.

Talking about the same scenario is a different matter. It is not enough to recognise the way the game plays itself out visually: the visual position of players and their materials, and the visual features of her picture. In order to explain the game, she must select and stay with the perspective of one player. She must recognise how that player's perspective is distinguished from the perspective of other players. That is, she must appreciate that each of the players has a distinct visual perspective, which makes them privy to different information from other players. The idea that each player *sees* and *knows* what other players do not see and know is fundamental to the aim of the game: guessing who. It is precisely this which puts Sally in a spin. She fails to distinguish my perspective from hers, and allow me to see and know what she must not.

Sally's difficulties with perspective are brought into relief when we compare the explanation of the game offered by 10-year-old Richard, whose words are far more limited and distorted than Sally's:

SC: What do I have to do?

R: [pɪɪn] card out. [pɪʔ] your card out. And we guess who you got the person. Someone – [juaju] guess – someone and [ə] winner.

SC: So what do we have to do first?

R: [pɪʔɪn] card out. No tell me, no. Put in there (pointing to my slot). [æʔs 'kʌntɪnz] (probably = 'ask questions').
[ɜ̃əʔ] you got – bald head – or not. Bald head or hair. [bə] him or her. Something else. Got hat – big eyes – and big nose.

SC: And how many questions can I ask?

R: [ɔ] – [ə] – [u] guess mine. [æ] turns. You, me, you . . .

For all the limitations of his language and his sometimes unclear references, Richard highlights just those differences in perspective that Sally obscures. He clearly takes my perspective in the game and he presents this consistently in relation to his perspective: he tells me to pick out a card, shows me where to put it, and instructs me not to tell him about it. His explicit references to 'guessing' and 'turn-taking' confirm his grip on who knows what and who does what. A further interesting difference between the two children emerges from the examples of questions they offer. All of Sally's examples pick on features of the characters which are purely visual. In contrast, Richard includes a question about the gender of the character ('him/her') which is not a simple visual feature.

The indications are that Sally, unlike Richard, experiences the world very differently from other children, and that the oddness of her utterances stems from *the oddness of the experience on which her language is built.* The suggestion is that her access to non-perceptual tiers of experience – to mental and affective tiers – is disturbed. We have seen that these tiers of experience are central to the meanings of many words; that they are central to discovering the meanings of words in general; and that they are central to appreciating the functions of words in utterances. A disturbance in these tiers can account for the mix of oddities observed in Sally's language: her tendency to echo other people's utterances; her limited comprehension and production of language; her unanchored references to people, events and times which make her spontaneous utterances so disorientating for the listener; and her confusion of perspectives.

Homing in on the mental/affective tiers of experience is really only the start of another story. The tiers of affective and mental experience are themselves complex (see Hobson 1993 and Mayes et al. 1993, for example), and may be disrupted to different degrees and in different ways. We have looked at data from three children who all appear to have difficulties with perspective, but the way these difficulties manifest themselves is by no means the same. Having identified perspective as the domain of difficulty, the wide differences between children who show difficulties in this domain invite us to look more closely at the complexities of affective and mental experience and the different ways in which such experience may be disrupted. Where children have some ability to understand and use language, their language is a potential source of evidence of the experience which lies behind it. In-depth investigation of carefully selected words in carefully devised scenarios could reveal more about the sorts of experience to which children are or are not sensitive. It could also reveal what they do with words which relate to experiences which elude them.

This type of psycholinguistic investigation has not yet been pursued with children like Sally whose difficulties with words lie in their meaning and use. From the data analysis in this chapter, the indications are that their words may provide a unique window onto the unusual quality of their experience and the unusual sense of the world to which this gives rise.

Endpoint and springboard

Some children can hear; they can speak; yet their language is not developing normally. The source of their difficulties is not immediately obvious. It lies beyond the auditory and motor ends of speech, in processes which are hidden from consciousness and from direct observation. This book has been a search into the mind of the child to uncover those hidden processes and to find out where they stop short.

The search sets out from the child's spontaneous language. In some cases, this provides leading clues. It reveals clear-cut strengths which eliminate certain components of processing from suspicion, and point a finger at others. Take the child whose output is unintelligible or near-unintelligible at first brush, but once deciphered, is found to contain the sorts of words and word combinations we would expect in that child. It can be confidently concluded that this child has no difficulties with the meaning of words or with their syntactic organisation into sentences, in either input or output. Difficulties with the phonological (rhythmic) organisation of sentences may also be eliminated. The problem is then confined to the phonological form of words. The question is: at what point (or points) in perceiving, representing or producing the sound patterns of words does the problem arise? We can probe the source of the problem further through input and output tasks which tap different sounds in different sound contexts.

Conversely, a child's output may be phonologically impeccable. Words may sound just as they should. They may also be appropriately organised into sentences, with appropriate rhythmic patterns. The child's output is nevertheless odd. The choice of words

262

and structures somehow jars with the social and semantic context. This points to problems with meaning. The child is not making sense of the world in the same way as other children, and so is attaching unusual meanings to the forms of language, these being no trouble in themselves. We would expect the peculiarities which show up in language to show up outside of language as well, in the child's response to scenarios and interactions which she experiences differently from other children. These initial observations drive further exploration. Systematic investigation into the child's language may reveal that she understands or uses words which tap certain types of experience but not others, say perceptual but not mental experience. Or it may reveal that the child understands or uses words in contexts which draw on some aspects of their meaning but not others, say perceptual but not affective aspects. By delving into subtle differences in the child's responses to words and contexts, we can throw more light on the oddness of her language and the experience of experience which underpins it.

While some children's output shows clearly polarised strengths and weaknesses, many children present a mixed picture:

- their words are limited, and the words they do produce may be off-beam phonologically or semantically
- their organisation of words into sentences is limited, and the sentences they produce may be characterised by omissions or errors in syntactic, phonological (rhythmic) and semantic structure

The incidence of such a scattered profile is not surprising. If a spanner falls into the middle of the works, the disruption is likely to be widespread. If a child has difficulties at crucial intersections in language processing, at or close to the point where form and meaning join, we might expect these to reverberate through the child's language.

We have seen that the union between the *processing of phonology* and the *processing of experience* is highly potent. In 'phonologising experience' – packaging experience into phonological chunks – language directs and controls our interpretation of that experience. Paradoxically, in tying down our experience, language

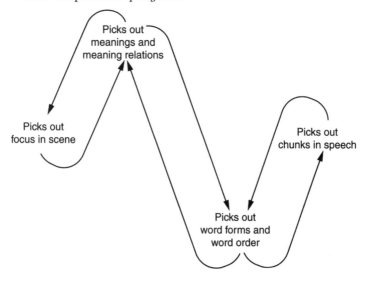

Figure 15.1 Interactions in mapping between form and meaning

affords us the freedom to manipulate and communicate experience in untold ways.

The 'phonologising of experience' relies on the child's facility for identifying phonological chunks within speech, and for identifying speaker focus within scenes. We have seen how each of these facilities acts as a **bootstrap** to the other. The chunks which the child finds in speech push the search for meanings which correspond to those chunks. The perspectives on scenes which the child picks out push the search for forms which correspond to those perspectives. The result may be seen as a push-me-pull-you relationship between form and meaning (see figure 15.1).

It is through these intertwining bootstraps that children construct the extraordinarily elaborate mapping between meaning and form which is language. Where there is a weakness at one or other end of the bootstraps, bootstrapping between form and meaning will be disrupted, and the child's mapping between these will be undermined.

Limitations in the child's ability to process rhythmic patterns, to pick out phonological chunks within these, or to hold onto the details of these chunks will limit the child's phonological grip on words. This limitation will roll along the bootstraps: it will affect the child's phonological bootstrapping to word semantics and to syntactic relations between words. We would expect to see limitations or distortions in word phonologies, but also in word semantics and in syntax. The extent of the gaps and errors will depend on

- the extent of the child's access to phonology
- the child's response to shortfalls in her processing, for example whether she includes information which is only partially specified or whether she leaves it out
- the extent to which the child is able to draw on strengths in processing to compensate for her limitations

The child's freedom to manipulate experience mentally, which comes with ready access to words and sentences, may to some degree be curtailed.

Limitations in the child's ability to identify speaker focus within scenes will again flow through the child's language processing, though with different effects. It will limit the child's semantic bootstrapping to the meaning which attaches to word phonologies and to the meaning relations which map onto syntactic structures. If the child's phonological and syntactic processing are intact, she may exploit these to the full and come out with words in sentences which sound positively sophisticated. But their meanings would extend only as far as her limited or odd abilities to experience allowed. This results in the polarised profile of strong word and sentence phonology and weak semantics which was described above. On the other hand, the child's limited semantic bootstrapping may cramp the connections she makes to phonology, leading her to ignore phonological and syntactic forms even if she has the capacity to process these.

Where the deviations in a child's output are scattered across phonology, syntax and semantics, our exploration of the child's processing will focus on each of these and their interconnections. This will mean selecting particular words or structures which are known to be problematic, in order to investigate what about them is more or less problematic. Can the child process the phonology which is needed for the form of the word or structure in question? Can the child process the types of experience which underlie the meaning behind that word or structure? Can the child process the connections between these? Through tasks judiciously chosen to tease out different aspects of a word or structure, we can expose the strengths and weaknesses in the child's bootstraps.

The children in this book have personified some of these profiles. They have provided the impetus for investigation into the processing behind the profile. They have illustrated the logic of psycholinguistic exploration, and the sort of techniques which can be used to uncover what the child can and can't do with words. This does not mean we will always recognise and understand the child's words, or fully appreciate the nature of experience to which those words give expression. Nor will we be able to 'restore' processing skills which the child does not naturally have. But our detection of strengths in the child's processing may point to ways round the weaknesses. We may highlight for the child what she *can* do with words, and encourage optimal use of her psycholinguistic resources. More than this, we may play into the child's strengths by adjusting our input to highlight those aspects of a target – phonological, semantic, syntactic – which the child *can* process. In this way, we may facilitate the child's access to aspects of a target which are not directly accessible.

As we refine our insights into the child's processing of language, we also come closer to the child's experience of language and language disability. Ruth, now 23, articulates the importance of such understanding:

> Some people don't understand it means. They don't understand what we going through like. And doctors don't. They know about it, but they don't know what caused it from . . . They should put something on TV. [ðəz] get people understand why we have it.

This book isn't TV, but it turns a spotlight on what Ruth has in mind.

Further reading

Language impairment in children
See **Bishop (1997)** and **Leonard (1998)** for comprehensive, in-depth and clear reviews of research into specific language impairment (SLI) in children, spanning:

- the nature and source of their difficulties with language and language processing
- other aspects of their cognitive processing
- genetic and neurobiological characteristics of children with SLI

Research studies documented in these texts also furnish further examples of techniques which may be used to tap different aspects of language and wider cognitive processing.
See **Lees & Urwin (1997)** for a clinical perspective on language-impaired children dealing with clinical assessment, treatment and management, and illustrating these with individual cases.

Speech impairment in children
See **Stackhouse & Wells (1997)** for extensive presentation and illustration of psycholinguistic investigation into speech processing in children with speech impairments.

Normal language development
See **Owens (1996)** for a comprehensive and clear review of research on the stages and processes of normal language development.
See **Fletcher & MacWhinney (1995)**, **Hirsch-Pasek & Golinkoff (1996)**, **MacWhinney & Bates (1989)**, **Morgan & Demuth (1996)**, **Tomasello & Merriman (1995)** and **Slobin (1985, 1997)** for further reading on aspects of language development focused on in this book.

Relationships between semantics, syntax and phonology

See **Saeed (1997)** for more on semantics in general, and **Pinker (1989)** for detailed analysis of the relationship between verb semantics and syntax.

See **Selkirk (1984)** and **Cooper & Paccia-Cooper (1980)** for extensive analysis and investigation into the relationship between the syntax and phonology of sentences.

Meaning in and outside language

See **Gumperz & Levinson (1996)**, **Jackendoff (1997)** and **Slobin (1997)** for extensive analysis and evidence of the relation between language and other cognitive structures in line with the thinking in this book.

Theories and models of language processing and wider cognitive processing

See **Aitchison (1994)**, **Harley (1995)** and **Levelt (1989)** for overviews of word and sentence processing.

See **Ellis & Young (1988)** and **Temple (1997)** for introductions to cognitive neuropsychology and extensive illustration of its application to cognitive impairments in adults and children respectively.

References

Aitchison, J. (1994). *Words in the mind: an introduction to the mental lexicon*. Oxford: Blackwell.

Aksu-Koç, A. A. & D. I. Slobin (1985). The acquisition of Turkish. In *The crosslinguistic study of language acquisition. Volume 1: The data*, edited by D. I. Slobin. Hillsdale, NJ: Lawrence Erlbaum Associates.

Ambalu, D., S. Chiat & T. Pring (1997). When is it best to hear a verb? The effects of the timing and focus of verb models on children's learning of verbs. *Journal of Child Language* 24: 25–34.

Anthony, A., D. Bogle, D. Ingram & M. W. McIsaac (1971). *The Edinburgh Articulation Test*. Edinburgh: Churchill Livingstone.

Baldwin, D. A. (1993). Infants' ability to consult the speaker for clues to word reference. *Journal of Child Language* 20: 395–418.

Baron-Cohen, S. (1995). *Mindblindness: An essay on autism and theory of mind*. Cambridge, MA: MIT Press.

Baron-Cohen, S., H. Ring, J. Moriarty & B. Schmitz (1994). Recognition of mental state terms: clinical findings in children with autism, and a functional neuroimaging study of normal adults. *British Journal of Psychiatry* 165: 640–9.

Baron-Cohen, S., H. Tager-Flusberg & D. J. Cohen (eds.) (1993). *Understanding other minds: perspectives from autism*. Oxford: Oxford University Press.

Berko, J. (1958). The child's learning of English morphology. *Word* 14: 150–77.

Bishop, D. V. M. (1983). *Test for Reception of Grammar*. Available from Age and Cognitive Performance Research Centre, Department of Psychology, University of Manchester.

Bishop, D. V. M. (1997). *Uncommon understanding: development and disorders of language comprehension in children*. Hove: Psychology Press Limited.

Bishop, D. V. M. (In press). Development of the Children's Communication Checklist (CCC): a method for assessing qualitative aspects of communicative impairment in children. *Journal of Child Psychology and Psychiatry*.

Bishop, D. V. M. & C. Adams (1989). Conversational characteristics of children with semantic-pragmatic disorder. II: What features lead to a judgement of inappropriacy? *British Journal of Disorders of Communication* 24: 241–63.

Bishop, D. V. M. & C. Adams (1991). What do referential communication tasks measure? A study of children with specific language impairment. *Applied Psycholinguistics* 12: 199–215.

Bishop, D. V. M. & L. Rosenbloom (1987). Classification of childhood language disorders. In *Language development and disorders. Clinics in Developmental Medicine No. 101/102*, edited by W. Yule & M. Rutter. London: MacKeith Press.

Bloom, L. (1970). *Language development: form and function in emerging grammars*. Cambridge, MA: MIT Press.

Bloom, L. & M. Lahey (1978). *Language development and language disorders*. New York: John Wiley.

Bortolini, U., M. C. Caselli & L. B. Leonard (1997). Grammatical deficits in Italian-speaking children with specific language impairment. *Journal of Speech and Hearing Research* 40: 809–20.

Boucher, J. (1998). SPD as a distinct diagnostic entity: logical considerations and directions for future research. *International Journal of Language and Communication Disorders* 33: 71–81.

Bowerman, M. (1982). Evaluating competing linguistic models with language acquisition data: implications of developmental errors with causative verbs. *Quaderni di Semantica* 3: 5–66.

Bowerman, M. (1996). The origins of children's spatial semantic categories: cognitive versus linguistic determinants. In Gumperz & Levinson.

Brett, L., S. Chiat & C. Pilcher (1987). Stages and units in output processing: some evidence from voicing and fronting processes in children. *Language and Cognitive Processes* 2: 165–77.

Bridgeman, E. & M. Snowling (1988). The perception of phoneme sequence: a comparison of dyspraxic and normal children. *British Journal of Disorders of Communication* 23: 245–52.

Brown, R. (1958). How shall a thing be called? *Psychological Review* 65: 14–21.

Brown, R. (1973). *A first language: the early stages*. Cambridge, MA: Harvard University Press.

Carey, S. (1978). The child as word learner. In *Linguistic theory and psychological reality*, edited by M. Halle, J. Bresnan & G. Miller. Cambridge, MA: MIT Press.

Chiat, S. (1979). The role of the word in phonological development. *Linguistics* 17: 591–610.

Chiat, S. (1983). Why *Mikey*'s right and *my key*'s wrong: the significance of stress and word boundaries in a child's output system. *Cognition* 14: 275–300.

Chiat, S. (1989). The relation between prosodic structure, syllabification and segmental realization: evidence from a child with fricative stopping. *Clinical Linguistics and Phonetics* 3: 223–42.

Chiat, S. (1994). From lexical access to lexical output: what is the problem for children with impaired phonology? In *First and second language phonology*, edited by M. Yavas. San Diego: Singular Publishing Group.

Chiat, S. & J. Hunt (1993). Connections between phonology and semantics: an exploration of lexical processing in a language-impaired child. *Child Language Teaching and Therapy* 9: 200–13.

Chiat, S., J. Law & J. Marshall (eds.) (1997). *Language disorders in children and adults: psycholinguistic approaches to therapy*. London: Whurr Publishers.

Clahsen, H. (1989). The grammatical characterization of developmental dysphasia. *Linguistics* 27: 897–920.

Clark, E. V. (1993). *The lexicon in acquisition*. Cambridge: Cambridge University Press.

Clark, E. V. (1997). Conceptual perspective and lexical choice in acquisition. *Cognition* 64: 1–37.

Clark, R. (1974). Performing without competence. *Journal of Child Language* 1: 1–10.

Cohen, D. J. (1980). The pathology of the self in primary childhood autism and Gilles de la Tourette syndrome. *Psychiatric Clinics of North America* 3: 383–402.

Constable, A., J. Stackhouse & B. Wells (1997). Developmental word-finding difficulties and phonological processing: the case of the missing handcuffs. *Applied Psycholinguistics* 18; 507–36.

Conti-Ramsden, G. & M. Gunn (1986). The development of conversational disability: a case study. *British Journal of Disorders of Communication* 21: 339–52.

Conti-Ramsden, G. & M. Jones (1997). Verb use in specific language impairment. *Journal of Speech, Language, and Hearing Research* 40: 1298–313.

Cooper, W. E. & J. Paccia-Cooper (1980). *Syntax and speech*. Cambridge, MA: Harvard University Press.

Crystal, D., P. Fletcher & M. Garman (1976). *The grammatical analysis of language disability: a procedure for assessment and remediation*. London: Edward Arnold.

Cutler, A. (1996). Prosody and the word boundary problem. In Morgan & Demuth.

de Villiers, J. G. & P. A. de Villiers (1973). A cross sectional study of the development of grammatical morphemes in child speech. *Journal of Psycholinguistic Research* 3: 267–78.

Dodd, B., J. Leahy & G. Hambly (1989). Phonological disorders in children: underlying cognitive deficits. *British Journal of Developmental Psychology* 7: 55–71.

Dromi, E., L. B. Leonard & M. Shteiman (1993). The grammatical morphology of Hebrew-speaking children with specific language impairment: some competing hypotheses. *Journal of Speech and Hearing Research* 36: 760–71.

Dunn, L. M. & L. M. Dunn (1981). *Peabody Picture Vocabulary Test – Revised*. Circle Pines, MN: American Guidance Service.

Dunn, L. M., L. M. Dunn, C. Whetton & D. Pintilie (1982). *British Picture Vocabulary Scale*. Windsor: NFER-Nelson.

Ellis, A. W. & A. W. Young (1988). *Human cognitive neuropsychology*. Hove: Lawrence Erlbaum.

Evelyn, M. (1996). An investigation of verb processing in a child with a specific language impairment. Unpublished MPhil thesis, City University, London.

Fisher, C., D. G. Hall, S. Rakowitz & L. Gleitman (1994). When it is better to receive than to give: syntactic and conceptual constraints on vocabulary growth. *Lingua* 92: 333–75.

Fletcher, P. & M. Garman (1979, 1986). *Language acquisition*. Cambridge: Cambridge University Press.

Fletcher, P. & B. MacWhinney (1995). *The Handbook of Child Language*. Oxford: Blackwell.

Fletcher, P. & J. Peters (1984). Characterizing language impairment in children: an exploratory study. *Language Testing* 1: 33–49.

Gathercole, S. E., C. S. Willis, A. D. Baddeley & H. Emslie (1994). The Children's Test of Nonword Repetition: a test of phonological working memory. *Memory* 2: 103–27.

Gerken, L. (1996). Phonological and distributional information in syntax acquisition. In Morgan & Demuth.

German, D. J. (1986). *National College of Education, Test of Word Finding*

(TWF). Allen, TX: DLM Teaching Resources.

German, D. J. (1987). Spontaneous language profiles of children with word-finding problems. *Language, Speech, and Hearing Services in Schools* 18: 217–30.

German, D. J. & E. Simon (1991). Analysis of children's word-finding skills in discourse. *Journal of Speech and Hearing Research* 34: 309–16.

Gleitman, L. R., E. L. Newport & H. Gleitman (1984). The current status of the motherese hypothesis. *Journal of Child Language* 11: 43–79.

Gopnik, M. & M. B. Crago (1991). Familial aggregation of a developmental language disorder. *Cognition* 39: 1–50.

Greenfield, P. & J. H. Smith (1976). *The structure of communication in early language development*. New York: Academic Press.

Gropen, J., S. Pinker, M. Hollander & R. Goldberg (1991). Affectedness and direct objects: the role of lexical semantics in the acquisition of verb argument structure. *Cognition* 41: 153–95.

Gumperz, J. & S. C. Levinson (eds.) (1996). *Rethinking linguistic relativity*. Cambridge: Cambridge University Press.

Harley, T. A. (1995). *The psychology of language: from data to theory*. Hove: Erlbaum (UK) Taylor & Francis.

Hayman, K. (1996). Phonological awareness therapy for a child with developmental word finding difficulties. Unpublished MSc thesis, City University, London.

Hirsh-Pasek, K. & R. M. Golinkoff (1996). *The origins of grammar: evidence from early language comprehension*. Cambridge, MA: MIT Press.

Hobson, R. P. (1993). *Autism and the development of mind*. Hove: Lawrence Erlbaum Associates.

Howard, D. & K. E. Patterson (1992). *Pyramids and Palm Trees*. Bury St. Edmunds: Thames Valley Test Company.

Huttenlocher, J. (1974). The origins of language comprehension. In *Theories in cognitive psychology*, edited by R. Solso. New York: Erlbaum.

Ingram, D. (1972). The acquisition of the English verbal auxiliary and copula in normal and linguistically deviant children. *Papers and Reports on Child Language Development* 4: 79–91.

Ingram, D. (1989). *First language acquisition: method, description and explanation*. Cambridge: Cambridge University Press.

Jackendoff, R. (1997). *The architecture of the language faculty*. Cambridge, MA: MIT Press.

Johnston, J. R. & T. K. Schery (1976). The use of grammatical morphemes by children with communication disorders. In *Normal and deficient child language*, edited by D. M. Morehead & A. E. Morehead. Baltimore:

University Park Press.

Jones, M. & G. Conti-Ramsden (1997). Verb use in children with SLI. *First Language* 17: 165–93.

Jusczyk, P. W. & D. G. Kemler Nelson (1996). Syntactic units, prosody, and psychological reality during infancy. In Morgan & Demuth.

Karmiloff-Smith, A. (1978). The interplay between syntax, semantics, and phonology in language acquisition processes. In *Recent advances in the psychology of language*, edited by R. Campbell & P. Smith. New York: Plenum.

Katz, N., E. Baker & J. Macnamara (1974). What's in a name? A study of how children learn common and proper names. *Child Development* 45: 469–73.

Kyle, J. G. & B. Woll (1985). *Sign language: the study of deaf people and their language*. Cambridge: Cambridge University Press.

Landau, B. & L. R. Gleitman (1985). *Language and experience: evidence from the blind child*. Cambridge, MA: Harvard University Press.

Lee, A., R. P. Hobson & S. Chiat (1994). I, you, me, and autism: an experimental study. *Journal of Autism and Developmental Disorders* 24: 155–76.

Lees, J. & S. Urwin (1997). *Children with language disorders*. Second edition. London: Whurr Publishers.

Leonard, L. B. (1992). Specific language impairment in three languages: some cross-linguistic evidence. In *Specific speech and language disorders in children*, edited by P. Fletcher & D. Hall. London: Whurr Publishers.

Leonard, L. B. (1998). *Children with specific language impairment*. Cambridge, MA: MIT Press.

Leonard, L. B., U. Bortolini, M. C. Caselli, K. K. McGregor & L. Sabbadini (1992). Morphological deficits in children with specific language impairment: the status of features in the underlying grammar. *Language Acquisition* 2: 151–79.

Leonard, L. B. & J. A. Eyer (1996). Deficits of grammatical morphology in children with specific language impairment and their implications for notions of bootstrapping. In Morgan & Demuth.

Leonard, L. B., J. A. Eyer, L. M. Bedore & B. G. Grela (1997). Three accounts of the grammatical morpheme difficulties of English-speaking children with specific language impairment. *Journal of Speech and Hearing Research* 40: 741–53.

Leonard, L. B., L. Sabbadini, J. S. Leonard & V. Volterra (1987). Specific language impairment in children: a cross-linguistic study. *Brain and Language* 32: 233–52.

Levelt, W. J. M. (1989). *Speaking: from intention to articulation*. Cambridge,

MA: MIT Press.

MacWhinney, B. & E. Bates (eds.) (1989). *The crosslinguistic study of sentence processing.* Cambridge: Cambridge University Press.

Markman, E. M. (1989). *Categorization and naming in children: problems of induction.* Cambridge, MA: MIT Press.

Marshall, J., M. Black, S. Byng, S. Chiat & T. Pring (1999). *The Sentence Processing Resource Pack.* Bicester: Winslow Press.

Marshall, J., T. Pring & S. Chiat (1993). Sentence processing therapy: working at the level of the event. *Aphasiology* 7: 177–99.

Mayes, L., D. Cohen & A. Klin (1993). Desire and fantasy: a psychoanalytic perspective on theory of mind and autism. In Baron-Cohen, Tager-Flusberg & Cohen.

McNamara, M., A. Carter, B. McIntosh & L. Gerken (1998). Sensitivity to grammatical morphemes in children with specific language impairment. *Journal of Speech, Language and Hearing Research* 41: 1147–57.

McTear, M. F. (1985). Pragmatic disorders: a case study of conversational disability. *British Journal of Disorders of Communication* 20: 129–42.

McTear, M. (1991). Is there such a thing as conversational disability? In *Child language disability, Volume II: Semantic and pragmatic difficulties,* edited by K. Mogford-Bevan & J. Sadler. Clevedon: Multilingual Matters.

Miller, J. & R. Chapman, (1982–7). *SALT: Systematic Analysis of Language Transcripts.* Madison: University of Wisconsin, Language Analysis Laboratory, Waisman Center.

Mogford-Bevan, K. & J. Sadler (eds.) (1991). Semantic and pragmatic difficulties or semantic-pragmatic syndrome? Some explanations. In *Child language disability, Volume II: Semantic and pragmatic difficulties,* edited by K. Mogford-Bevan & J. Sadler. Clevedon: Multilingual Matters.

Moore, M. E. & J. R. Johnston (1993). Expressions of past time by normal and language-impaired children. *Applied Psycholinguistics* 14: 515–34.

Morgan, J. L. & K. Demuth (eds.) (1996). *Signal to syntax: bootstrapping from speech to grammar in early acquisition.* Mahwah, NJ: Lawrence Erlbaum Associates.

Nelson, K. (1973). Structure and strategy in learning to talk. *Monographs of the Society of Research in Child Development* 38, No. 149.

Newport, E. L., H. Gleitman & L. R. Gleitman (1977). Mother, I'd rather do it myself: some effects and non-effects of maternal speech style. In *Talking to children: language input and acquisition,* edited by C. E. Snow & C. A. Ferguson. Cambridge: Cambridge University Press.

Oetting, J. B. & J. E. Horohov (1997). Past-tense marking by children with and without specific language impairment. *Journal of Speech and Hearing Research* 40: 62–74.

O'Hara, M. & J. Johnston (1997). Syntactic bootstrapping in children with specific language impairment. *European Journal of Disorders of Communication* 32: 189–205.

Owens, R. E. (1996). *Language development: an introduction.* Fourth edition. Needham Heights, MA: Allyn & Bacon.

Peters, A. M. (1983). *The units of language acquisition.* Cambridge: Cambridge University Press.

Pinker, S. (1989). *Learnability and cognition: the acquisition of argument structure.* Cambridge, MA: MIT Press.

Rapin, I. & D. A. Allen (1987). Developmental dysphasia and autism in preschool children: characteristics and subtypes. *Proceedings of the First International Symposium on Specific Speech and Language Disorders in Children.* London: AFASIC.

Renfrew, C. (1980). *Word-finding vocabulary scale.* Oxford: C. E. Renfrew.

Rescorla, L. A. (1980). Overextension in early language development. *Journal of Child Language* 7: 321–35.

Rice, M. L. & J. V. Bode (1993). GAPS in the verb lexicons of children with specific language impairment. *First Language* 13: 113–31.

Rice, M. L., J. C. Buhr & M. Nemeth (1990). Fast mapping word learning abilities of language-delayed preschoolers. *Journal of Speech and Hearing Disorders* 55: 33–42.

Rice, M. L. & J. B. Oetting (1993). Morphological deficits of children with SLI: evaluation of number marking and agreement. *Journal of Speech and Hearing Research* 36: 1249–57.

Rom, A. & L. B. Leonard (1990). Interpreting deficits in grammatical morphology in specifically language-impaired children: preliminary evidence from Hebrew. *Clinical Linguistics & Phonetics* 4: 93–105.

Sachs, J. & L. Truswell (1978). Comprehension of two-word instructions by children in the one-word stage. *Journal of Child Language* 5: 17–24.

Saeed, J. I. (1997). *Semantics.* Oxford: Blackwell.

Selkirk, E. O. (1984). *Phonology and syntax: the relation between sound and structure.* Cambridge, MA: MIT Press.

Shatz, M., H. M. Wellman & S. Silber (1983). The acquisition of mental verbs: a systematic investigation of the first reference to mental state. *Cognition* 14: 301–21.

Shipley, E. F., C. S. Smith & L. R. Gleitman (1969). A study in the acquisition of language: free responses to commands. *Language* 45: 322–42.

Slobin, D. I. (1973). Cognitive prerequisites for the acquisition of grammar. In *Studies of child language development*, edited by C. A. Ferguson & D. I. Slobin. New York: Holt, Rinehart & Winston.

Slobin, D. I. (ed.) (1985). *The crosslinguistic study of language acquisition, Volumes 1–2*. Hillsdale, NJ: Erlbaum.

Slobin, D. I. (1996). From 'thought and language' to 'thinking for speaking'. In Gumperz & Levinson.

Slobin, D. I. (ed.) (1997). *The crosslinguistic study of language acquisition, Volume 5*. Hillsdale, NJ: Erlbaum.

Snow, C. E. (1977). The development of conversation between mothers and babies. *Journal of Child Language* 4: 1–22.

Snow, C. E. (1995). Issues in the study of input: finetuning, universality, individual and developmental differences, and necessary causes. In *The handbook of child language*, edited by P. Fletcher & B. MacWhinney. Oxford: Blackwell.

Stackhouse, J. & B. Wells (1997). *Children's speech and literacy difficulties: a psycholinguistic framework*. London: Whurr Publishers.

Tager-Flusberg, H. (1993). What language reveals about the understanding of minds in children with autism. In Baron-Cohen, Tager-Flusberg & Cohen.

Temple, C. (1997). *Developmental cognitive neuropsychology*. Hove: Psychology Press.

Tomasello, M. (1987). Learning to use prepositions: a case study. *Journal of Child Language* 14: 79–98.

Tomasello, M. (1995). Joint attention as social cognition. In *Joint attention: its origins and role in development*, edited by C. Moore & P. J. Dunham. Hillsdale, NJ: Lawrence Erlbaum Associates.

Tomasello, M. & M. Barton (1994). Learning words in nonostensive contexts. *Developmental Psychology* 30: 639–50.

Tomasello, M. & J. Farrar (1986). Joint attention and early language. *Child Development* 57: 1454–63.

Tomasello, M. & A.C. Kruger (1992). Joint attention on actions: acquiring verbs in ostensive and non-ostensive contexts. *Journal of Child Language* 19: 311–33.

Tomasello, M. & W. E. Merriman (1995) *Beyond names for things: young children's acquisition of verbs*. Hillsdale, NJ: Lawrence Erlbaum Associates.

Tomasello, M., R. Strosberg & N. Akhtar (1996). Eighteen-month-old children learn words in non-ostensive contexts. *Journal of Child Language* 23: 157–76.

Tomasello, M. & J. Todd (1983). Joint attention and lexical acquisition style. *First Language* 4: 197–212.

Van der Lely, H. K. J. (1993). Specific language impairment in children: research findings and their therapeutic implications. *European Journal of Disorders of Communication* 28: 247–61.

Van der Lely, H. K. J. & M. Harris (1990). Comprehension of reversible sentences in specifically language impaired children. *Journal of Speech and Hearing Disorders* 55: 101–17.

Watkins, R. V., M. L. Rice & C. C. Moltz (1993). Verb use by language-impaired and normally developing children. *First Language* 13: 133–43.

Weismer, G., D. Dinnsen & M. Elbert (1981). A study of the voicing distinction associated with omitted, word-final stops. *Journal of Speech and Hearing Disorders* 46: 320–7.

Wepman, J. M. & W. M. Reynolds (1987). *Wepman's Auditory Discrimination Test.* Second edition. Los Angeles: Western Psychological Services.

Wiig, E. H., W. Secord & E. Semel (1992). *Clinical Evaluation of Language Fundamentals – Pre-school.* Sidcup, Kent: The Psychological Corporation.

Index

Note: References to figures, tables and notes are given as follows: e.g. 80*f*, 219*t*, 87n.

279